New Playwrights: The Best Plays of 2010

D1241002

NEW PLAYWRIGHTS

The Best Plays of 2010

Edited and with a Foreword by
Lawrence Harbison

Introduction by
Rajiv Joseph

CONTEMPORARY PLAYWRIGHTS SERIES

A Smith and Kraus Book
HANOVER, NEW HAMPSHIRE

A Smith and Kraus Book
Published by Smith and Kraus, Inc.
177 Lyme Road, Hanover, NH 03755
www.SmithandKraus.com

First Edition: August 2011
10 9 8 7 6 5 4 3 2 1

Manufactured in the United States of America
Cover design by Emily Kent, emilygkent@gmail.com
Book design by Rachel Reiss, rachelreiss@verizon.net
Photo on title spread © iStockphoto.com/Joseph Luoman

ISBN-10 1-57525-775-0
ISBN-13 978-1-57525-775-4
ISSN 2162-8084

Contents

Foreword

In November of the 2008–2009 season, a group of women play-wrights set up a public discussion with the Artistic Directors of several prominent New York theatre companies. The issue under discussion was the paucity of productions of new plays by women. The statistics were truly appalling. Of the major theatres in New York, not one had as yet that season produced a play by a woman. During the previous season, 12.8% were by women.

There are several reasons why New York theatre-goers see so few plays by women. Some of these were discussed during the abovementioned forum, some weren't (because to do so would have opened up a politically-incorrect Pandora's box); but the practical effect was that there were a lot more plays by women on New York City stages—and, in fact, all around the country—during the 2009–2010 season. Primary Stages' entire line-up was plays by women. Some of the fine plays I saw were by seasoned veterans such as Theresa Rebeck (she had two—*Our House* and *The Understudy*) but many were by less well-known playwrights, which was great for me because I had so many more terrific plays by women than in previous seasons to consider for this book.

Generally, my *New Playwrights* anthology is top-heavy with plays I saw in New York. I have more access to these plays; but I do try to include plays which have not yet seen the light of a New York stage. This year's sole example is Allison Moore's hilarious *Slasher*, a send-up of so-called "slasher films" which premiered at Actors Theatre of Louisville's Humana Festival before going on to productions in Los Angeles and elsewhere around the country. *Slasher* is not just a spoof, though; it's also a searing indictment of our fascination with these kinds of films, most of which feature gruesome things done to women in the name of "entertainment."

Annie Baker scored with two plays—*Circle Mirror Transformation* at Playwrights Horizons and *The Aliens* at Rattlestick Playwrights Theatre. *Circle Mirror Transformation* is a satire about an adult-education class in "creative drama," which becomes more about group therapy than it does about theatre. The play develops its plot in a most unusual way, which I found fascinating. When you read the play, you'll see what I mean.

The exemplary Women's Project had a good year overall, the high point of which was Liz Duffy Adams' delicious comedy *Or*, whose central character is the first woman to make her living by her pen, Aphra Behn, who becomes a spy for King Charles II and manages to get it on with his chief mistress, Nell Gwynne, at the same time. Ms. Adams somehow manages to create a cleverly modern Restoration comedy, which appealed to audiences even if they had no idea of the characters and their historical context.

Lincoln Center Theatre has set up a producing division called LCT3, devoted to plays by up and coming playwrights, which is where I saw Ellen Fairey's superb comic drama *Graceland*, about an adult brother and sister who convene for the funeral of their father, who committed suicide. This sounds like a bummer, but it's not.

And now, for the guys' plays.

Geoffrey Nauffts' *Next Fall*, actually managed something which is all too rare these days: a transfer to Broadway of a play acclaimed off Broadway, and a respectable run on the so-called "Main Stem." At its dramatic center is a most unusual relationship between a 40-ish man who's a cynical atheist and a much younger man who is a "hardcore" Christian. It's a delightfully off beat gay play which has added poignancy because as the play begins the younger man is in a coma, and may not come out of it.

Finally, Scott Organ's *Phoenix* is a two-character comic drama which deals with two sticky-wicket subjects; the difficulty so many of us have in getting serious about our lives and loves, and the abortion issue. It premiered at the Humana Festival and very soon thereafter was done in New York by the Barrow Group.

I chose these plays because I feel they represent the work of playwrights who I have no doubt will all go on to become a lot better known. I'm not guaranteeing any will become the next Tennessee Williams or Arthur Miller, but you never know...

I promise you, you're in for six great reads!

Lawrence Harbison
Brooklyn, NY

Introduction

Spoiler Alert: By the end of this introduction, I will have successfully compared playwrights to ninjas. And you, the reader, if you are a playwright, will be so excited, because you'll think to yourself, "Man! I am just like a ninja."

One of my favorite people and playwrights, Theresa Rebeck, gathers a group of writers every year at her home in Vermont and gets them drunk so they say stupid things that make her laugh. There is also time to work on new plays and share work with others, but this always seems secondary.

Once, when I was there, we got to talking about the concept and fear of "selling out" as a playwright. I probably used the term while discussing the specter of television writing in my future, or the specter of writing anything that wasn't my next play. Theresa, being exceptionally wise, told me that thinking like this was self-destructive. Writers write, she told me, and writers try to make a living writing, and it's hard enough to do this without saddling yourself with unnecessary guilt.

But as a good Catholic boy, I am not one to let a fine prospective nugget of guilt get away without a fight. I insisted that it wasn't self-destructive, it was self-preservation! If I was going to be a playwright, I had to believe it was the *most honorable thing ever*! I said all this as Theresa nodded and quietly poured more vodka into my glass.

As we talked (and drank) we began to realize that in the case of playwrights, the fear of selling out was particularly real, because if you are the type of crazy person who decides to write plays, you are also the type of crazy person who thinks theatre is important and vital and necessary. And if you are this type of crazy person, and have jumped head first into the unpredictable waters of the American Theatre, you have done so because you believe in an archaic art form, and the power of live performance, and the thrill of theatricality and metaphor over the literal one-dimensionality of the screen. And also because you are crazy. And so in a weird way, you've sort of taken an oath to uphold a sacred tradition. You have decided to be a warrior for a cause that people have been dismissing as "dead" for centuries, and you believe that, in spite of this, your powers remain potent and dangerous and worthy.

And this is why you are like a ninja.

I think Theresa is right. I don't believe any longer that exploring other dramatic forms for money or excitement or whatever is a sell out move. But I like to think that as a playwright, I'm part of an ancient caste of warriors. And that we, the warriors, the playwrights, are mysterious and weird and unpredictable. And honorable.

The writers in this collection make it seem so easy, but it's not, it only seems that way because they are adept masters of their craft and just when you think you have them figured out, they will flip you, ninja-style. And so we should be thankful—that these seven scribes are keeping the faith and tackling the big things in the world with zeal and courage and strength. Call it crazy, call it what you will, but the ancient tradition continues.

Circle Mirror Transformation

Annie Baker

This play is dedicated to Reed Birney, Tracee Chimo, Peter Friedman, Sam Gold, Didi O'Connell and Heidi Schreck.

PLAYWRIGHT'S BIOGRAPHY

Annie Baker's full-length plays include *Circle Mirror Transformation* (Playwrights Horizons, OBIE Award for Best New American Play, Drama Desk nomination for Best Play), *The Aliens* (Rattlestick Playwrights Theater, OBIE Award for Best New American Play), *Body Awareness* (Atlantic Theater Company, Drama Desk and Outer Critics Circle nominations for Best Play/Emerging Playwright) and *Nocturama*. Her work has also been produced and developed at the Bush Theatre in London, New York Theatre Workshop, MCC, Soho Rep, the Orchard Project, the Ontological-Hysteric, Ars Nova, the Huntington, Victory Gardens, Z-Space/Theatre Artaud, the Magic Theater, the Cape Cod Theatre Project, the Bay Area Playwrights Festival and the Sundance Institute Theatre Lab in Utah and Ucross, Wyoming. Annie is a member of New Dramatists, MCC's Playwrights Coalition and EST, and she is an alumna of Youngblood, Ars Nova's Play Group and the Soho Rep Writer/Director Lab. Recent honors include a New York Drama Critics Circle Award, a Susan Smith Blackburn Prize nomination, a Lilly Award, a Time Warner Storytelling Fellowship, and a MacDowell fellowship. An anthology of her work, The Vermont Plays, is forthcoming from TCG in 2011. MFA, Mac Wellman's playwriting program at Brooklyn College.

ORIGINAL PRODUCTIONS

Circle Mirror Transformation was developed, in part, with assistance of the Sundance Institute Theatre Program, with additional support from the Sundance Institute's Time Warner Storytelling Fellowship.

Circle Mirror Transformation had its world premiere at Playwrights Horizons in New York City opening in October 2009. It was directed by Sam Gold; scenic and costume design by David Zinn; lighting design by Mark Barton; sound design by Leah Gelpe; and the production stage manager was Alaina Taylor.

CAST

Schultz . . . . Reed Birney
Lauren . . . . Tracee Chimo
James . . . . Peter Friedman
Marty . . . . Deirdre O'Connell
Theresa. . . . . Heidi Schreck

CHARACTERS

Marty, 55
James, 60
Schultz, 48
Theresa, 35
Lauren, 16

SETTING

*A windowless dance studio in the town of Shirley, Vermont.
There is a wall of mirrors. There is a big blue yoga ball.
Summertime.*

NOTE

The week titles (Week One, Week Two, etc.) should somehow be
projected and/or displayed onstage, but not the scene numbers (I,
II, etc).

AUTHOR'S NOTE

To anyone interested in putting on a production of this play:
Please heed the pauses and the silences. They are of great impor-
tance—they are just as important as the dialogue—and every one of
them was placed in the script with extreme care. If you skip over or
rush through these silences, you are performing a different play.
There will be a point in the rehearsal process where it seems like
these pauses and silences are slowing the play down. The actors will

worry that the play is boring—that they'll lose the audience's attention—that what they need to do is *pick up the pace.*

All I can say is, this is an inevitable feeling and you must fight against it.

Without its silences, this play is a satire, and with its silences it is, hopefully, a strange little naturalistic meditation on theater and life and death and the passing of time.

A "pause" should be approximately two seconds long, a "short pause" should be approximately one second long, a "silence" should be approximately five seconds long, and a "long silence" should be at least seven seconds long.

▮ Circle Mirror Transformation

PROLOGUE

> *Lights up.*
> *Marty, James, Theresa, Lauren and Schultz are all lying on the floor, in various positions.*
> *After at least fifteen seconds of silence:*

THERESA: One.
> *A long silence.*

JAMES: Two.
> *Silence.*

LAUREN/SCHULTZ: Three.

MARTY: Start again.
> *Silence.*

SCHULTZ: One.

MARTY: Two.

JAMES: Three.
> *Another long silence.*

LAUREN: Four.

MARTY: . . . Five.

JAMES: Six.
> *Silence.*

THERESA/SCHULTZ: Seven.

SCHULTZ: Shoot.

MARTY: Start again.
> *Silence.*

SCHULTZ/JAMES: One.

LAUREN: . . . Oh my god.

MARTY: Okay. Wait.

We're not getting it.
>   *(pause)*

Let's all . . . everyone take a deep breath.
>   *(pause)*

Okay.
>   *About five seconds go by.*

JAMES: One.
>   *Silence.*

THERESA/LAUREN: Two.

MARTY: Start again.
>   *Blackout.*

Week One

I

>   *James is standing center stage, facing the audience. The rest of the class sits downstage facing James, their backs to the audience.*

JAMES: Hi.

My name is Marty Kreisberg. Short for Martha, but they've been calling me Marty since I was born.

Ah . . .
>   *(he scratches his head, then grins)*

My husband is supposed to do this, ah, monologue about me but he doesn't really know what to—
>   *(Marty is trying to signal something to him. James looks off)*

Why can't I do that?
>   *(he shakes his head)*

Allrightallright.

I'm 55 and I'm, ah . . . I live in Shirley, Vermont. I'm co-executive director here at the Community Center and I also teach a bunch of classes . . . ah . . . pottery, jewelry-making, Creative Drama for youth . . . I've been pushing for an adult Creative Drama class for a while and I'm . . . I'm really glad they let me do it.
>   *(pause)*

Okay.

Ah . . . I'm from New Jersey. Originally. I don't have any kids, but I'm a great stepmother.

My husband is named James. He's in the class too.

Ah . . . let's see. I'm really into nontraditional healing and sort of . . . unconventional, ah . . .

(he scratches his head again)

I'm 55 years old. I really love the Southwest. I hope to move there some day.

Did I already say that?

Okay.

Blackout.

II

Theresa, Schultz, Lauren and James are all walking around the room in different directions, sock-footed. This should last at least thirty seconds. Everyone is taking this seriously. Marty is sitting on her yoga ball, watching.

MARTY: . . . Faster.

They all walk a little faster, still going in different directions.

MARTY: . . . Even faster.

They start zooming around the room, except for Lauren, who tries to keep a safe distance away from everyone.

MARTY: Now . . . I want you to slow down.

(pause)

Start noticing everyone around you.

They all keep walking while making an effort to notice everyone around them. About 20 seconds pass.

MARTY: . . . And I want you to find people and shake their hand.

They obey. About 20 more seconds pass.

MARTY: Now say your name when you shake hands!

About 30 seconds of walking/shaking hands/saying your own name.

MARTY: Okay! Good.

Great.

Stop.

They stop and look at her. She smiles at them.

MARTY: How'd that feel?

An awkward silence.

THERESA: Great   SCHULTZ: Weird.
                                      . . . Good.

MARTY: Okay.

    (she gets up off her ball)

Um.

  Well.

  Welcome.

    (pause)

I just . . . I'm so excited to get to know all of you.

    (an even longer pause)

I um . . . I don't want to talk too much, because that's . . .

    (she makes a vague gesture with her hands)

But. Um. I just hope that you all feel, um, safe here. And open.

  And willing to *go* with it.

  Ah . . . okay.

  Let's keep going!

    Blackout.

III

Marty, Theresa, Lauren, James and Schultz are sitting in a semi-circle.

MARTY: I

THERESA: Took

LAUREN: This

JAMES: Class

SCHULTZ: Because

MARTY: It

THERESA: Was

LAUREN: In

JAMES: The

SCHULTZ: . . . Paper.

    A weird pause.

MARTY: Love

THERESA: . . . Truth!

LAUREN: Um . . . discovery

JAMES: Self-Actualization

SCHULTZ: . . . Friends

MARTY: Were

THERESA: Part

LAUREN: Of

JAMES: All

SCHULTZ: The

MARTY: Mess!

THERESA: And

LAUREN: *(pause)* Stuff.

JAMES: . . . Enormous.

   A confused pause.

SCHULTZ: I

MARTY: Feel

THERESA: Fantastic!

LAUREN: Period.

MARTY: Oh. Hey. Yeah. I forgot to—we don't have to . . . you don't
  have to say "period." You can just keep—

JAMES: Pain

SCHULTZ: Um . . . ah . . . Loneliness

MARTY: Are

THERESA: Feeding

LAUREN: Me

JAMES: . . . Sky.

   Pause.

SCHULTZ: Evil

MARTY: . . . Blue

THERESA: Birds

LAUREN: Fly

JAMES: Over

SCHULTZ: Head.

   Pause.

MARTY: Green

THERESA: Wondrous

LAUREN: Um . . . sunshine

JAMES: Washes

SCHULTZ: Over

MARTY: My

THERESA: Little

LAUREN: Tiny

JAMES: Face

>*Pause.*

SCHULTZ: . . . Hopefully.

>*Pause.*

MARTY: Okay.

>Great.

>*(pause)*

Maybe next week we'll try to make it a little more like a real story.

>*Blackout.*

IV

>*Breaktime.*

>*Schultz and Theresa are the only people in the room. Theresa is squatting in the corner, listening to a cell phone message. Schultz is drinking from a bottle of water and eyeing her.*

SCHULTZ: How long did she say?

>*Theresa holds up one finger and mouths "Sorry." After a few seconds she snaps her phone shut.*

THERESA: Sorry. What?

SCHULTZ: How long did she . . .

>*(a pause while he tries to reformulate his thoughts)*

Ah . . .

>How long is the break?

THERESA: I think she said ten minutes?

>*Schultz nods, embarrassed, and goes back to drinking water. Theresa watches him drink and smiles at him. He puts down the water and smiles back at her.*

SCHULTZ: I'm sorry. You have . . .

>Sorry. Do you ah—

THERESA: What?

SCHULTZ: I just ah . . .

> I was going to say that you have very . . . you have very alive *eyes.*

THERESA: Oh. Wow. I—

SCHULTZ: But that sounds kind of—

THERESA: No! Thank you.

SCHULTZ: I don't mean it in a, uh . . . in a weird way.

THERESA: No. It's a—it's a compliment.

> *They smile at each other. A pause.*

SCHULTZ: What's your deal?

THERESA: Oh. God. I um—

SCHULTZ: I just mean . . . I haven't seen you around. It's a small town, so—

THERESA: I moved here like five months ago.

SCHULTZ: All right.

> *A pause.*

THERESA: Do you live near here? Or do you—

SCHULTZ: I live in the Brook.

THERESA: I'm . . . what? Sorry. The—

SCHULTZ: They're condos. The Brook. It's on Hitchcock? Right off 7. Across from the—

THERESA: Oh yeah. I know where that is.

> *A silence, during which Theresa notices his wedding ring.*

THERESA: So do you live there alone or do /you—

SCHULTZ: I live there alone.

> *(pause)*

> My wife and I recently . . . we're divorced. That's why I live in the, uh . . . I moved out about a year ago.

THERESA: Oh. Okay.

SCHULTZ: She lives in our house. It's a great house. With a . . . I spent years working on the garden.

THERESA: Huh.

SCHULTZ: The Brook is . . . it's very corporate. Very corporate-feeling.

> *Theresa smiles sympathetically at him. Another silence.*

THERESA: I was just confused because you um . . . you're still wearing your wedding ring.

> *Schultz looks down at his hand.*

SCHULTZ: Yes. Yes I am.

Lauren enters, her cell phone pressed to her ear. She eyes them suspiciously, then goes over to her bag, rummages through it, removes something, slips it into her pocket, and then leaves. They watch her.

SCHULTZ: I should probably take it off.

THERESA: Yeah. I don't know. What's the rush, I guess.

Pause.

SCHULTZ: Would you be interested in—

Marty and James enter, in the middle of talking.

JAMES: So *she* called *you.*

MARTY: Yeah. We just—

JAMES: What'd you talk about?

MARTY: Nothing really.

(she looks up and smiles at Theresa and James)

We've got about three more minutes, you guys.

James walks out of the room. A weird silence. Maybe we can hear the very faint sound of James peeing in the bathroom offstage. Marty's cell phone rings. She takes it out and looks at it, then puts it back in her pocket.

SCHULTZ: *(to Theresa)* So you're a . . . you like to hula hoop!

THERESA: Um. The correct term is actually hooping.

SCHULTZ: Oh god. I'm sorry.

THERESA: No, no. It's a common, um . . . but "hula hooping" is, actually, um . . . it's a misnaming.

SCHULTZ: Ah.

Schultz keeps staring at the hoop. The sound of the toilet flushing offstage. James reenters and stands near the doorway, watching Schultz and Theresa.

SCHULTZ: It's big.

THERESA: The big ones are actually easier to use.

Wanna see?

MARTY: We're about to start. Whenever Lauren gets back.

THERESA: It'll take two seconds.

Theresa runs over to the corner, gets the hoop, and runs back to the center of the room. Schultz stands aside while she raises the hoop to her hips and then, with a few small, deft tilts of her pelvis, begins hooping.

SCHULTZ: . . . Wow.

Theresa continues hooping. After a while:

THERESA: The key is actually less movement.

SCHULTZ: Uh huh.

THERESA: As opposed to more movement.

> *Now Marty and James are watching, too. Everyone is a little hypnotized.*

SCHULTZ: Jesus.

> *Theresa stops and gracefully catches the hoop before it falls to the ground.*

THERESA: *(to Schultz)* Try it.

SCHULTZ: Oh. No. I can't. I ah—

THERESA: It's actually really easy.

> *Schultz shakes his head.*

THERESA: Schultz.

SCHULTZ: Nope.

> *Lauren reenters, turning off her cell phone.*

MARTY: Oop! You know what? Everyone's back. Let's get started.

JAMES: *(suddenly)* I'll try it.

THERESA: Yeah James!

> *James walks over to Theresa. She hands him the hoop, and he steps into it.*

JAMES: What do I do?

THERESA: Okay. Just um . . . put one foot forward.

> *James puts one foot forward.*

JAMES: Uh-huh.

THERESA: Now just . . . try it. Don't think too much.

> *James throws his pelvis forward and sends the hoop aloft. It crashes to the ground in about three seconds.*

JAMES: *(shaking his head)* Ah.

THERESA: Try again. It's just a little motion. Like a little . . . spin.

> *James tries again. He sends the hoop aloft, awkwardly swinging his hips back and forth.*

THERESA: Good! Oh my god! That's awesome!

> *Everyone watches James, half-impressed, half-aghast. The hoop crashes to the ground. Schultz and Theresa and Lauren all applaud. James hands the hoop back to Theresa.*

MARTY: That was amazing.

> *Blackout.*

V

Lights up. They are all sitting in a circle. Marty is in the middle of a story. Everyone is rapt.

MARTY: And it was at this . . . this wedding was like . . . it was a real hippie wedding. We were all sleeping on the floor of . . . we were sleeping in the lobby of this old abandoned hotel in Eureka. And I spread out my little straw mat . . . this was at the end of the night, and we were all a little drunk, and we'd been dancing, and singing, and I was about to go to sleep, but then I looked over . . . and next to me, lying on his little straw mat, was this, um, this *guy.*

    (pause)

This really cute guy. I'd seen him earlier that night dancing with all . . . I mean, he was constantly surrounded by women.

And I hadn't gotten a chance to talk to him, but I'd noticed him.

    (pause)

So we were all lying in the dark, so I couldn't quite tell if . . . but then my eyes started adjusting and I said: holy . . . this guy lying next to me is . . . this adorable guy is just staring at me and smiling at me.

And we just lay there smiling at each other for the next couple of hours.

Not touching or . . .

I don't even remember when we fell asleep.

And the next morning we woke up, smiled at each other again, and he said: I'm James.

SCHULTZ: *(softly)* I knew it.

MARTY: And I said: I'm Marty.

And he said . . . . I couldn't believe the . . . without any kind of . . . he just said, with total . . . "Wanna go camping with me tomorrow? I'm driving north to Arcata."

I couldn't believe the nerve of this guy! And I had all these obligations back in . . . .

But I found myself saying . . . I just said:

"Sure. Why not."

    James grins, embarrassed. Schultz applauds a little. A long pause.

CIRCLE MIRROR TRANSFORMATION

THERESA: That is really really cute.

Another pause.

MARTY: Okay. Who else has a story? And don't forget to really listen, you guys. We're gonna have to remember these.

Pause.

THERESA: I'll go.

MARTY: Perfect.

Theresa stands up, somewhat unnecessarily.

THERESA: Okay. Well. This one time when I was still living in New York? I was on the . . . there was this old Jewish guy in my subway car. I knew he was Jewish because . . . well, he was stereotypically Jewish. I mean, not that all Jews look this way, obviously, but he had this humongous nose and this long like white beard with these big glasses and he had this accent like an old Jewish Yiddish-y Brooklyn accent and these . . . um . . . suspenders kind of pants.

Anyway.

The point is he was very clearly Jewish and he was sitting there talking to these old black guys. Who seemed kind of crazy. They all seemed crazy. But he was holding these pamphlets and he was yelling at them not angry just kind of yelling all this stuff and they were nodding and saying like Totally Man or like You're So Right and I started listening and he was talking about this Jewish Conspiracy and he used the phrase "Jew S.A." And then he was like: "Do you think the World Trade Towers came down by themselves?" And then he was talking about how, you know, the Jews killed Christ, and then . . . ah . . . what else. Oh. Something about World War II. How that happened because Jews were running Wall Street and Wall Street paid for Germany or something?

A very long, weird silence. No one knows what to do.

THERESA: I guess that's it.

She sits down.

MARTY: What made you think of that story?

THERESA: Um. I don't know. I think about it when . . . you know. The issue of self-hate or whatever.

Silence.

MARTY: That man may not have been Jewish.

THERESA: Oh. Um. I'm pretty sure he was.

MARTY: He may have fit your stereo . . . he may have fit your stereo-
  type of a Jewish person but he may not have been Jewish.
      Another silence. Finally Marty looks at her watch.
  Okay. It looks like we're out of time!
      Everyone starts getting up.
MARTY: Thanks, you guys.
  I think this was a really really great start.
      *They all start going over the corner to get their bags, put on
      their shoes, turn on their cell phones, etcetera.*
MARTY: Hey—Lauren? I almost forgot. Just before you—I think you
  still owe me a check?
LAUREN: My mom was supposed to mail it to you.
MARTY: I don't think I . . . would you be willing to remind her?
LAUREN: Um. Yeah. Sure.
      Blackout.

Week Two

I

  *Lauren is standing center stage, facing the audience. Everyone else sits
  downstage, their backs to the audience.*

LAUREN: Hi.
  My name is Schultz.
  I'm a carpenter.
  And I don't just . . . I mean, I do regular carpenter things but I
  also make these amazing chairs that are like . . . this one chair has,
  like . . . like the headrest is the sun and the whole thing is gold?
      (Lauren looks nervously at Schultz)
  It's kind of hard to explain.
  There's this other chair that looks like a cloud.
  Um . . . I'm forty-eight years old.
  I grew up in Maryland and my mom died when I was really
  little. She was an elementary school teacher. I always wanted to
  be a baseball player.
  Um . . .

I'm really nice to everyone.
(pause)
I met my wife Becky right out of college and we . . .
(Schultz is saying something we can't hear)
Yeah. I know. I was gonna—
We just separated. Divorced.
I'm in a lot of pain about it.
But, um, to look on the bright side, I have more time now to work on my chairs and maybe find a way for them to um, spread out to um, more people.
(pause)
I am an artist.
I am a really good artist.
Blackout.

II

Schultz, James, Theresa and Lauren are playing a particularly confusing and chaotic version of Explosion Tag while Marty stands in the corner and watches. Explosion Tag is basically regular tag except you're supposed to "explode" when tagged. When you're tagged you also become It, and as It you're supposed to be exploding constantly. When the lights come up Lauren is It. Everyone is awkwardly darting around the room. Lauren is exploding vocally, not physically (she keeps saying "powccchrrrpowpow"), and half-heartedly scurrying after people. Everyone has a different way of eluding her, although it is not very difficult. This can last up to a minute. Finally Lauren tags Schultz on the elbow. It is unclear whether or not he purposely let this happen.

LAUREN: You're it.

> *Schultz makes a melodic falling-bomb sound ("NEEEEEEE-eeeeeerrrr") while sinking to his knees. There is a long pause while he remains there, still. Everyone stops and watches.*
> *Finally Schultz explodes: silently, beautifully, atomically. His arms are thrust out, his eyes are wide open, his mouth is gaping open in a silent scream.*

MARTY: . . . Gorgeous.

> *Schultz falls backwards onto the floor and lies on his back. There is a long silence while everyone remains standing, watching him.*

MARTY: You're It now, Schultz.

SCHULTZ: *(sitting up)* Oh. Sorry.

> *Schultz reaches out, quick as a snake, and grabs James's
> ankle.*

JAMES: Ah! Jesus.

SCHULTZ: You're it.

> *Blackout.*

III

> *Breaktime.*
> *Marty and Theresa are squatting by their bags in the corner, talk-
> ing quietly. Schultz is lurking in the other corner, drinking from his
> water bottle.*

THERESA: It's natural.

MARTY: It *is?*

THERESA: Weird, right?

MARTY: Well. It's beautiful.

THERESA: Thanks.

MARTY: Have you . . .

> *(a pause)*

. . . I just . . . I saw them in CVS the other day, and I . . . have you
seen these things?

THERESA: Wait, what are you talking about?

MARTY: These um . . . they're like these little packets of dye, but
they're . . .

> *(she giggles, then whispers)*

. . . they're for . . . it's for *pubic* hair.

THERESA: Oh my god.

MARTY: They were in their own little section, and I was: I said: Oh. My.
God. and I called James over and he said: what's the big deal?

THERESA: Well. Of course. He—

MARTY: And I was in a huff about it, I was in this big huff, and then I
thought . . .

> *Marty stops talking and glances over at Schultz.*

THERESA: *(giggling)* Can you hear us, Schultz?

> *Schultz lowers his water bottle.*

SCHULTZ: What? No.
> *Marty and Theresa dissolve into more giggles. Schultz looks tormented.*

SCHULTZ: I have to check my uh . . . my phone messages.
> *Schultz takes his cell phone out of his pocket, crosses to the front corner of the room, and pretends (convincingly) to listen to a message.*

THERESA: So you were really angry—

MARTY: I was in a big huff about it, but then I . . . oh god. You probably don't have to worry about this. You're too young. But my um . . . that hair is half-*gray* now and it drives me crazy . . . and I thought—

THERESA: Did you buy it?

MARTY: I'm thinking about it.

THERESA: Oh my god. Awesome.

MARTY: But then James will . . . I know he's going to accuse me of being a hypocrite.

THERESA: I bet he'll like it.

MARTY: Theresa.

THERESA: I bet he will.
> *Marty shakes her head.*

MARTY: I have to pee.
> *Marty gets up and exits. Silence. Schultz is still listening to the imaginary message. Theresa smiles at him.*

THERESA: Hey.
> *Schultz snaps his phone shut.*

SCHULTZ: Hi.

THERESA: How was your week?

SCHULTZ: It was okay.
> *Pause.*

SCHULTZ: How was your week?

THERESA: It was good.
> *(pause)*

I bought a plant!

SCHULTZ: Oh yeah? What kind?

THERESA: Um . . . I don't know. The tag says that it's a "money plant"? Like if you put it under—if you put it in the window you'll make a lot of money or something.

SCHULTZ: Wow.
> *Silence.*

THERESA: Who called you?

SCHULTZ: My friend.

THERESA: Oh.
> *Another silence. Theresa looks at the door, then back at Schultz.*

THERESA: So what do you think?

SCHULTZ: I ah . . . ?

THERESA: About the class.

SCHULTZ: Huh. Well . . .
> *(he glances nervously towards the door)*

Uh . . . I like it. I don't feel . . . I guess I'm having a little trouble feeling totally comfortable?

THERESA: Yeah.

SCHULTZ: I feel pretty self-conscious.

THERESA: You'll get the hang of it.

SCHULTZ: You seem so . . . you're so good at everything.

THERESA: Well. I'm /actually—

SCHULTZ: You do everything in such a . . . you're so graceful.

THERESA: Oh god. That's . . .
> *She shakes her head and grins. They look at each other. A long silence.*

THERESA: Schultz.

SCHULTZ: What.

THERESA: Do you maybe wanna get a cup of coffee after class? Or um . . . .
> *Schultz stands there, speechless. Theresa is confused. After a pause:*

THERESA: I'm sorry. Did I do something wrong?

SCHULTZ: No.

I mean yes.

Didn't I say yes?

THERESA: You didn't say anything.

SCHULTZ: Oh god. Yes.

I'm sorry. I thought I said yes.

Yes!
> *Blackout.*

IV

> *James, Schultz, Theresa and Lauren are sitting up against the stage right wall. Marty is in the center of the room, facing them.*

MARTY: Okay. So I'm going to use myself as an example.
> *They all nod. Marty taps her chin thoughtfully.*

MARTY: Schultz.

SCHULTZ: Yes.

MARTY: Will you be my father?

SCHULTZ: Gladly.
> *He stands up. She takes hold of his arm and leads him into the center of the room.*

MARTY: *(to the group)* Don't be afraid to physically take hold of people and guide them. That's the point. Okay.
> *(pause, to Schultz)*

All right. Um . . . let's see. You are . . . .you're . . . you're a very condescending . . .

You're always kind of quietly Looking Down on everyone. So maybe . . .
> *(Marty manipulates Schultz's arms until they're folded across his chest. Schultz is thoroughly enjoying himself)*

And also . . . you have this certain . . .
> *(she reaches up and pushes his eyebrows)*

You have a condescending sort of . . .
> *(Schultz raises his eyebrows in exaggerated contempt)*

Perfect.

Okay. Stay that way.
> *(she turns back to the group)*

Now. Theresa. I want you to be my mother.

THERESA: Awesome.
> *Theresa leaps up. Marty guides her towards the center of the room and puts her next to Schultz.*

MARTY: Okay. You are . . . you're very angry. You're this very aggressive, very dominating woman . . . .people have always asked so much of you and not respected your intelligence and so you're really . . .
> *(Marty manipulates Theresa's hands so that she's clutching her own hair)*

And if you could turn toward Schultz . . . your husband . . .

(Theresa turns towards Schultz)

And . . .

(Marty takes hold of Theresa's mouth. This surprises Theresa a little)

And just . . . you're screaming at him.

Good. Good.

And Lauren?

LAUREN: *(not getting up)* Yeah.

MARTY: You're me.

A pause.

MARTY: Can you get up?

Lauren gets up. This time Marty doesn't go over and take her arm. Instead Lauren slowly walks towards the center of the room.

MARTY: I want you to sit on the ground.

Lauren sits cross-legged on the ground.

MARTY: Except I want you to hug your knees.

Lauren obeys.

MARTY: Yep. And kind of bury your head in . . .

Yep.

Marty observes for a while.

MARTY: That looks great.

She looks over at James, who is still seated against the wall.

MARTY: Don't they look great?

He nods. Silence.

MARTY: Wow.

Okay. You can relax.

Theresa and Schultz exhale and let their arms drop to their sides, laughing. Lauren lifts her head up a little but doesn't move otherwise.

SCHULTZ: Can I go next?

MARTY: Of course! Yes. Everyone back at the wall.

Everyone starts heading back to the wall.

MARTY: And this is just the beginning! Next week we start reenactments.

Blackout.

V

They are all lying on the floor again. The lights are dimmed.

SCHULTZ: One.

MARTY: Two.

THERESA: Three.

> *Long silence.*

THERESA: Four.

> *Silence.*

SCHULTZ: FIVE.

> *Silence.*

JAMES: Six.

> *Silence.*

SCHULTZ/LAUREN: Seven.

MARTY: Start again.

> *Silence. Blackout.*

Week Three

I

Schultz, center stage, facing the audience. Everyone else sits downstage, their backs to the audience.

SCHULTZ: My name is Theresa.

> Ah . . . I am a very special person.
>
> *(he looks tenderly at Theresa)*

I am 35 years old.

> I'm very passionate. About all things. I care about things very deeply.
>
> *(pause)*

I grew up in a small town in New Hampshire. I have a younger brother named Brendan. He's getting married next summer.

> Ah . . . I lived in New York for about . . . for many years. I was . . . I am an actress. The decision to move to Vermont was a difficult but I think ultimately positive one. There was a competitiveness and a claustrophobia that was very difficult for me

in New York . . . also this sense that people didn't really care about each other.

(he shoots another tender look at Theresa)

I have always wanted to make a difference. I have an amazing soul, an amazing warmth, that, that, that people can sense the minute they meet me. I had hoped to reach people through theater, but the realization that maybe this was impossible caused me to reevaluate and try living in a, a smaller place, where I could work, uh, directly with people. I'm studying for a certificate in acupressure and, ah . . .

Shoot.

Rolfing.

Rolfing.

About six months before I left New York I broke up with my boyfriend, Mark. He was not very good to me. Sometimes I guilt myself out and convince myself that I ruined something and that I made a mistake, but those, uh, my friends and people who are close to me know that I did the right thing. That was a toxic relationship.

My father has prostate cancer. It's a, ah, blessing to be only a few hours away from him and to be able to see him on the weekends. I'm also worried about my mother.

I don't want my parents to die.

(a long pause while he thinks deeply about this)

Yeah. Okay. That's it.

Blackout.

II

Theresa, James and Lauren are standing against the wall. Schultz is standing in the center of the room, whispering to Marty. She nods, smiling.

MARTY: . . . Okay.

Yeah.

Yes. Beautiful.

He thinks, then whispers something again.

MARTY: Sure.

She turns and smiles at Theresa, James and Lauren.

MARTY: We're just figuring this out.

> *Schultz whispers something to her again.*

MARTY: Well. Either way.

> *Schultze nods. Marty walks back to the wall and stands against it with Lauren, Theresa, and James. A long silence while Schultz stands there, looking around the room, troubled.*

MARTY: Why don't you start with your bed.

SCHULTZ: *(to James)* Will you be my bed?

JAMES: Ah . . .

> *(he looks at Marty)*

Sure.

> *James steps forward.*

MARTY: What did your bed look like?

SCHULTZ: . . . It was small.

> *(pause)*

It was next to my window.

MARTY: Can you describe some of the . . . some of its special qualities to James?

> *A silence.*

SCHULTZ: Small.

> *(pause)*

Soft.

> *Marty looks at James. Slowly, a little creakily, James gets on his hands and knees. They all watch him.*

MARTY: Great. What's next?

SCHULTZ: Ah—

MARTY: What's something you loved about your childhood bedroom?

SCHULTZ: . . . The tree outside my window.

MARTY: Perfect.

SCHULTZ: *(to Theresa)* Will you be the tree?

THERESA: Of course.

> *Theresa steps forward.*

THERESA: What kind of tree?

SCHULTZ: Ah . . . maple.

THERESA: Am I large or small?

SCHULTZ: Large.

> *Theresa stands near James and strikes a beautiful Tree pose.*

SCHULTZ: Oh. Yeah.

Schultz and Theresa smile at each other. To Lauren:

SCHULTZ: Ah . . . will you be my baseball glove?

LAUREN: Um . . .

MARTY: What are some of the qualities of your baseball glove that you'd like Lauren to embody?

SCHULTZ: Uh . . .

Lauren plops down on the ground, cross-legged.

SCHULTZ: Yeah. Okay.

MARTY: What else, Schultz? What else did you love about your bedroom?

SCHULTZ: Ah . . .

> *(pause)*

My stuffed snake.

MARTY: Your—

SCHULTZ: Right before she died my mother, uh . . . she gave me this stuffed animal. A, ah . . . a stuffed snake.

Silence.

MARTY: Do you want me /to—

SCHULTZ: Yeah.

MARTY: Where do you want me to go?

SCHULTZ: Will you sit on my bed?

Marty nods. She sits on James's back, and mimes, as best she can, the position of a stuffed snake.

MARTY: *(still in stuffed snake position)* Okay. Now . . . take a step bac . . . and look at your bedroom.

Schultz takes a step back. They all freeze in their positions. He looks at them for a while.

MARTY: What are you feeling?

SCHULTZ: Ah . . .

> *(pause)*

It doesn't really . . .

> I'm sorry.

> *(pause)*

I ah . . .

> It doesn't really look like my bedroom.

MARTY: Does it feel like your bedroom?

Schultz shakes his head. A sad silence.

MARTY: . . . Well. Okay.

SCHULTZ: Sorry.

MARTY: No. No. It's fine.

> *She gets off of James's back, a little embarrassed.*

MARTY: Let's um . . . we can all . . . everybody can relax.

> *James and Lauren get up immediately. Schultz smiles at Theresa.*

SCHULTZ: You were great.

> *Blackout.*

III

> *Breaktime.*
>
> *Theresa is by herself, sitting by her bag, listening to her messages. Schultz enters. He walks over to her, touches her hair, then knees down and tries to kiss her.*

THERESA: Hold on. I have to finish listening to my—

> *Schultz keeps trying to kiss her.*

THERESA: Schultz. Hold on a second.

> *Schultz stops and waits. After a second she snaps her phone shut. They look at each other. After a second, he leans in again and they kiss. She stops and looks nervously around the room.*

SCHULTZ: They're out feeding the meter.

THERESA: What about Lauren?

SCHULTZ: *(softly)* I thought about you this morning.

In the shower.

> *They begin to kiss again. After a few seconds Lauren walks in, sees them, freezes, and walks out.*

THERESA: . . . Oh god.

Okay.

We have to stop.

> *Schultz looks at his watch.*

SCHULTZ: We have three more minutes.

THERESA: Schultz.

SCHULTZ: Come into the bathroom with me.

THERESA: I think that's probably a bad id—

SCHULTZ: Just for a minute.

Just for a minute.

He starts walking out the door. A little reluctantly, Theresa follows. The room is empty for twenty-five seconds. Then Lauren reenters, looking a little traumatized. She puts her bag down. She isn't sure what to do. She stands facing the mirrors, looking at herself. She frowns, then walks closer and inspects a pimple on her chin. After a little while Marty enters, looking at her phone. She sees Lauren and smiles.

MARTY: Hey Lauren.

LAUREN: . . . Hey.

MARTY: Are you excited about school starting in a few weeks?

LAUREN: Um.

I'm not sure.

Marty laughs a little.

MARTY: That's understandable. I guess school is a mixed bag.

A long pause while Marty smiles at Lauren. Then Marty walks over to her bag in the corner and starts rummaging through it.

LAUREN: *(suddenly)* Hey.

Um.

I have a question.

MARTY: *(looking up)* Yes.

LAUREN: Um . . .

A long silence.

LAUREN: Are we going to be doing any real acting?

Another silence.

MARTY: . . . What do you mean by Real Acting?

LAUREN: Um . . .

(pause)

Like acting out a play. Or something. I don't know.

(pause)

Like reading from a . . .

(she trails off)

MARTY: Um. Well. Honestly? I don't think so.

Another silence.

LAUREN: Okay.

MARTY: Did you . . . were you looking forward to that?

LAUREN: Um . . . I signed up for this class because I thought we were gonna act.

MARTY: We are acting.

LAUREN: . . . Yeah.

> *(pause. she sighs.)*

Okay. Thanks.

> *Lauren exits. Marty watches her go. After a few seconds James enters.*

JAMES: She won't pick up. Her phone is on. She just won't pick up.

MARTY: Do you want me to call her?

JAMES: No. That's absurd.

> *(pause)*

She's so fucking *ungrateful.*

MARTY: I don't know if I agree with that assessment.

JAMES: Okay. Could you please—

> *Schultz and Theresa enter holding hands. Theresa drops Schultz's hand the second she sees other people in the room, then goes over to her bag and starts looking through it. Schultz is smiling. James looks at Schultz.*

JAMES: What.

SCHULTZ: Sorry?

JAMES: You're smiling like something . . . like something hilarious just happened.

SCHULTZ: Oh. Ah . . . no. Sorry.

> *Blackout.*

IV

> *James and Theresa, standing, facing each other. Schultz and Lauren and Marty watch.*

JAMES: *(hello)* Ak Mak.

THERESA: *(hello)* Goulash.

JAMES: Ak Mak?

THERESA: Ah . . . .goulash. Goulash.

JAMES: Ak. Mak.

> *James giggles.*

MARTY: Stay in it.

THERESA: *(becoming serious—"I have something to tell you")* Goulash . . . goulash goulash goulash.

JAMES: *(what is it)* Ak Mak.

THERESA: *(sometimes, at night, I feel incredibly lonely)* Goulash, goulash, goulash goulash goulash.

JAMES: *(I don't understand what you're saying)* Ak mak, Ak mak.

THERESA: *(I lie in bed staring at the ceiling, and I think about couples and families, like you and Marty)* Goulash goulash goulash goulash, goulash goulash goulash goulash, goulash goulash goulash goulash.

JAMES: *(You are very beautiful.)* Ak mak, ak mak ak mak ak mak.

THERESA: *(are you sad too?)* Goulash?

JAMES: *(I am attracted to you)* Ak mak.

THERESA: *(you're sad, too. I knew it)* Goulash goulash goulash. Goulash.

JAMES: *(I feel really guilty when I think about how attracted I am to you)* Ak mak ak mak ak mak ak mak

A long silence.

THERESA: *(I feel like you understand me)* Goulash goulash.

JAMES: *(I feel like you actually understand me)* Ak mak ak mak.

They gaze at each other.

MARTY: Okay. Good. Stop. What were they communicating?

SCHULTZ: . . . They seemed very connected.

MARTY: Uh-huh. Good.

LAUREN: They were in love.

A silence.

LAUREN: It seemed like they were in love.

Another silence.

MARTY: Huh.

Okay.

Um . . . what was actually happening, though? What was being sad? Sorry. Said. What was being said?

Silence.

SCHULTZ: Uh . . . well . . . I mean, the sentiment /was—

LAUREN: At first she seemed upset.

SCHULTZ: It seemed like she was sharing a secret.

LAUREN: Yeah. Like a . . .

SCHULTZ: But I thought that . . . it felt like James understood her.

THERESA: *(softly)* I'm sorry. Excuse me.

She quickly walks out of the room and shuts the door. Silence.

JAMES: Should someone—

SCHULTZ: I will.

MARTY: No. That's okay.
        I'll be right back.

> *She walks out of the room and shuts the door. Blackout.*

V

> *The group stands in a circle. Theresa starts swinging her arms back and forth and making a corresponding sound.*

THERESA: WOOP.
         WOOP.
         WOOP.
         WOOP.

MARTY: Let's all mirror it back to her!

> *Everyone mirrors the gesture/sound back to Theresa, in unison. After a few seconds of this:*

MARTY: Now Lauren! Transform it!

> *Lauren, after a second of hesitation, transforms the gesture/sound into a different gesture/sound. The whole group mirrors it back to her. They go around the circle, twice, playing Circle Mirror Transformation. This is the only improvised part of the play. Except: the exercise should end with Schultz transforming someone's else gesture into a form of solemn and silent davening. Everyone silently davens on their knees for a while.*
>
> *Blackout.*

Week Four

I

> *Schultz enters the room, in darkness. He is the first one there. He switches on the lights. He puts his backpack down, drinks some water, gives himself a long look in the mirror, and then starts doing knee bends and touching his toes.*
>
> *Theresa enters, carrying her hula hoop. She starts a little when she sees Schultz.*

THERESA: Hey.

SCHULTZ: Hey.

> *A very long, agonizing silence.*

THERESA: I'm sorry I didn't call you last—

SCHULTZ: You don't need to apologize.

> *Silence.*

THERESA: I know I don't.

> *Silence.*

THERESA: But I'm sorry I didn't call you back.

SCHULTZ: Twice.

THERESA: What?

SCHULTZ: You didn't call me back twice.

THERESA: . . . I'm sorry.

> *Schultz shrugs and takes a long drink from his water. Theresa watches him for a while.*

THERESA: You seem angry.

> *Schultz lowers the water and sighs.*

SCHULTZ: Um . . . I think I'm . . . I think I'm a little disappointed. In you.

But. Uh. I'm not *angry*.

> *A long silence.*

THERESA: Well. You shouldn't be disappointed in me.

(pause)

Because I've made it . . . I've made it really, really clear that I can't—

SCHULTZ: Yes. Thank you. Okay.

THERESA: Schultz.

SCHULTZ: It's just . . . it's funny. The not-calling.

Because a week and a half ago you were calling me every day.

> *Pause.*

THERESA: Yeah.

SCHULTZ: So . . . it's just . . .

(pause)

I'm at a really vulnerable place in my life right /now, and—

THERESA: So am I!

SCHULTZ: —and the, uh, I really don't need someone who—someone who's going to be inconsistent?

Silence.

THERESA: I'm sorry.

Schultz convulses in horrible, strained, silent laughter.

THERESA: I won't be ... I won't be inconsistent anymore.

I think we ... I think the best thing might be for ... maybe we should take a break from seeing each other. Outside of ... and then I won't have to—

The door opens. It's Marty and James and Lauren. They all come in together, with their purses, backpacks, etc. Lauren and Marty are in the middle of a tense exchange.

LAUREN: She said she mailed it to you three weeks ago.

MARTY: Okay. Sure. But I never got it.

LAUREN: Maybe it got lost in the mail.

MARTY: All right. Fine. But then she has to cancel it and ...

Marty notices Theresa and Schultz.

MARTY: Is everything okay?

THERESA: *(after a pause)* Mmhm.

Blackout.

II

Theresa, center stage, beaming, facing the audience. Everyone else sits downstage, their backs to the audience.

THERESA: I'm James.

I grew up in a lot of different places because my father was in the army. Um ... Germany. Chicago. Florida. I spent the last, um, three years of high school in Long Beach, California, so that was nice cause I got to graduate with people I knew and make real friends.

I went to school at UC Santa Barbara, which was pretty crazy in the late sixties! I learned a lot about myself during college. One, it was pretty hard to break away from my father and all his expectations for me. I also learned a lot about women and men and sexual politics.

Um ... I have a really funny story about avoiding the draft ...

(she glances briefly at James and grins)

... but, um, okay.

I traveled around a lot after college. I lived in Monterey. I lived at this crazy campground and I had to um, when I did my laundry I would hang my clothes out on the tree branches. Um . . . I went to law school. That was a really different world. But I got really interested on my own in, um, Marxist philosophy, and, um, oh . . . I met my first wife there. Her name was Sylvia. We got married a couple of years later. Um . . . what else. Oh god.

There's just a lot of good stuff.

I'm really interesting.

(she giggles)

Um. Okay. I got through law school and I landed myself this really like great job at a firm in Berkeley and then the day of the bar exam came and I went there and I sat down at the desk and I looked down at the paper in front of me and then I just, like, put down my pencil and I walked out.

Because I realized at that moment that I didn't want to participate in that. In the system. I didn't want to contribute to like a fundamentally flawed . . .

(a pause)

Oh god. Okay. Sorry. I'll stop um . . . .

I have a daughter! Her name is Erin. She's my only child but I wish we were a little closer . . .

(Theresa sobers up a little)

. . . and that's hard for me.

She's close with Marty. Marty is my wife.

(she grins)

Marty is *awesome*.

We live in this amazing house near the center of town painted these really amazing colors. It's like purple and orange and yellow and people stop their cars and take pictures of it. We have a cat named Coltrane.

Coltrane only has three legs.

(she giggles again)

Um . . . okay.

I am . . .

(she sobers up and thinks again)

I am a very strong man. By strong I don't mean physically strong, although, um, that too. I've been through a lot. My first wife was an alcoholic. My whole family is alcoholics. Alcoholic. My father was emotionally abusive to my mother and although I'm not that way I feel a lot of his anger inside of me. I feel it and I think instead of dealing with it I push it, um, I push it deep down inside me and repress it.

> *(a pause)*

But the truth is ... I mean, I haven't said this. But ...

I think the problem is not my father so much as my fear of being my father. Like if I run away too hard from him I will become something else that is also problematic.

Because actually?

I'm an amazing person.

> *(she grins)*

Okay. Thank you.

> *Blackout.*

III

Lights up. Theresa, Marty, Schultz and James stand in a line in front of the wall of mirrors. Lauren is facing them, her back to the audience.

LAUREN: Um.

> *Silence. Lauren steps forward. She taps James on the shoulder.*

LAUREN: You're my dad. Neil. You're Neil.

JAMES: Okay.

LAUREN: Just ... um ...

> *She takes him by the arm and leads over to a different spot in the room.*

LAUREN: This is um. You're ... um. You're in an armchair. You're reading.

> *James nods and pretends to be studying an invisible newspaper. Lauren walks back over to Theresa and Marty and Schultz.*

LAUREN: Um.

> *Lauren taps Marty on the shoulder.*

LAUREN: Will you be my mom?

> *Marty nods, smiling. Lauren leads her to a spot in the room across from James.*

LAUREN: *(to Marty)* You're um . . .
    You're angry.
MARTY: Why am I angry?
LAUREN: Um . . . because he's angry?
        A confused pause.
JAMES: Should I just . . .
LAUREN: You should /just—
JAMES: Wait—what you said before? About /the—
LAUREN: Yeah.
MARTY: Why don't we start? And Lauren . . . you can stop us at any
    time.
        Lauren nods, then steps back. Silence.
MARTY: Neil.
        James continues reading his invisible newspaper.
MARTY: Neil. I need to talk to you about something.
        *A pause while James studies his invisible newspaper. Then he
        looks up.*
JAMES: *(to Marty and Lauren)* I'm sorry. I'm having a little—I'm kind
    of drawing a blank.
MARTY: Can you just go off what Lauren told you?
JAMES: I don't really . . . I don't really know who this guy is.
MARTY: . . . Can you try?
JAMES: Can I try to *what*?
        Marty sighs. A pause.
JAMES: Never mind.
    Start again.
        He goes back to reading his newspaper.
MARTY: James. I mean Neil.
    Neil.
    I need to talk to you.
JAMES: I'm busy.
MARTY: You're reading the newspaper.
JAMES: The newspaper is important to me.
MARTY: Please pay attention to me, Neil.
        After a second, James puts down his newspaper.
JAMES: What is it?
MARTY: I'm lonely.
JAMES: Well, fine. I'm lonely too. We're all lonely.

MARTY: Then why do you ignore us? Why do you insist on ... why are you always reading at the dinner table? Or watching TV when you should be talking to Lauren?

> *A pause.*

MARTY: Why don't you engage with me anymore?

JAMES: You're too neurotic.

LAUREN: *(from the corner)* He wouldn't say that. I mean, he wouldn't think that.

MARTY: What would he think /was—

LAUREN: He would say that she's always nagging him.

JAMES: *(to Marty)* You're always nagging me.

MARTY: Maybe I'm nagging you because you're ignoring me!

> *James stands up.*

JAMES: Maybe I'm ignoring you because you're driving me crazy!

> *A pause.*

MARTY: Then leave, Neil.

Why don't you just leave?

> *Another pause.*

JAMES: I'm stuck.

MARTY: Well, I'm stuck, too.

JAMES: And I, uh ...

> *He is in pain. A long pause.*

MARTY: But what about Lauren? Just because you're mad at me doesn't mean you should ... you can still be nice to your daughter!

> *Another pause.*

JAMES: *(softly)* I'm worried she's going to judge me.

MARTY: She's not going to judge you. She loves you.

JAMES: I'm worried she's going to ...

> *James starts rubbing the spot between his eyes. It's unclear whether or not he's going to start crying.*

JAMES: I, uh ...

MARTY: What? Be straightforward for once!

JAMES: ... I feel ashamed.

MARTY: Of what?

JAMES: Of what I've ...

> *(a very long pause)*

... Of my life.

MARTY: But Lauren isn't judging you, Neil.
>   *(pause)*
> She just wants you to love her.
>> Neil. Look at me.
>> *James looks up, tears in his eyes.*

MARTY: Lauren just wants you to love her and pay attention to her.
>   *(pause)*
> That's all you need to do.
>> *After a while, James nods. He and Marty look at each other sadly. After a while Marty breaks and looks at Lauren.*

MARTY: Well?
>> *Lauren purses her lips, thinking. Everyone waits nervously for her response. After a long silence:*

LAUREN: That was pretty good.
>   *Blackout.*

IV

> *Breaktime.*
>> *Theresa is alone, drinking from her Nalgene. The door opens. It's Schultz. He sees her, sees that she's the only one in the room, and then darts away, shutting the door behind him. Theresa sighs. The door opens again. It's James.*

THERESA: Hi.

JAMES: Hi.
>> *James steps into the room and shuts the door behind him.*

JAMES: . . . That was intense.

THERESA: Yeah.
>   *A pause.*

THERESA: You got pretty—

JAMES: I got kind of worked up.

THERESA: I mean, I think that's great. Maybe that's what Lauren needed.

JAMES: Yeah.

THERESA: She's a really sweet kid.

JAMES: Yeah.
> She reminds me of my daughter. In some . . . in certain ways.

THERESA: Erin?

JAMES: Yeah. Good memory.

THERESA: Oh god. I never forget stuff like that. I mean, about people that I . . . people that I find interesting.

> *(pause)*
>
> My ex-boyfriend . . . I like totally memorized his entire life. I'd bring up some girl he kissed in high school and he'd be like: "Who?" and I'd be like: "Lopie Grossman, you made out with her twenty years ago" and he'd be like—
>
> Jesus. That's actually her name.
>
> See? I still remember.

JAMES: That's amazing.

THERESA: It's actually horrible.

> *(pause)*
>
> I'm like haunted by these . . .
>
> *A pause.*

JAMES: So are you and Schultz . . . ?

THERESA: Oh. No.

> Yeah. No.

JAMES: Huh.

> *Pause.*

THERESA: We were. For a little while. I mean, we went out on a couple of—

JAMES: Yeah. I mean, I knew that.

> *Pause.*

THERESA: That was a . . . I feel like such an asshole. It was a mistake and now . . . and now things are really weird. I shouldn't be talking to you about it.

> *Theresa glances toward the door.*

JAMES: He said that you were still hung up on Mark?

THERESA: Schultz said that?

JAMES: Yeah.

THERESA: So he—

JAMES: He called me and Marty the other night. He was really upset. He hadn't heard back from you and he—

THERESA: Oh god. That's . . .

> Oh god. Poor Schultz. I'm such a . . .
>
> *She shakes her head.*

JAMES: What?

THERESA: It's just . . . I mean, I *am* really screwed up about Mark. But it's like . . . I mean . . . I would . . . I would like to be, to try being in a relationship right now, you know?

> *(pause)*

Just not with Schultz.

Oh god. I hate myself.

JAMES: You shouldn't hate yourself.

> *(pause)*

Was it . . . did you feel like he was too old for you?

THERESA: Oh. God. No. I always date older guys.

> *An awkward silence. Theresa goes back to drinking her Nalgene. James watches her.*

JAMES: You shouldn't hate yourself.

> *Theresa smiles at him.*

THERESA: Aw. James. Well . . . thanks.

You're really cool.

> *James looks down.*

THERESA: You and Marty are like the coolest couple ever. I loved hearing all your . . . your stories and . . . it made me really happy. I was just like: this couple is so cool!

JAMES: Yeah. She—

> *Lauren enters.*

LAUREN: Hi.

THERESA: Hey, Lauren.

> *James nods. Lauren goes over to the corner, sits down, riffles through her backpack, and pulls out a wrapped sandwich. She slowly opens the sandwich and begins eating it, while curiously looking over at James and Theresa. They are self-conscious. After a while:*

THERESA: So tell me about Erin!

JAMES: Oh. Ah . . .

> *James rubs his forehead.*

THERESA: How old is she?

JAMES: She's twenty-three.

THERESA: Okay. Cool.

JAMES: She actually ah . . . she refuses . . . she's refusing to, ah, *speak* to me right now.

Lauren, still in the corner, stops chewing. James clears his throat.

THERESA: Oh no. Um . . . can I ask why—

JAMES: Marty ah . . .

> *(he shakes his head)*

I guess it's not really Marty's fault.

THERESA: Uh-huh.

JAMES: Ah . . .

> *(he lowers his voice)*

About two months ago, she—Marty—told her something I wish she hadn't . . . Marty didn't—I don't know *why* she—but Marty didn't realize that Erin . . .

> That I hadn't told Erin about, ah . . . this ah . . . this, ah . . .
>
> *(his voice drops even lower and quieter)*
>
> . . . very minor infidelity that I, ah, committed during my marriage to, ah, Erin's mother—

THERESA: Oh. Okay.

JAMES: —And ah . . . anyway Marty sort of brought it up on the phone in this sort of casual—I don't know *why* she—but that's beside the—and Erin said: Who's Luisa?

THERESA: Oh. God.

JAMES: And now she's not speaking to me.

THERESA: Oh James.

JAMES: She is speaking to Marty.

THERESA: Well. That makes sense.

JAMES: Yeah. Ah . . . does it?

THERESA: I'm sorry.

JAMES: Yeah. I just ah . . .

THERESA: It'll get better.

> *James nods. Lauren chews her sandwich and stares at them from her spot in the corner. Blackout.*

V

> *They are all lying on the floor again. The lights are dimmed.*

THERESA: One.

JAMES: Two.

Silence.

MARTY: Three.

SCHULTZ: Four.

Silence.

SCHULTZ: Five.

Silence.

LAUREN: Six.

MARTY: Seven.

Silence.

JAMES: Eight.

THERESA/SCHULTZ: Nine.

A very long, disappointed silence.

JAMES: One.

Silence.

LAUREN: Two.

Silence.

SCHULTZ: Three.

Silence.

MARTY: Four.

LAUREN: *(still lying on her back)* I don't get it. I don't get what the point is.

MARTY: Lauren, maybe you should wait until after class to talk to me about this.

Lauren sits up abruptly.

LAUREN: *(to Theresa)* You were like a real actress. Why aren't you the teacher?

Still lying down, Theresa shuts her eyes and shakes her head.

LAUREN: What's the point of counting to ten?!

MARTY: The point is being able to be totally present. To not get in your head and second-guess yourself. Or the people around you.

LAUREN: I want to know how to become a good *actress.*

MARTY: That is how you become a good actress.

THERESA: She's right, Lauren.

Lauren looks at Theresa, wounded. After a few seconds she lies back down. A long silence.

THERESA: One.

JAMES: Two.

Silence.

LAUREN: Three.

MARTY/SCHULTZ: Four.

Blackout.

Week Five

I

Marty, center stage, facing the audience. She has a Band-Aid on her forehead. Everyone else sits downstage, their backs to the audience.

MARTY: My name is Lauren Zadick-White.

I'm sixteen.

I was born right before midnight, on October 24th. Um . . . I'm a Scorpio, and my mother says that accounts for why I'm such a hard worker.

Also why I'm so stubborn!

Ah . . . this fall I'll be a junior at Shirley High. School is okay, but I can't wait to go to college and start doing what I love, which is theater and dance. I'm also really interested in going to veterinary school. We'll see. I don't have to make any decisions right now, even though I think I do.

(she gazes pointedly at Lauren)

I don't enjoy talking that much about my family and my, um, background, but it's actually fascinating and just . . . really, really interesting.

My mother is Lebanese, and my father is Irish. Both of them were born outside of the states and they met at the University of Iowa.

Um . . . my grandmother lives with us. We call her "Sitti." That's Lebanese for "grandma." I'm really close with her. Everyone says we look alike.

(pause)

I have agreed to let all of you know that in the past couple of years my father has had some problems with the, um, law. I hope that this will remain strictly confidential. It has been really hard for my whole family, especially my mother and grandmother, who have always had such high expectations. My grandmother thinks my mother should leave my father. They fight about it.

(pause)

I'm not going to go into any more detail.

(pause)

It is really hard for me to talk about it and I should be so proud of myself for sharing it with all of you.

(pause)

Oh. Also. This fall they're doing "West Side Story" at the high school and I would really like to get the part of Maria. It's my dream role. I signed up for this class so I would be, um, better prepared for it.

(pause)

I hope that I, . . .

Maybe one day I can stop putting so much pressure on myself.

Blackout.

II

James and Lauren and Marty are watching Theresa and Schultz, who stand in the center of the room facing each other.

THERESA: I want it.

SCHULTZ: You can't have it.

    Silence.

THERESA: I want it.

SCHULTZ: You can't have it.

THERESA: I WANT IT.

SCHULTZ: You can't have it.

THERESA: I WANT IT.

SCHULTZ: You can't have it.

MARTY: Come on, Schultz. Really get into it.

THERESA: I want it.

SCHULTZ: Well, you can't have it.

THERESA: But I want it.

SCHULTZ: You can't have it.

THERESA: I FUCKING WANT IT!

>   *Silence.*

SCHULTZ: Jesus.

>   *Schultz wipes his mouth with his sleeve, a little upset. He puts his hands on his hips.*

SCHULTZ: *(shaking his head)* You can't have it.

MARTY: Switch phrases.

THERESA: I want to go.

SCHULTZ: . . . Wait, what do I say?

MARTY: "I need you to stay."

SCHULTZ: I need you to stay.

THERESA: Well, I want to go.

>   *Schultz regards Theresa sadly.*

SCHULTZ: I need you to stay.

THERESA: I want to go.

SCHULTZ: I need you to stay.

THERESA: But I /want to—

SCHULTZ: I need you to stay.

>   *(after a short pause)*

>   I need you to stay.

MARTY: Good.

THERESA: I want to go.

SCHULTZ: I. Need. You. To. Stay.

THERESA: I want to go.

>   *Schultz steps forwards and grabs Theresa by the shoulders.*

SCHULTZ: I NEED YOU TO STAY.

MARTY: Okay, no touching.

THERESA: I want to go.

>   *(to Marty)*

>   I'm sorry. I need to go the bathroom.

>   *(to James)*

>   Will you step in for me?

JAMES: . . . Sure.

>   *Theresa exits quickly. Schultz and James stand facing each other.*

>   *Blackout.*

III

Lauren and James are standing, facing each other. Theresa is hovering nearby, watching them. Schultz and Marty are leaning against the mirrors.

LAUREN: Stop haunting me, Mark.

    A pause.

JAMES: You shouldn't have broken up with me.

    You made a mistake.

LAUREN: No I didn't.

JAMES: Yes you did.

LAUREN: No I didn't. You were domineering and you made me feel . . . you made forget Who I Am.

JAMES: Who cares? Now you're going to be alone forever.

LAUREN: No I'm not.

JAMES: Yes you are.

LAUREN: No I'm not.

JAMES: Yes you are.

LAUREN: No I'm not.

JAMES: Yes you are.

    Silence.

LAUREN: No I'm not.

MARTY: *(from the corner)* Okay. Let's make it a little /more—

LAUREN: I'm not going to be alone forever.

JAMES: I'm the best guy you'll ever have, Theresa. I was the best guy you'll ever have.

LAUREN: You don't know that. Have you . . . have you, like, met all the guys in the world?

    Pleased with herself, Lauren glances over at Theresa.

JAMES: No one will ever love you the way that I do.

LAUREN: You were too possessive.

JAMES: That was one of the things you secretly liked about me.

LAUREN: *(glancing over at Theresa)* No it wasn't?

    Theresa shakes her head.

LAUREN: Yes it was. Okay, yes it was, but that doesn't mean it was good for me. I am a beautiful um really cool woman and I'm really attractive and there are lots of men out there who will like me and be nice to me.

JAMES: You're fooling yourself.

A pause. Lauren sighs.

LAUREN: I don't know I'm supposed to say.

Theresa speaks up from the corner.

THERESA: I don't want to be with a man who threatens me.

JAMES: I'm not threatening you. I'm telling you the truth.

THERESA: *(stepping forward)* No. That's not . . . it's because you're insecure, Mark. You could never just let me love you and be free. You were so . . . you were so judgmental and moralistic. You were always lecturing me. If you really love someone, you don't make them feel bad about themselves! All this negative stuff you're saying . . . it's just . . . it's just further proof that you don't really care about me the way that you say you do. If you really loved me, you'd want me to feel okay about the future. You'd want me to be optimistic.

Silence. Then James smiles.

JAMES: I'm speechless.

Theresa grins.

THERESA: Whew!

MARTY: That was great.

LAUREN: *(to Theresa)* Sorry.

THERESA: No! You were awesome.

LAUREN: *(to Marty)* He was starting to make me feel really bad.

Theresa gives James a high five.

THERESA: That was so crazy, man! You totally reminded me of him!

James beams. Schultz watches all of this, expressionless. Blackout.

III

Breaktime.

Marty is alone in the room, standing in front of the mirrors, looking at her reflection and fussing a little with the Band-Aid on her forehead. After a while Schultz enters. He looks at her.

SCHULTZ: What happened?

MARTY: Oh. God. Yeah. It's . . . I fell out of bed. Two nights ago. If you can believe it.

SCHULTZ: Why?

MARTY: . . . Why what?

SCHULTZ: Why did you fall out of bed?

MARTY: Oh. Um . . . I don't know. I'm not sure what happened. I just woke up and I was on the floor. It's happened to me a bunch of times in the past couple of years.

SCHULTZ: Are you a restless sleeper?

MARTY: Um—

SCHULTZ: Do you talk a lot? Wake up screaming?

MARTY: Well, James says I do. And the other week I—

SCHULTZ: Night terrors.

MARTY: What?

SCHULTZ: You probably have night terrors.

> *Marty smiles.*

SCHULTZ: It's a real thing, Marty.

MARTY: What is it?

SCHULTZ: Becky used to get them. They're uh . . . they're different from dreams because they're just . . . they're just fear. And they can make you have these like, these little seizures. And sometimes you fall out of bed.

MARTY: Huh.

SCHULTZ: Were you abused as a child?

MARTY: I'm sorry?

SCHULTZ: Were you abused as a child?

MARTY: . . . No. Um. No. I don't think so.

SCHULTZ: Okay. Cause it's a common symptom among abuse survivors.

MARTY: Huh.

> *Pause.*

SCHULTZ: Night terrors.

MARTY: Huh. Yeah. Maybe. I don't know what it was.

SCHULTZ: It was night terrors.

MARTY: Yeah.

SCHULTZ: Becky went on medications for . . . she went on some kind of epilepsy medication. It helped her.

MARTY: Huh.

Pause.

MARTY: And it's a real—

SCHULTZ: It's a real thing. It's a real thing. Look it up online.

MARTY: Okay. Yeah. Thanks.

Silence.

MARTY: How're you doing, Schultz? Are you okay?

Pause.

SCHULTZ: Uh . . . I don't know.

(pause)

How are you?

James suddenly enters, exuberant, with a bottle of water.

JAMES: I hooped.

I hooped for over a minute.

MARTY: . . . Wow.

Great.

JAMES: Now Theresa is giving Lauren a massage. In the parking lot.
It's hilarious. You guys should go take a look.

Marty and Schultz both attempt to smile.

MARTY: . . . That's great.

*James suddenly grabs Marty in his arms and gives her a kiss.
It's a little awkward. Marty smiles at Schultz, embarrassed.*

Blackout.

IV

The entire group is sitting in a circle.

MARTY: When I go to India . . . I'm going to bring my purple shawl.

LAUREN: Wait. I've played this before. Isn't it California? "When I go
to California"? We played this in fifth grade.

MARTY: This time we're playing it with India.

When I go to India I will bring my purple shawl. Schultz?

SCHULTZ: I don't understand what—

LAUREN: Say what she said and then add something.

(after a pause)

"When I go to India I'm gonna bring my purple shawl and a"
like another object. Then the next person lists all the other
things and adds on something new.

SCHULTZ: Ah . . . when I go to India I'm gonna bring my purple shawl and ah . . .

> *A long silence.*

MARTY: Whatever you want.

> *Another long silence.*

SCHULTZ: Philip's head screwdriver.

MARTY: Okay.

LAUREN: When I go to India I'm gonna bring a purple shawl and a Philip's Head screwdriver and a . . . a toothbrush.

MARTY: Theresa! Quick! And get creative!

THERESA: When I go to India I'm going to bring a purple shawl and a Philip's Head screwdriver and a toothbrush and . . . a tiny velvet cape.

LAUREN: *What?*

THERESA: Sorry. Just a cape. A velvet cape.

MARTY: Good! Keep going! James!

JAMES: When I go to India I'm gonna bring a . . . a . . . a purple shawl and a Philip's Head screwdriver and a toothbrush and a velvet cape and . . . ah . . .

> The Bible.

MARTY: WhenIgotoIndiaI'mgonnabringapurpleshawlandaphilip's-headscrewdriverandatoothbrushandavelvetcapeandacopyofthe-Bibleand . . . a bottle of red wine!

> *(pause)*

Schultz!

SCHULTZ: Okay.

> I can do this.

> *(pause)*

When I go to India I'm gonna bring a purple shawl and a Philip's Head screwdriver and a toothbrush and a and a and a and a copy of the Bible and a . . . and a big ol' bottle of red wine! Yes! Oh. And a battle axe!

> *A long pause.*

LAUREN: You forgot the velvet cape.

SCHULTZ: . . . I did?

> *A pause.*

MARTY: Did he?

> Who remembers?

LAUREN: He forgot.

JAMES: I didn't notice.

MARTY: Me neither.

> *A silence, during which Theresa grapples with an ethical dilemma. Finally:*

THERESA: Um . . . I think he forgot.

> *A wounded silence.*

MARTY: Okay. Um. Schultz, you're out.

SCHULTZ: What does that mean?

MARTY: You're just . . .

You have to leave the circle.

> *After a while Schultz gets up. He stands there for a few seconds, then walks away from the circle. He wavers on his feet, clenching and unclenching his fists.*

MARTY: Whose turn is it?

LAUREN: Me.

Um . . . When I go to India I'm gonna bring a purple ca—a purple shawl, a Philip's Head screwdriver, a toothbrush . . .

> *While Lauren is talking Schultz walks over to the wall of mirrors and stands there, making direct eye contact with his own reflection. He remains there, unmoving.*

LAUREN: . . . a velvet cape, a copy of the Bible . . . a bottle of red wine . . . and um . . . . a battle axe.

And a calico kitten.

(pause)

I did it! Right? I did it!

> *Marty, who has been glancing over in Schultz's direction, clears her throat.*

MARTY: You know what? I want us to try something different.

LAUREN: But—

SCHULTZ: *(still facing his reflection, not moving)* It's fine, Marty.

MARTY: No. No. I . . . I just forgot how competitive this game is. And it's . . . this . . . what we're doing in this class is really not about competition.

> *Silence.*

MARTY: Schultz.

Please come back and join us in the circle.

> *Schultz slowly turns around and rejoins the circle.*

MARTY: Great. So this next exercise is . . . hm. Wait. We need paper.

*Marty gets up and hurries over to her backpack. She takes
out a flyer and hurries back into the circle. She begins tear-
ing the flyer into five strips.*

MARTY: Okay. We're going to . . . uhp. You know what? We also need
pencils.

*She gets up again and hurries back over to her backpack,
then rummages through it. They all watch her.*

MARTY: I've got one . . . two . . . three . . . this is useable, I guess . . . four . . .

JAMES: I've got a pen.

MARTY: Okay. Perfect.

She returns to the circle.

MARTY: So. Everyone take a . . .

Marty hands out the pencils/pens.

MARTY: Okay. So I want everyone to take your scrap of paper and
write on it . . . I want you to write down a secret that you've
never, ever told *anyone*.

LAUREN: Whoa.

MARTY: And . . . you don't have to be specific. We don't need to know
it's you. In fact, we *shouldn't* know it's you. This is an opportunity to have people . . . to be able to air a secret in front of a
group without feeling like you have to . . . like you have to answer to it. Or someone.

Silence.

THERESA: What if we don't have any secrets?

MARTY: You must have *one*.

THERESA: I don't know. I've been pretty open in all my relationships.
I basically tell my partners everything.

MARTY: Okay. Well, if you can't—just try to think of something that .
. . something that's hard for you to talk about.

Theresa nods.

MARTY: Okay. So. Just . . . don't take too long. Write down the first big
thing that comes into your mind. Even if it's scary.

They all nod.

MARTY: All right. Go for it.

*Everyone (including Marty) starts writing/thinking/chew-
ing on their pens/scootching away to a different part of the
floor to have right amount of privacy to write/think/chew on
their pens. Silence and then the sound of scribbling for about
45 seconds.*

MARTY: Is everyone done?

LAUREN: Just . . . hold on.

SCHULTZ: Yeah. I need a few more seconds.

Mary waits for about 10 more seconds.

MARTY: Okay. Now fold up your paper into four—fold it twice into a little square and give it back to me.

They all obey.

MARTY: And let's all sit together again.

They return to the circle.

MARTY: Okay.

(she takes the little pieces of paper and shakes them in her cupped hands)

. . . We're each gonna pick one. And we're gonna stand in front of the group and read it silently to ourselves, and then we're gonna read it out loud to the group. In a very sincere . . . in a meaningful way.

SCHULTZ: What if you pick your own?

MARTY: Just read it anyway. We won't know.

(pause)

Okay?

Trust me, guys.

Lauren.

Pick one.

Lauren picks a square of paper.

MARTY: Okay . . . now . . .

(she hands the papers out)

Schultz . . .

James . . .

Theresa . . .

Okay.

And I guess this one is for me.

(pause)

Um . . . Schultz. Can you stand up?

Schultz stands up.

MARTY: Will you deliver your secret, please?

Schultz opens his piece of paper, reads it silently, and then looks up.

SCHULTZ: My father may have molested me.

A slightly shocked silence.

MARTY: Okay. Thank you.
>   *Schultz sits down.*
MARTY: Theresa?
>   *Theresa stands up. She unfolds and looks at her piece of paper.*
THERESA: I secretly think I am smarter than everyone else in the world.
>   *A pause. Lauren giggles.*
MARTY: Lauren.
>   Great, Theresa. Good job.
>   *Theresa sits back down.*
MARTY: James?
>   *James slowly stands up, unfolds and then reads directly from his paper.*
JAMES: I have a problempossibleaddiction
>   *(he looks up)*
>   ... that's written as one word ...
>   ... with internet pornography.
>   *Lauren covers her mouth with her hand.*
MARTY: Great. Thank you.
>   *James sits back down.*
MARTY: Lauren?
>   *Lauren stands up. She reads her paper, then stuffs it into her pocket. She looks out at the group.*
LAUREN: I think I might be in love with Theresa.
>   *A very long silence. Lauren is still standing.*
LAUREN: Um ...
MARTY: You can sit down. Thank you.
>   *Lauren sits down. Another horrible 10-second silence. Schultz frowns, then looks traumatized, then stares angrily at James, then looks traumatized again.*
MARTY: Okay. Ah ...
>   I guess it's my turn.
>   *Marty stands up. She unfolds her piece of paper and reads it out loud, not taking her eyes off the paper. Her voice is shaky.*
MARTY: Sometimes I think that everything I do is propelled by my fear of being alone.
>   *A very long silence. Marty finally crumples the paper in her fist. She refuses to make eye contact with anyone.*

MARTY: Great job, you guys.

> *Blackout.*

V

> *They are all lying on their backs in the semi-darkness. Silence for a while.*

MARTY: *(dully)* Okay. Next week is our last class. So let's really try to . . .

> *A long silence.*

LAUREN: One.

> *Silence.*

JAMES: Two.

> *Silence.*

LAUREN: Three.

> *Silence.*

THERESA: Four.

JAMES: Five.

> *A long silence.*

SCHULTZ: Six.

> *Silence.*

JAMES: Seven.

THERESA: Eight.

MARTY: Nine.

> *A very very long silence.*

LAUREN: Ten.

> *No one moves. Blackout.*

Week Six

I

> *The room, in darkness. The sound of footsteps in the hallway. Marty enters the room, her bag over her shoulder, and turns on the lights. She stands there for a while, tired. She walks over to the corner of the room and puts her bag down.*

> *She walks over to the Pilates ball, and sits down. She bounces there, sadly, for about 15 seconds.*
> *The door opens. James enters.*
> *Marty stops bouncing.*
> *James walks over to the corner and puts his bag down. He stands there in the corner, looking at her. She stays on the ball and looks at him. They look at each other for a while.*

MARTY: You came.

JAMES: Of course.

> *She nods. Silence for a while.*

JAMES: I talked to Erin the other night. Finally.

> *Marty nods.*

JAMES: She said you didn't call her back this week. That she left you five—

MARTY: So that's good. So you talked to each other.

> *He nods. More silence.*

JAMES: How's Phyllis?

MARTY: Fine.

> *Silence.*

JAMES: So what are you . . .

Are you on the *couch* /or—

MARTY: There's an air mattress.

> *More silence.*

JAMES: Come home, Marty.

MARTY: No fucking way.

> *Another silence.*

JAMES: You . . . did you want this to happen or something?

MARTY: Did I *what*?

JAMES: Having us write out—

Did you *want* me to—

MARTY: Okay. See. That's exactly. That's exactly the problem. That right there.

> *The door opens. It's Schultz, with his backpack.*

SCHULTZ: Hi, guys.

JAMES: Hey, Schultz.

> *Schultz steps inside and starts putting his backpack down in the corner.*

SCHULTZ: How were your—did you guys have a good week?

*Marty and James both nod. Awkward silence for a little
while. Schultz unzips his backpack and takes out a little box.*

SCHULTZ: Ah . . . Marty?

MARTY: Mmhm?

SCHULTZ: I wanted to, uh . . .

Schultz walks over to Marty and hands her the little box.

SCHULTZ: . . . Thanks.

MARTY: Oh Schultz.

SCHULTZ: For everything. It's been a great class.

Marty looks down at the box.

MARTY: Should I—

SCHULTZ: Yeah. Open it.

Marty rips off the paper and takes the lid off the box.

MARTY: Oh wow.

She stares at the box's contents.

SCHULTZ: Yep.

MARTY: This is really great.

SCHULTZ: Do you already have one?

MARTY: Um . . . well, yes, I do, but it's bigger, and not as nice. It's in
the living room.

JAMES: *(from across the room)* What is it?

SCHULTZ: It's a dream catcher.

MARTY: We can put this one . . .

I can put this one in the . . .

*Marty trails off. She lifts the dream catcher out of the box
and holds it up to the light.*

MARTY: I love the little purple—

SCHULTZ: Ah man. I was hoping you didn't already have one.

MARTY: No. No. I love it. I love it.

Marty puts it back in the box.

SCHULTZ: The Native Americans used them to uh . . .

An awkward silence. He has forgotten.

MARTY: Thank you so much, Schultz.

SCHULTZ: Maybe it'll help with the night terrors.

MARTY: Mmhm.

SCHULTZ: Night terror catcher.

Schultz looks at James.

SCHULTZ: Did she tell you about those?

James shakes his head. Blackout.

II

They are all sitting in a circle.

MARTY: If

LAUREN: I

SCHULTZ: Wanted

THERESA: To

JAMES: Become

MARTY: A

LAUREN: . . . Actress

SCHULTZ: I

THERESA: Would

JAMES: Just

MARTY: Go

LAUREN: *(pause)* Home.

SCHULTZ: . . . I

THERESA: Have

JAMES: Learned

MARTY: So

LAUREN: Um . . . .Much.

SCHULTZ: *(pause)* I

THERESA: Will

JAMES: Try

MARTY: To

LAUREN: Realize

SCHULTZ: The

THERESA: Gigantic-ness!

JAMES: Of

MARTY: Capabilities!

LAUREN: And

SCHULTZ: The

THERESA: Way

JAMES: I

MARTY: Express

LAUREN: Anger

SCHULTZ: Is

THERESA: . . . Indescribable.

JAMES: Peace

MARTY: Is

LAUREN: Just

SCHULTZ: Okay

THERESA: For

JAMES: Everybody

MARTY: But

LAUREN: We

SCHULTZ: Will

THERESA: Succeed

JAMES: Always

MARTY: If

LAUREN: We

SCHULTZ: Try

THERESA: And

JAMES: Become

MARTY: . . . Flowers.

> *Silence.*

MARTY: That was perfect.

> *Blackout.*

III

> *They are all sitting in a circle.*

LAUREN: Okay. Um.

I was on the subway. In New York. And there was this old guy. Who was . . . who was maybe Jewish.

He had a beard.

A-and . . .

> *(a pause)*

He was totally anti-Semitic.

> *Lauren sighs.*

MARTY: It's okay, Lauren.

LAUREN: I don't remember anything else.

> *Lauren sits back down.*

MARTY: Does anyone else remember something from the first day?

> *A pause. No one says anything.*

MARTY: Okay. Well. I think maybe we'll do one more exercise and then call it a—

SCHULTZ: Wait! I do.

> *Schultz stands up. He clears his throat.*

SCHULTZ: Uh . . . okay.

I was at a wedding. In, ah . . . .Eureka, California.

Right near the Oregon border. Where there are a lot of redwoods. It's really beautiful up there.

This is nineteen-eighty . . . something.

There was this big wedding. Two of my friends were getting married in this big old hotel. And we . . . uh . . . we were all sleeping on straw mats. In the lobby. Of the hotel.

We were all drunk. And we'd been dancing.

And uh . . . there was this guy. I'd been looking at this guy all night. This really attractive, really beautiful guy who just . . . who caught my attention. But I didn't think anything would happen because he was just surrounded by women. All the women liked him.

> *(pause)*

He was one of those guys. Those guys that get all the women.

> *(pause)*

Then I was getting ready to go to sleep on my straw mat and I noticed that he was sitting . . . that he was lying next to me. On his straw mat. And even though they'd turned off all the lights I could tell that he was looking at me.

And I felt . . .

I felt seen.

And he smiled at me. I could feel him smiling in the dark.

And then I smiled back.

And neither of us had to say anything, because we knew that we would spend the rest—

MARTY: Schultz?

SCHULTZ: —of our lives together.

MARTY: That was great. Thank you.

SCHULTZ: I'm not finished.

MARTY: The thing is . . . it's quarter till, and I want to make sure we can squeeze in the last exercise.

SCHULTZ: . . . Oh. Okay.

> *Silence.*

THERESA: That was beautiful, Schultz.

> *Schultz can't quite bear to look at Theresa, but he nods.*

SCHULTZ: Yeah. Thanks.

> *Blackout.*

IV

> *Schultz and Lauren stand in the center of the stage, facing each other. Marty, James, and Theresa stand against the wall of mirrors, watching.*

SCHULTZ: *(to Marty)* Five years?

MARTY: Ten years. Ten years from now.

> *Schultz takes a deep breath.*

SCHULTZ: Okay.

> *Schultz walks away from Lauren, then turns around and feigns surprise.*

SCHULTZ: Lauren?

LAUREN: Yeah?

SCHULTZ: Is that you?! !

LAUREN: Yeah. Hi, Schultz.

SCHULTZ: Hey!

> *Silence.*

SCHULTZ: What are you doing here in . . . Burlington?

LAUREN: Um . . . I live here now.

SCHULTZ: Weird. So do I!

> *(pause)*

I live here with my wife.

LAUREN: You got married again?

SCHULTZ: Yeah. Yeah. She's fantastic.

LAUREN: That's so cool.

> *(pause)*

What's her name?

SCHULTZ: Ah . . . Susan.
>   Yeah.
>   She's a, uh . . .
>   She's a seamstress.
LAUREN: Wow.
>   *Silence.*
SCHULTZ: How are you?
LAUREN: I'm, um, I'm okay.
SCHULTZ: How old are you now?
LAUREN: I'm . . .
>   *(a pause while she calculates)*
>   . . . twenty-six.
SCHULTZ: Oh. Man. That's awesome.
>   *Silence.*
LAUREN: I live here with my boyfriend.
SCHULTZ: Aw. Great.
LAUREN: Todd.
SCHULTZ: That's great.
LAUREN: He's a, um . . . he's a doctor. Veterinarian.
>   We run a veterinary clinic together.
SCHULTZ: What happened to acting?
LAUREN: Oh. Yeah.
SCHULTZ: I thought you wanted to be an actress.
LAUREN: No. I . . . I did a lot of acting in college. I was, like . . . I starred
>   in a lot of . . . but now I'm a veterinarian.
SCHULTZ: That's great.
LAUREN: I really like it.
>   *Silence.*
SCHULTZ: So you're happy?
LAUREN: Yeah. I think so.
SCHULTZ: Yeah.
LAUREN: Are you happy?
SCHULTZ: I am. I am. I'm very happy. Susan is just . . . she's changed
>   my life around. And business is going really well.
LAUREN: Are you still making your chairs?
SCHULTZ: Oh yeah. Oh yeah.
>   *(pause)*

Have you heard from any of the others?

LAUREN: Oh. Um—

SCHULTZ: Do you know how Theresa is doing?

> *Marty opens her mouth and starts to step forward to interrupt them, but Theresa stops her.*

LAUREN: Um. Yeah.

> *(she glances over at Theresa)*

She's like a really successful massage therapist. In Putney.

SCHULTZ: Oh, that's good.

LAUREN: Yeah. And she married this like actor. He's kind of famous.

> *Theresa giggles from the back wall.*

LAUREN: I forget his name. He's really good-looking.

SCHULTZ: Huh. That's good.

> *(pause)*

Man. She really screwed with my head.

LAUREN: . . . Yeah.

SCHULTZ: But ah . . . I don't really think about her that much any more.

LAUREN: Yeah.

SCHULTZ: Have you heard from Marty or James?

> *Still standing at the back wall of mirrors, Marty shakes her head. Lauren thinks for a while.*

LAUREN: Um . . . yeah. A couple of years ago. I got um . . . I got like a Christmas card from Marty.

SCHULTZ: What'd she say?

> *Over the next minute, the lights fade so that Marty, James, and Theresa eventually disappear, and only Lauren and Schultz remain, in a spotlight.*

LAUREN: Oh. She um. She moved to New Mexico.

SCHULTZ: Oh wow.

LAUREN: Yeah. She started some kind of like arts program? For poor kids? Some kind of like drama thing?

SCHULTZ: Huh.

LAUREN: Yeah. She lives in Taos. In this really beautiful, um, adobe hut. She sent me a picture.

SCHULTZ: So you two kept in touch.

LAUREN: Yeah. A little. I got . . . it's funny. I didn't get the lead in West Side Story that fall, but I got the um . . . I got the part of Anita? Which was actually—

SCHULTZ: Aw. I wish I'd known.

LAUREN: Yeah. I called Marty and told her. She came to see it.

> *Silence.*

SCHULTZ: So she and James aren't together anymore?

> *Lauren shakes her head.*

SCHULTZ: Do you know where he—

LAUREN: I think he's still in Shirley. At the college. Teaching economics.

SCHULTZ: Huh.

> *Silence.*

SCHULTZ: How's your family?

LAUREN: Oh. Um . . . my parents got divorced this past fall.
Yeah.
After um . . . after thirty years of marriage.

SCHULTZ: I'm so sorry.

LAUREN: Yeah. No. I mean, I think it was a good decision.

> *An awkward silence.*

LAUREN: Hey. Um. This is kind of a weird—but do you ever wonder how many times your life is gonna end?

> *Another silence.*

SCHULTZ: Uh . . . I'm not sure I know what /you—

LAUREN: Like how many people you're . . . like how many times your life is gonna totally change and then, like, start all over again? And you'll feel like what happened before wasn't real and what's happening now is actually . . . *(she trails off)*

SCHULTZ: Uh . . . I don't know.
I guess I feel like my life is pretty real.

LAUREN: . . . Yeah.

> *Silence.*

SCHULTZ: Well. Uh. It's great seeing you.

LAUREN: Yeah.
You too.

SCHULTZ: I always really liked you, Lauren.

LAUREN: Yeah. I liked you too.

> *They smile awkwardly at each other and do not move. Then, very faintly, we hear the sounds of a street in Burlington: people talking, a car honking, plates clinking at an outdoor restaurant. The spotlight goes out.*
>
> *End of play.*

Graceland

Ellen Fairey

Dedication: For Parker

Special thanks to Matthew Miller, Henry Wishcamper, Jenny Mercein, Paige Evans, Jason Mandell, Laura House and everyone at Profiles Theatre.

PLAYWRIGHT'S BIOGRAPHY

Ellen Fairey is the author of the hit play Graceland which recently finished its New York premiere as part of Lincoln Center's LCT3 series and previously enjoyed an extended six-month run at Chicago's Profiles Theatre. Graceland was awarded the 2010 Joseph Jefferson Award for Best New Work and *The New York Times* named Ellen one of their Faces to Watch for Spring 2010. Her first play, GIRL 20, was named one of the top ten plays of 2006 by Chris Jones of the *Chicago Tribune*, and nominated for two *LA Weekly* theatre awards. Her short plays have been part of Collaboraction's Sketchbook Festival and Chicago Dramatists Saturday series as well as Edward Albee's Last Frontier Theatre Conference in Valdez, Alaska. She is a graduate of the School of the Art Institute of Chicago.

ORIGINAL PRODUCTIONS

Graceland was originally produced by Profiles Theatre in Chicago, Illinois, May 2009. It was directed by Matthew Miller. Set designed by William Anderson. Costumes designed by Ricky Lurie. Lights designed by Jess Harpenau. Sound and original music designed by Mikhail Fiksel.

CAST

Sara . . . . Brenda Barrie
Miles . . . . Jackson Challinor
Joe . . . . Darell W. Cox
Anna. . . . . Somer Benson
Sam . . . . Eric Burgher

Graceland had its New York premiere at Lincoln Center's LCT3 in May 2010. It was directed by Henry Wishcamper. Set designed by Robin Vest. Costumes designed by Anne Kenney. Lights designed by Matthew Richards. Sound designed by Bart Fasbender. Projections by Aaron Rhyne.

CAST

Sara . . . . Marin Hinkle
Miles . . . . David Gelles Hurwitz
Joe . . . . Brian Kerwin
Anna. . . . . Polly Lee
Sam . . . . Matt McGrath

CHARACTERS

Sara 40
Sam 37
Miles 15
Joe 45
Anna. 30

SETTING

Chicago's Graceland Cemetery.
The living/dining room of a low-end high-rise.
The roof of the high-rise.

▌ Graceland

Act I

SCENE 1

> *Gram Parsons and Emmylou Harris sing 'In My Hour of Darkness.'*
> *Song fades.*
> *Lights rise:*
> *Late afternoon. Brother and sister Sam and Sara stand in*
> *Chicago's Graceland cemetery—a picturesque and historical resting*
> *place.*
> *They are dressed in the usual funeral garb—Sam's jacket looks*
> *like he slept in it, Sara wears pants, not a dress. They both hide behind*
> *their sunglasses.*

SAM: So, when are you leaving?

SARA: What?

SAM: I just wondered when you were going back. Maybe you need a
ride or something . . . to the airport.

SARA: I'm here for the weekend, Sam.

SAM: Okay.

SARA: We have some things to figure out.

SAM: I know.

SARA: Like who's going to take care of the dog.

SAM: The dog. Right . . . how about you?

SARA: I work. In another city

SAM: I work.

SARA: You deliver fruit.

SAM: I deliver *arrangements* made of fruit, it's different.

SARA: I thought you wanted to teach fucked up kids.

SAM: Yeah, well, I'm sticking to what my advisor said is a tendency to-wards 'violent underachieving'. Speaking of, how's the table store?

SARA: It's called Sur la Table.

SAM: Excuse moi, 'Taahbluh', how is it?

SARA: It's fine . . . it's great actually. I'm the manager now, so . . . you know, that's a big deal.

SAM: Good for you.

SARA: It is.

(Sam takes out a one-hitter, loads it, smokes.)

SARA: He called me.

SAM: Who?

SARA: Dad.

SAM: Oh.

SARA: The day. That day. He left a message, he was at Deacon's. You want to hear it? I saved it.

SAM: No thanks.

SARA: It was probably only a few hours before.

SAM: I'm good.

(Beat.)

SARA: Did she really have blood on her fur?

SAM: What?

SARA: The dog. You said . . . when you called.

SAM: I guess. How's the hotel—where are you staying again? The Blackstone?

SARA: It's fine.

SAM: I heard they fixed it up. Is there a mini-bar?

SARA: I have no idea.

SAM: When they fix them up they usually put mini-bars in.

SARA: Are you sure you don't want to hear the message?

SAM: If you ate and drank everything in the mini-bar it would proba-bly cost more than your room.

SARA: I'll put it on speaker. Hold on.

She scrolls through her cell phone menu. Finds something.

MAN'S VOICE: 'Yo girl—what's up?'

SARA: Shit—not that.

She forwards to the next message.

MAN'S VOICE: 'Hey baby doll, how you doin?'

SARA: Dammit.

SAM: How *old* is that guy?

SARA: Shut up. Here it is.

    They listen.

MAN'S VOICE: 'Sara, it's Dad, Jesus Christ—you believe this bullshit smoking ban? What's happening to this fascist Nazi country? Son's of bitches. Oh well, at least you go home smelling good. Where is everybody? I'm at Deacons, I'm sick of this place anyway.'

AUTOMATED PHONE VOICE: 'To save, press nine.'

    She presses nine, closes the phone.

SARA: So. I guess that was his, you know, 'note': 'Sick of this place— see ya'.

    Neither of them speak.

SARA: Twenty-two.

SAM: What?

SARA: The guy—the voice you heard. He's twenty-two.

SAM: Congratulations.

SARA: Don't be an asshole.

SAM: What am I supposed to say, 'how was it'?

SARA: He had tattoos of birds on his body. Swallows.

SAM: *(sarcastic)* Neat.

SARA: I'm just giving you a visual.

SAM: Please don't.

    He takes a big hit of weed.

SARA: *(remembering)* It was fun.

SAM: I'm glad.

SARA: I didn't *know* he was *twenty-two*.

SAM: I'm glad you had good time.

SARA: He was *happy*. Who in the world is so *happy* like that?

SAM: No idea.

    Beat.

SARA: Hey, where's Anna, by the way?

SAM: What?

SARA: Your girlfriend.

SAM: I don't know.

SARA: What do you mean you don't know?

SAM: We're not together . . . right now, anymore, so.

SARA: What?

SAM: We broke up.

SARA: Are you kidding?

SAM: Nope.

SARA: Are you alright?

SAM: I'm great.

SARA: Does she even know about Dad?

SAM: Yeah, can we not—

SARA: Because you know how they liked each other—

SAM: Can we not talk about Anna?

SARA: God, I hated how they would sing those Warren Zevon songs together—Ahoooooooo!

SAM: Sara!

SARA: *Sorry.*

> *Beat.*

SAM: The dog's on drugs.

SARA: What?

SAM: She takes Doggie Xanax. Or Valium. For anxiety.

SARA: Jesus.

SAM: She's anxious.

> *Beat.*

SAM: So what are we supposed to do next here?

> *Sara pulls an invitation from her purse.*

SARA: 'Gene Marciniak and family' are having a thing.

SAM: Who?

SARA: Some guy he sold wine with.

SAM: Is it mandatory?

SARA: No, it's not mandatory, it's just what people do when someone dies.

SAM: Do these people even know who we are?

SARA: The guy with the moustache asked if I was Dad's 'lady friend'. So no, I guess not.

> *Sam flinches. Sara looks to the sky.*

SARA: This sunshine is pissing me off.

> *A distant rumble . . .*

SARA: What's that noise?

A group of fighter jets scream through the sky.

SARA: Holy *SHIT!*

SAM: Air show!

> *Another jet buzzes the cemetery.*
> *The planes disappear. Silence.*

SARA: I need a drink.

SAM: Hey, didn't you lose your virginity here? Chuck what's-his-name? By the Marshall Field tomb? You thought you should get a ten percent lifetime discount.

SARA: Yeah well, Marshall Field's is gone. Let's get a drink.

SAM: I'm not going to this Marciniak guy's house.

SARA: So we'll go to a bar.

SAM: Where are we gonna go?

> *Beat.*

SARA: Deacons?

SAM: Yeah, that sounds real fun.

SARA: He'd like it, us going to his bar.

SAM: *Would've* liked.

SARA: Yes, I'm aware. *Would have.* What time is it?

> *Sam pulls a pocket watch out of the pocket of his jacket.*

SAM: Almost five.

SARA: Let me see that.

> *He hands it to her, she examines it.*

SARA: 'Lone star'. Everything had to be about Texas. Where did you find this?

SAM: You know, in his stuff.

SARA: Remember we carved our own stars on the back? With that handheld engraver thing?

SAM: That thing took off one of my fingernails.

SARA: I know, I remember, there was blood everywhere.

> *Beat. Sam walks away.*

SARA: Can I hold on to this for a while?

SAM: I don't care. I mean, you know, don't lose it.

SARA: I'm not going to lose it.

SAM: Good. Let's go.

SARA: Deacons?

SAM: Deacons. Why not.

Another fighter jet rips through the sky.

Lights.

SCENE 2

Later that night. One of those low-end high rises on north Lake Shore Drive.
    Joe enters. A less composed Sara follows. Alcohol has been consumed.

JOE: *(a la 'Honey I'm home')* Runny! I'm foam!
    Drunk laughter.

SARA: Wow, a *turntable*!

JOE: You don't like my vintage stereo?

SARA: No, it's great . . . *records.*

JOE: Vinyl. Nothin' like it.
    He goes to the fridge. She pulls a random album from his collection—Neil Diamond

SARA: Neil!
    She continues to pick through the albums.

SARA: What time is it? Oh wait, I have a watch!
    She plops onto the couch—takes out the pocket watch.

SARA: Father Time . . . that's funny.

JOE: Okay—beverage! What's your pleasure?

SARA: Surprise me.
    He saunters back to the outdated stereo system. She sets the watch on the coffee table.

JOE: Need some tuneage! Like a morgue in here!

SARA: *(to no one)* Thank God I'm drunk.
    She struggles with her coat.

JOE: Rough day?

SARA: No. No. Great day.
    Joe puts on Nina Simone's 'Do I Move You', breaks out some moves.

SARA: Wow.

JOE: That's right.

SARA: This is good.

JOE: Ms. Nina Simone . . . yow!

Joe deals with beverages—sings along.
Sara moves to the music—stays seated.

SARA: So is Deacon's like, 'your bar' or something?

JOE: I've been known to log some hours in over at Deacons, sure.

SARA: You ever see this man in there—tall, drinks gimlets? Tells bad jokes?

JOE: *(at the fridge)* You already asked me that sweetie. Can't say that I have.

SARA: Smokes Pall Malls?

JOE: Nope.

> *Joe pours some booze in a glass—brings it to her.*

JOE: I need to worry about this tall guy or what?

SARA: Huh? Oh no . . . no.

> *She drinks.*

JOE: Pall Malls. Sounds old school. I can appreciate that.

SARA: He's from Texas.

JOE: A tall Texan . . . uh oh.

> *She gets up—dances a little.*

SARA: So, what are your feelings on the smoking ban?

JOE: Probably for the best, right? Why, you smoke?

SARA: No. Once in a while.

JOE: Carbon monoxide, baby. Put years on ya.

SARA: Thanks for the information.

JOE: Be a shame to damage that otherwise lovely face.

> *She drains her glass.*

JOE: Someone's thirsty.

> *He notices the pocket watch on the couch—picks it up.*

JOE: This yours?

> *She takes it from him.*

SARA: Actually, it belongs to a dead man.

JOE: Really. Wow. Someone has a dark side.

SARA: Someone.

JOE: Pardon?

SARA: My name's Sara.

JOE: I know baby, I know. Sara.

SARA: How old are you?

JOE: How old do you want me to be?

She thinks.

SARA: I don't know. Twenty two?

JOE: That's funny.

SARA: Twenty three?

JOE: Sorry, girlfriend. I's a grown up man.

SARA: Too bad. Just kidding. Do you have any Warren Zevon?

JOE: Can't say that I do.

> *The next song on the Nina Simone album comes on: 'Do I Move You?'*

JOE: Why don't you come a little closer here, darlin'.

> *She dances a little closer to him.*

JOE: Beautiful.

SARA: Right.

> *She moves away, dances more.*

JOE: I'm serious: cheekbones!

SARA: *(to herself)* Yay cheekbones.

> *To Joe-*

SARA: Why are you smiling?

JOE: Why do you think, baby?

> *He pulls her in. She lets him.*

JOE: Why do you think?

> *Lights fade. Music rises.*

SCENE 3

> *Joe's place. The next morning.*
> *The front door opens. Miles, a mass of awkwardness and energy in the shape of a teenage boy, enters. He heads to the fridge.*
> *A toilet flushes in the background.*
> *A hung over Sara emerges from the bathroom, clad in an oversized Chicago Bears jersey.*
> *She sees Miles, freaks.*

SARA: Oh!

MILES: Whoa!

SARA: Shit!

MILES: Sorry.

SARA: Sorry.

She tugs her shirt down.

MILES: Nice ... shirt.

    Small beat.

MILES: I'm the son.

SARA: What?

MILES: He didn't tell you he had a son.

SARA: No.

MILES: Cramps his style.

    Miles inspects the crackers on the coffee table.

MILES: 'Australian Water Wheel Wafers'. Wow.

    He shoves one in his mouth.

MILES: Don't feel weird, this happens a lot. So what's your name? Wait, can I guess?

SARA: I should—

MILES: —Is it Mandy? Nine times outta ten it's Mandy.

SARA: No.

MILES: I bet I could guess your age—no offense. Sorry, I'm Miles.

    Pause.

SARA: Nice ... meeting you.

MILES: Nice meeting you, too, 'sad-woman-wearing-Dad's-shirt'. Hey! That could be like your Indian name.

    He sees an album on the floor.

MILES: Uh oh.

SARA: What?

MILES: Did he play you Nina Simone?

SARA: I guess. I don't know.

MILES: Yikes.

SARA: Is there something you're trying to tell me?

MILES: No.

SARA: It just seems like, look—if your dad is some kind of *lady killer* or something—I mean, it's not anything I'm worried about.

MILES: 'Lady killer'?

SARA: Player. Whatever. It doesn't matter.

MILES: Cool.

SARA: And my name is Sara.

MILES: Cool, Sara.

SARA: And I'm not sad.

She punctuates this with a forced smile.

MILES: Good.

SARA: Do I look sad?

MILES: You look...really...fancy crackers are a good sign, by the way. It means he's trying. You wanna hear Dad's manifesto on females?

SARA: Not really.

MILES: Okay! One: Always tell them they're beautiful even if they're not. Two: Never let them pay, duh. Three: If you want them to sleep with you play Miles Davis, if you want them to fall in love with you play Nina Simone. Four: Always carry a copy of Jack Keorouac's On The Road—chicks love drifters—and Five: Always make them an egg or eggs in the morning. Are you thirty?

> *Beat.*

SARA: No.

MILES: Thirty-two?

> *Nothing.*

MILES: Four?

> *Sara remains mute.*

MILES: What, *six?*

SARA: What do you *want?*

MILES: Holy crap, don't tell me you're *forty.*

> *She heads for the bedroom.*

SARA: Nice meeting you.

MILES: Does my Dad know?!

SARA: Do you—is there some aspirin here?

MILES: Huh? Yeah, hold on a sec.

> *Miles leaps over the couch—runs to the bathroom.*
> *Sara quickly retrieves her bra from the couch.*
> *Miles returns with aspirin.*

MILES: Wal-bu-profin. You look really good for forty.

SARA: Gee, thanks.

> *He runs to the kitchen to get some water.*

MILES: *(O.S.)* Are you into my dad?

SARA: What?

MILES: *(O.S.)* Are you interested in my father?

SARA: I don't really have a strong opinion on the matter.

MILES: You think you guys will hang out again?
> *Miles returns with a glass of water.*

SARA: I have no idea.
> *Sara takes the aspirin.*

MILES: Oh, I get it. You're like what's-his-chops from On The Road, all 'don't tie me down, man'. That's cool.

SARA: No, I just . . . don't really make plans.

MILES: Why not?

SARA: Because it's easier that way. I need to go back—

MILES: Is it just with people or is it with everything? I mean, like, do you look forward to things? Like, if you ordered a burrito would you let yourself be psyched for it or would you not expect anything at all and just deal with it when the waitress brought it to you?

SARA: What?

MILES: I'm just wondering if you're a Buddhist.

SARA: No.
> *Miles studies her.*

MILES: Well you could be. If you wanted.
> *A fighter jet blazes through the outside sky.*

MILES: *(re: the planes)* You know The Blue Angels like, *synchronize their heartbeats* to keep from crashing?

SARA: No.

MILES: Kind of badass when you think about it.
> *An animal-like voice booms from the bedroom.*

JOE: *(O.S.)* Helloooo?

MILES: *(to Sara)* I'm not here.

SARA: *(to Joe)* Um . . . hello?

JOE: *(O.S.)* You left me!

MILES: Hangovers make him needy.
> *Miles puts his backpack on—heads for the door.*

MILES: See ya.
> *Miles exits.*
> *Another jet flies over—loud. Sara's hangover comes rushing back.*
> *Joe steps out of the bedroom—scratches himself.*

JOE: Ugh! What is this, freakin' Fallujah? Holy Christ.

SARA: It's the air show. Planes . . .

JOE: Sounded like they were landin' in the god damned *kitchen*. I
     don't know how those poor slobs deal with this shit over in
     wherever, ya know? Where it's for real? Wow, wait a second,
     somebody looks good in the morning—come here.
          He pulls her in.
SARA: My head.
JOE: Poor baby—bottle flu?
SARA: I guess.
JOE: I make you some eggs? I'll make you an egg sandwich!
SARA: I should get going.
JOE: What? Why? Let me take care of you.
SARA: Huh? Oh, no, that's okay.
JOE: Aw.
SARA: I've kind of got a family . . . thing.
JOE: Okay honey, that's fine. Family first, right? Family first.
SARA: Yeah.
          She exits to the bedroom.
JOE: *(to himself)* Egg sandwich . . .
          Joe stumbles off to the kitchen. Lights.

SCENE 4

     Graceland. Noon. Sam stands in the cemetery.
     Blue Angels fly overhead, die-down.
     Miles enters with a rake. He is dressed in Graceland groundskeep-
     ing clothes.

MILES: *(re planes)* Pretty intense, huh?
          Sam turns.
SAM: What?
MILES: The planes.
SAM: Oh . . . yeah.
          Miles comes closer.
MILES: You need help with something?
SAM: Waiting for my sister—always late.
MILES: Chicks.
SAM: *(amused)* Right.

Beat.
Miles takes a pack of cigarettes from his back pocket.

MILES: You got a light by any chance?

SAM: Sure.

Sam lights Miles' cigarette for him.

MILES: You hear about the smoking ban?

SAM: Yeah.

MILES: Figure it's okay to smoke in here what with everyone already being dead . . . Sorry, no disrespect.

Sam shrugs.

MILES: You lose someone close?

SAM: Not especially.

Beat.

SAM: *(re cigarettes)* You got another one of those, man?

MILES: Huh? Oh yeah, sure.

Miles gives Sam a smoke.

SAM: So, how does someone end up working at a cemetery?

MILES: Truth?

SAM: Uh . . . yeah.

MILES: I kind of use to be one of those kids that was into dead shit or whatever. You know like 'woe is me, let's listen to the Smiths twenty-four seven.' So like . . . workin' in the cemetery kind of completed the picture. Plus, I mean, twelve bucks an hour's not bad. No one bugs you. Nature.

Sam looks around.

SAM: It is really pretty here.

MILES: What do you do?

SAM: Um, I'm kind of in between jobs, it's . . . yeah, I fuckin' deliver fruit arrangements, man.

MILES: No shit?

SAM: Edible Creations.

MILES: I've seen that truck!

SAM: That's me.

MILES: Those things any good?

SAM: Strawberries dipped in chocolate. How bad can it be?

MILES: Women must love that stuff—show up with a bunch of flowers that they can *eat*.

SAM: I guess. I don't know.

MILES: So what kind of music do *you* like? Seem like maybe a Radio-head guy. Or old school Blues.

> *Sam shrugs.*

MILES: Dylan! Bob Dylan! Blood On The Tracks is the best break-up album ever, FYI.

SAM: I haven't been listening to anything much lately.

MILES: Man, when I stop listening to music I know shit is seriously messed up.

> *Sara enters, sees Miles—freezes.*

SAM: *There* you are.

MILES: Oh. Wow. *Okay.* Um. Hi?

SAM: Where where you?

SARA: Nowhere.

SAM: Well, your late.

SARA: Sorry.

SAM: This is my friend—

MILES: Miles. Hi.

SAM: Miles. Cool name.

SARA: You . . . work here?

MILES: Yes ma'am. Since ninth grade. Half day of school, half day at the bone orchard. Like me so much they let me stay all summer.

SAM: *(to Sara)* 'Bone orchard.'

SARA: Shut up. what are we doing?

SAM: We're supposed to look around and find examples of what we like monument-wise.

MILES: You should go uncut.

SAM: Sorry?

MILES: Uncut gravestones. Like the Burnhams. They have their own island with these big ass rocks for their headstones.

SARA: Fascinating.

MILES: It is! It's kind of like . . . organic or whatever.

SARA: *(as in: get lost)* Okay, so, anyway, have a good day. At work.

> *Blank looks.*

SAM: Don't mind her, she's rude when she's late.

MILES: Oh no, it's totally fine.

> *Miles starts to leave.*

SAM: Dad's watch stop working or something?
>> *She searches her purse.*

SARA: Shit.

SAM: What?

SARA: Nothing.

SAM: What are you looking for?

SARA: Nothing.

SAM: Where's Dad's watch?

SARA: It's—

SAM: You lost it already?

SARA: No!

MILES: Maybe you left it somewhere.
>> *She glares at him.*

MILES: Anyway, see ya, man. Bye . . . Sara.
>> *Miles exits.*

SARA: We should go.

SAM: What about the headstone?

SARA: What was he saying to you?

SAM: Nothing. Why were you so rude?

SARA: I wasn't. I just don't want some *troubled teen* looming around while we're figuring all this out.

SAM: That's funny coming from you. Where's Dad's watch?

SARA: It's . . . on the night stand at the hotel.

SAM: Tell me you didn't go home with that one guy.

SARA: What one guy?

SAM: The one who talked REALLY LOUD ABOUT HATING CATS?

SARA: I left right after you.
>> *Sam's cell vibrates. He pulls it out.*

SAM: Shit, I gotta go to work. Can you do this?

SARA: What?

SAM: The headstone!

SARA: Do I have to?

SAM: What is wrong with you?

SARA: Nothing. Go!
>> *Sam exits.*

SARA: *(to herself)* Fuck.

She looks around—nervous. Pulls out her cell, puts it back in her bag.
She briefly examines a headstone, quickly loses interest.
Miles returns.

SARA: What?

MILES: Sorry. I just wanted to say if you think you left your watch at our place I can totally look for it when I get home . . . Or not. I don't know. Sounded like it was important.

SARA: It is.

MILES: I have this T-shirt my mom used to wear—Neil Young After the Gold Rush—I'd be seriously bummed if I lost it.

SARA: Just—*go away.*

MILES: I'm really sorry about your dad. Your dad died, yeah?

SARA: Yeah.

MILES: How did—

SARA: *(quickly)*—Heart attack. When can I come pick up the watch?

MILES: Whenever you want. I'm home anytime after six.

SARA: Fine. Tell your father I'm coming, I don't have his number so just let him know if you don't mind.

MILES: *(teasing)* You remember how to get there?

SARA: Yes. I do.

MILES: I'll get out of your way.

He starts to walk away—stops.

MILES: Hey, it's super nice over by the Marshall Field tomb. There's lavender. It's calming.

Miles walks off. Sara watches him go.

Music cue: The Smiths 'How Soon Is Now' transitions to the next scene.

SCENE 5

Joe's place. Later. Miles dances to The Smiths 'How Soon Is Now'.
He checks the microwave, gets plates out of the cupboard.
The buzzer goes off—he buzzes whoever it is in, cracks the door open and turns off the stereo
A moment later there Sara is standing there.

MILES: Oh . . . I thought you were someone else.

SARA: Is your dad here?

MILES: No! I'm making pizza puffs.

SARA: Where is he?

MILES: He's in Detroit for the weekend. Trade show—bath mats—I mean textiles. Come on in.

SARA: Do you have the watch?

MILES: Uh, no. Dad's room is kind of a black hole. And I mean, I'm sure it's in there but I haven't found it yet, so why don't you just come in and take a look, we can both look.

SARA: I'll wait.

MILES: For what?

SARA: While you look for it again.

MILES: Oh. Okay . . . Are you hungry?

SARA: No.

MILES: That's cool.

> *He heads to the bedroom.*
> *Sara goes to the couch, searches the cushions.*

MILES: *(O.S.)* What kind of watch is it again?

SARA: A pocket watch . . . it has a star on it, stars . . .

> *Miles returns, watches Sara for a moment. He smells his wrists.*

MILES: My dad swears by this stuff—'Brut' something or other—what do you think?

> *He holds his wrist out.*

SARA: Yeah. Did you find it?

MILES: Not yet. Doesn't mean it's not there. Look, let's just go step by step. When did you see it last?

SARA: Last night.

MILES: What were you guys doing, while you were here?

SARA: Nothing. We had a drink.

MILES: Then what?

SARA: I'm not going to do this.

MILES: Do what?

SARA: Can I go look? I'm going to go look, alright?

> *She heads to the bedroom, all business.*

MILES: Yeah, sure . . .

> *Miles pulls the pocket watch out of his jeans . . .*

MILES: *(to himself)* Look . . .

He stuffs it back in his pocket—sings the Smiths song.

MILES: 'I am human and I need to be loved . . . just like everybody else does.'

He grabs a beer from the fridge—opens it.

MILES: *(yells)* So your dad was a pretty popular guy, huh?

SARA: *(O.S.)* No, why?

MILES: Red headed chick crying by his thing today after you left.

SARA: *What?*

She bolts out of the bedroom.

MILES: *(re the beer)* This is for you, it's made by monks.

SARA: What chick? When?

MILES: Today. I don't know. She had red hair, she was crying . . . a lot. You know her?

SARA: Yeah, unfortunately.

MILES: Your dad's girlfriend or something?

SARA: No! God, no.

MILES: Oh. Well, I mean, it's an emotional place, Graceland. Loss and what have you.

SARA: She didn't lose anything.

Sara grabs the beer from him.

MILES: I read once that people in their forties are either super depressed or super calm and wise.

SARA: Did you *talk* to her?

MILES: You seem like you're kind of a combo plate. No, I didn't talk to her. Why, who is she?

SARA: My brother's ex girlfriend—forget it. I should go.

MILES: My dad went out with this chick once that stole his shoes. All of them. He wept.

The microwave beeps.

MILES: Pizza puffs!

Miles goes to the kitchen—dumps the pizza puffs onto two plates.

MILES: They're from Trader Joe's.

He sets the plates on the coffee table.

MILES: After you.

SARA: I'm fine.

MILES: You say that a lot.

He sits—pops a puff in his mouth.

MILES: *(real pain)* Ouch! Hot! Can I have the—
> *He motions for the beer. She hesitates—gives it to him. He drinks.*

SARA: How old are you?

MILES: Eighteen. Dix-huit. That's French.
> *Painful silence.*

MILES: This is fun. It would be funner if you sat down but it's totally cool if you want to stand.
> *She gives in—sits on the edge of a living room chair—far from him.*

MILES: You know what I thought when I saw you standing in the living room this morning?

SARA: No, what?

MILES: I thought, finally—proof of God.

SARA: Right.

MILES: I'm serious! Then you were at Graceland this afternoon and now here you are now, and, I don't know, it's mildly religious.
> *She tries not to smile.*

MILES: What did you think when you saw me?

SARA: I wanted to run.

MILES: Oh. Okay.

SARA: Why are you doing this?

MILES: Doing what?

SARA: Talking to me? Sitting here with me? I mean, shouldn't you be out stealing bikes or something?

MILES: Is that a joke?

SARA: No.

MILES: Hasn't anyone ever liked talking to you?

SARA: Of course, lots of people.

MILES: Well, add me to the list.
> *Beat.*

SARA: *(re: his shirt)* Is that your mom's shirt you were talking about?

MILES: Oh. Yeah. Neil Young.

SARA: Where is she?

MILES: Uh . . . well . . . she's dead.

SARA: Oh, shit. I'm sorry.

MILES: It's okay.

SARA: Your father didn't say anything.

MILES: Rule number six: 'Be discreet with the details, the less they know the better.'

SARA: Rule number six ...

MILES: Mystery.

SARA: Great.

MILES: So, do you have like, 'rules' or anything when it comes to the male of the species?

SARA: No.

MILES: Really?

SARA: Why, what would you suggest?

MILES: Um. What about ... rule number one: 'If he doesn't treat you like the amazing goddess that you obviously are, run for the hills and don't look back.'

SARA: I'm not a goddess.

MILES: Rule number two: 'Know how fucking great you are.'

SARA: Who are you? I mean, seriously.

MILES: I'm Miles.

> *Small beat.*

MILES: Can I ask you something? And please don't think I'm being disgusting, this is purely like, to obtain family knowledge but .. . is my dad, you know, good in bed?

SARA: *Excuse me?*

MILES: I'm totally not trying to be sick.

SARA: I knew it.

MILES: Knew what? All he said was that you had soft skin!

SARA: Oh my God.

MILES: The softest actually!

SARA: You're disgusting.

MILES: Why is that disgusting? I think it's nice! He never said 'I slept with Sara and it went like this.'

SARA: I don't want to know!

MILES: From the amount of women that stream through this place I'm guessing he's not bad.

> *She gets up—heads to the door.*

SARA: I *really* don't want to know, okay?

MILES: *(blurts out)* I've never been in love!

She stops.

SARA: *What?*

MILES: I was wondering if you could tell me what it's like.

SARA: Are you kidding?

MILES: No . . . Yes . . . Yes I am! Totally kidding.

He gets up, a little frantic.

MILES: I'm gonna make tea. Don't go. I'll make us tea. We have this stuff that has fortunes, quotes, on each bag, you'll love it, they're deep. Like Buddhist deep.

He scrambles to put a kettle on.

SARA: I didn't sleep with your father.

MILES: I'm sorry, I just thought—

SARA:—And if I did, it's none of your business.

MILES: I know. I'm an asshole. Okay? Flat out.

She says nothing.

SARA: Did he say he slept with me?

MILES: No! He just said you had soft skin. Please don't go. Just . . . have some tea. I won't ask any more dumb questions.

He busies himself with tea preperation.

MILES: *(re box of tea)* 'Elysian Fields'. Wonder what that tastes like.

SARA: It's like drugs.

MILES: What?

SARA: Love. It's like being on drugs.

MILES: What kind of drugs?

SARA: The kind that make you feel like shit.

Beat.

MILES: That sucks.

SARA: I wouldn't recommend it.

Miles thinks.

MILES: "Love is a fog that burns with the first daylight of reality."

SARA: Your dad said that?

MILES: No. Bukowski. I saw it on YouTube. I like to research things. You ever call the Answers line?

SARA: I don't know what that is.

MILES: Public library. They have this number you can call and ask whatever you want. It's awesome. Like—Who invented hot dogs: most likely the Viennese or the Germans. Or How do you

say 'I'm sorry' in Navajo: actually there is no word for I'm sorry
in Navajo but '*Yanisin*' means 'I am ashamed'.

>   *Beat.*

MILES: We totally reamed the Native Americans, I plan on apologizing if I ever meet one.

SARA: I'm sure they'll appreciate that.

MILES: It's really cool—the Answers line—you should try it.

SARA: I like Google.

MILES: There's no one to talk to at Google. The Answers Line has
people, you talk to real people.

>   *The kettle starts to whistle. Miles runs to make tea.*

MILES: Hey, maybe I'll call them and ask for answers about you.

SARA: Let me know what you find out.

MILES: I will.

SARA: Good.

MILES: Great.

>   *Miles makes tea—hands her a cup.*
>   *He reads the quote on his tea bag.*

MILES: *(re tea bag quote)* 'Recognize that the other person is you'.
Heavy.

>   *Beat.*

MILES: What's yours say?

SARA: *(reads)* 'You are infinite.'

MILES: I'm pretty sure that means you'll never die.

SARA: Wonderful.

MILES: What was your dad like?

SARA: *(off guard)* What?

MILES: Your dad—what was he like?

SARA: Like a dad, I don't know . . .

>   *They drink their tea. She thinks.*

SARA: He liked country music.

MILES: Like Johnny Cash?

SARA: Yeah, and old hymns, stuff like that.

MILES: I don't even know what a hymn sounds like.

SARA: *(sings, barely)* 'Will the circle, be unbroken . . . ' you know.

MILES: Keep going.

SARA: I'm tone deaf.

MILES: No you're not.

SARA: 'By and by lord, by and by'. Anyway.

MILES: I like that.

SARA: We didn't really see each other that much.

MILES: Why?

SARA: Because I live in New York.

MILES: Holy shit, I love New York, that's amazing! What do you do there?

SARA: Sell knives.

MILES: What!?

SARA: I work at a gourmet cookware store. I manage it, it's—is this an interview?

MILES: No. Sorry. I'm just interested.

> *They sip their tea.*

SARA: I'm . . . sorry about your mom.

MILES: Oh no, it's fine. You know who you remind me of?

SARA: Please don't say your mother.

MILES: No! Shit. No, you remind me of . . . one of those French actresses. You know how they like, live alone and wear dresses all the time and they're not all perfect? And they walk around in the rain with sunglasses on.

> *She smiles.*

MILES: Not perfect is good by the way.

SARA: I don't wear dresses.

MILES: That's too bad.

> *Beat.*

MILES: You don't know how pretty you are, do you?

> *Beat.*

MILES: That's cool. It makes you prettier—not knowing.

SARA: I should—

MILES: Hey, I found out how the Blue Angels—

SARA: Go . . . What?

MILES: I found out how the Blue Angels synchronize their heartbeats. It's all breathing. Check it out.

> *He goes to the middle of the living room, reaches his hand out.*

MILES: Come here.

SARA: What.

MILES: Come here. You'll love this.
>	*She goes to him. He tries to take her hand.*
MILES: Okay, so, the deal is . . . here . . . just walk with me.
>	*They slowly circle the living room together—side by side.*
MILES: Now breathe.
SARA: I am breathing.
MILES: With me.
>	*They synchronize their steps.*
MILES: In—two—three—four. Out—two—three—four. See?
SARA: No.
MILES: Okay, let's just try the breathing.
>	*They stop. Miles takes her hands. They are facing each other.*
MILES: In—two—three—four. Out—two—three—four—that's when they do the barrel rolls—In—two—three—four. Out—two—three—four. One guy counts and they all just get on the same exact rhythm. In—two—three . . .
>	*They continue—silent.*
MILES: Just counting and breathing.
>	*A moment.*
SARA: The watch.
MILES: Wait, can I just see something?
>	*He takes her wrist.*
SARA: What are you doing?
MILES: Just don't say anything.
>	*He checks her pulse.*
>	*Silence.*
>	*A moment.*
>I think it worked.
>	*Beat.*
>	*She moves toward him . . . a kiss. Slow and awkward at first, then thing heat up.*
>	*He maneuvers her to the couch—gets on top of her kissing her the whole time.*
>	*Then:*
>	*The front door opens.*
>	*Joe enters-*
>	*Miles and Sara scramble for composure.*
JOE: What the *fuck?!*
MILES: Dad!

SARA: Shit!

JOE: You gotta be kidding me!

SARA: Shit!

MILES: What about Detroit?

JOE: Show was empty, no one gives a shit. What are you doing to my son?

SARA: Nothing!

MILES: She left a watch here!

JOE: Why aren't you at your mother's?

MILES: What?

SARA: *What?*

MILES: Wait!

SARA: I thought your mother was dead?

JOE: HA! Is that what he told you? Hardly. She lives on the 10th floor.

MILES: Sara, I'm—

sara:—Fuck! I'm leaving, I'm out of here. Do you have my watch?

JOE: What the hell were you doing to my son?

SARA: Nothing!

JOE: Man, you weren't kidding when you said you like 'em young! You know I could call the cops on you, right? Fifteen? You need to brush up on your statutory limits.

SARA: Fifteen?!

MILES: *(screams)* No! Dad!

SARA: Fifteen?

JOE: I'm not calling the fuckin' cops, Jesus Christ. All she needs.

SARA: What do you mean all I need?

JOE: I mean I don't think ya need the fucking cops called on ya four days after your old man blew his head off.

    Everything stops.

MILES: What?

    Silence.

MILES: Is that true?

JOE: Oh it's true, alright. Hit me this morning: Tall. Gimlets. Pall Malls? I knew the guy! Caruso, right? Don Caruso. Everybody's talkin' about it. Bought the bar a round, paid the tab, went home and blew himself away. Some bleak shit, some real bleak shit. I think I can cut you a break here, but you need to go.

SARA: Were you there? At the bar, that day?

JOE: No honey, I wasn't there.

SARA: But you know people who were?

JOE: Yeah sure.

SARA: What did they say?

JOE: Said he bought the bar a round. I told ya—

SARA:—WHAT DID THEY SAY!?

JOE: I WASN'T THERE! I told ya what I know. Now I think you need to pack up your stuff here and leave. We're sorry for your loss. Truly. I can't imagine.

> *Miles moves towards her.*

MILES: I'll walk you.

SARA: Stay the *FUCK* away from me.

JOE: Son—dignity.

SARA: *(to Joe)* Where is my father's watch?

JOE: Oh man, you gotta be kidding me! I don't have your old man's watch, okay?

> *There is a KNOCK at the door.*

JOE: Holy hell, now what?

MILES: Don't get it.

> *Joe flings the door open.*
> *Sam stands holding a 'flower arrangement' made of fruit.*

SARA: *Sam?*

MILES: Oh shit.

SAM: *Sara?*

SARA: What are you doing here?

SAM: Delivering a Strawberry fucking Fields . . . What are *you* doing here?

JOE: Think you got the wrong place buddy.

MILES: *(quiet)* No he doesn't.

JOE: You ordered this horseshit?

SAM: Sara?

MILES: I asked for the early delivery!

SAM: We're behind—air show barbecues—Sara?

JOE: *(looks at invoice)* Forty bucks. I'm in the wrong business.

SAM: What the fuck is going on?

SARA: Dad's watch. I came to get Dad's watch.

JOE: And a few "other things".

MILES: Dad!

SAM: You didn't.

SARA: It's not—

SAM: —Why would Dad's watch be here?

SARA: Because I left it here.

SAM: When?

JOE: Okay, I think you both need to go.

> *To Sara*

JOE: Your dad liked 'em young too if I recall. Him and that redhead, shoulda figured you go after—

> *Sam throws the fruit arrangement. Joe ducks. Strawberries everywhere.*
> *Sam lunges at Joe—from here on out things border on mass hysteria.*

SAM: Don't you fuckin' talk to her like that!

> *Adlib chaos.*

MILES: Dad! Dad!

> *Miles pulls them apart.*

SAM: Jesus *Christ*, Sara.

> *Sam shakes himself loose of Miles.*

SAM: Let's go.

SARA: What's he talking about?

SAM: Now!

SARA: What red head?!

> *Blackout*

SCENE 6

> *Graceland cemetery—dawn. Sam and Sara are curled up on the ground. An empty bottle of Jameson's lies nearby.*
> *Sam opens his eyes, realizes where he is. He nudges Sara's foot with his own.*

SAM: Hey.

> *Beat.*

SAM: Sare.

> *Beat.*

SAM: Hey.

> *He nudges her.*

SARA: Dad?

SAM: No.

> *She opens her eyes.*

SARA: Oh . . .

SAM: You alright?

SARA: What time is it?

> *He checks the clock on his cell.*

SAM: Almost six.

> *She looks around.*

SARA: Really?

SAM: We jumped the fence last night.

SARA: Oh yeah . . .

> *Beat.*

SARA: Why?

SAM: You were convinced Anna was going to be here.

SARA: Was she?

SAM: No. Just us and some raccoons. Apparently there's an infestation.

> *Sara sits up, sleepy.*

SARA: I dreamt I was living in a house made of vodka gimlets . . . and Dad was watering the lawn with Roses Lime Juice.

> *Beat.*

SARA: Remember how no one could make his gimlets the way he liked? They always put too much Roses in?

SAM: 'Light on the Roses'.

SARA: I use to think he was talking about flowers.

> *Sara yawns.*

SARA: We jumped the fence?

SAM: You did. I kind of just threw myself over.

SARA: Just like the old days.

SAM: Stairway to Heaven . . .

SARA: Zeppelin.

> *She looks around.*

SAM: You want to go get some breakfast?

SARA: Do you have any pot?

SAM: Uh . . . . yeah

SARA: *(matter of fact)* Can I have it?

SAM: Okay . . .

> *He pulls a baggie out of his pocket—loads a pipe—hands it to her.*

SAM: It's stronger than the stuff we use to get in—

> *She lights up.*

sam:—Okay, you're fine.

SARA: I smoke pot.

> *Exhales.*

SAM: I can see that.

SARA: In New York.

SAM: Nice of you to give me such grief about it when you visit.

> *She smokes.*

SARA: I didn't know he was fifteen.

SAM: I know.

> *Beat.*

SARA: What happened?

SAM: Kid ordered an arrangement, we got backed up.

SARA: Not that—Anna, Dad and Anna.

SAM: I told you already.

SARA: Tell me again.

SAM: *(a list:)* Dad's birthday. Deacons. She brought her guitar. She played a Linda Rondstadt song. Dad told her she was timeless . . . They sang harmonies and I went home.

SARA: You left them there.

SAM: I don't know how to sing harmonies.

> *Beat.*

SAM: I had class in the morning. 'Emotional Disturbances of Adolescence'.

SARA: I thought you quit school.

SAM: I did. A couple of weeks later.

> *Beat.*

SARA: Why would you date someone like that?

SAM: Probably for the same reason you date people that are half your age and completely inappropriate.

SARA: I don't date people who are half my age.

SAM: Sorry, a third. I'm so bad at math.

SARA: It wasn't a date.

SAM: I don't want to know. I'm starved. You coming?

> *Beat.*

SARA: Were they in *love* or something?

SAM: I don't know.

> *Beat.*

SARA: Were you?

SAM: I . . . don't know.

SARA: Do you even care that this happened?

SAM: What do you think?

SARA: I don't know, you don't seem like you give a shit.

SAM: Trust me.

SARA: Well get mad then. Yell or something. Fuck something up.

> *She picks up the empty Jamesons bottle.*

SAM: What are you doing?

SARA: *(mischief)* I break things.

SAM: Uh huh.

> *She waves the bottle around.*

SARA: At work . . . On purpose. It's fun.

> *Sam looks worried.*
> *Sara yells—a demonstration.*

SAM: Would you not do that?

SARA: Try it.

SAM: No.

SARA: Come on.

> *She yells again.*

SAM: Sara! Stop it!

SARA: I will, when you do it!

> *She yells again. He finally joins in. Loud and fun.*
> *A fighter jet interrupts them.*
> *They stop, watch it.*

SAM: Maybe she made him happy.

> *Sara looks at him—'are you kidding me?'.*

SAM: I mean, obviously not happy enough.

> *She pokes him with the Jameson's bottle.*

SARA: Come on.

> *Another fighter jet rips through the sky as they leave.*

SCENE 7

Joe's apartment. Later that morning. Joe concocts some kind of 'health shake' in a powerful blender, it's green. Miles enters—tries to avert his father's gaze.

JOE: *(re the shake)* Colon blow?

MILES: No thanks.

JOE: Don't know what your missin'.
> *Joe pours his shake.*

JOE: I'll be in the john in ten minutes tops.

MILES: *(under his breath)* Good for you.

JOE: Damn straight it is. You outta try it.
> *Miles begins gathering his things.*

JOE: So?

MILES: What?

JOE: One for the books, huh?

MILES: Uh huh.

JOE: Cuckoo for Cocoa Puffs.
> *Miles shrugs.*

JOE: You wanna talk about it?

MILES: Not really.

JOE: Alright, discretion. Classy.
> *No response.*

JOE: What do ya got goin' on today?

MILES: Nothing. Work.

JOE: Must be saving up some cheese all the hours you put in.
> *Joe chugs more of his shake.*

JOE: Think I'll head over to the gym, maybe check out Gina's class. Remember Gina?

MILES: Nope.

JOE: With the hips?
> *Beat.*

JOE: Curls my toes the way those gals can bend.

MILES: Maybe I'll check it out sometime.
> *Beat.*

JOE: So what, she do some kind of Mrs. Robinson thing?

MILES: I don't know what that is.

JOE: Flash her wares?

> *Puzzled look from Miles.*

JOE: You know, seduce you?

MILES: She wanted her dad's watch.

JOE: Uh huh. Well it's hard to resist the crazies, that's for sure.

> *No response.*

JOE: I remember—I was a little older than you—there was this *stewardess*, back when they were still incredible . . . she had this *orange* uniform, size of a postage stamp . . .

> *Joe reminisces.*

JOE: Wait a minute.

MILES: What?

JOE: I think I'm startin' to figure this out.

MILES: Okay.

JOE: I'll say. *You* seduced her . . . didn't you?

MILES: We talked, Dad.

JOE: Oldest trick in the book—talking. Hell, I taught ya that.

> *Joe steps back.*

JOE: I'll be a sonofabitch. Christ, I'm gettin' old.

MILES: No you're not.

JOE: Yeah I am. I don't even know what kind of jeans I'm supposed to wear anymore.

> *Beat.*

JOE: What's it like?

MILES: What's what like?

JOE: You know, all of it. I can't remember.

MILES: Why are you being so intense?

JOE: Called gettin' old buddy. C'mere, let me look at you.

MILES: I'm right here.

JOE: Get over here. Now.

> *Miles moves closer to his father.*

JOE: God, I'd kill to be you. You have no idea. You're just flyin', you know? Got nothin' to worry about.

MILES: I worry, Dad.

JOE: Oh yeah? What do you think about when you wake up in the middle of the night?

MILES: I don't wake up in the middle of the night.

JOE: That's what I thought. Now come here—

> *Joe grabs Miles for what appears to be a hug but turns into a noogie.*

JOE:—So I can kick your ass!

MILES: Stop. Dad.

> *Miles wriggles free.*

JOE: I don't know whether to congratulate you or beat the crap outta ya. You know some dad's might not take too kindly to their son moving in on their woman.

MILES: You think she's your woman?

JOE: I'm just saying. Watch yourself, Bud. Some mythological shit you're messin' with there.

> *Miles doesn't react.*
> *The buzzer goes off.*
> *A Blue Angels jet buzzes over.*

JOE: For the love of God.

> *Joe goes to the buzzer.*

JOE: Yeah?

VOICE: It's Sam Caruso.

JOE: Who?

VOICE: Sam Caruso.

MILES: Her brother.

VOICE: Do you have a minute?

JOE: This should be good.

> *Joe buzzes Sam up.*

MILES: I should go.

JOE: Just hold on a minute. I might need ya for some back-up.

MILES: What are you talking about?

JOE: Come on, it'll be fun. Sit down.

> *Miles sits on the chair—perturbed.*
> *Joe 'covers' the couch area—ready to rumble.*
> *Sam enters.*

SAM: Hey.

MILES: Hi.

SAM: You okay?

MILES: Fine.

JOE: What, no banana bouquet?

SAM: Uh, no. It's . . . about my sister.

MILES: What happened?

SAM: Nothing. I just wanted to make sure everything was cool over here.

JOE: Funny you should ask, we were just discussing the lady, weren't we son?

MILES: No.

SAM: She's been under a lot of stress. I don't think she meant any harm.

JOE: Debateable.

MILES: Dad.

SAM: I know you mentioned the police.

MILES: He's not calling—

JOE: —Technically something illegal *may have* occurred. Though I'm not getting much info out of this one. Miles? Thoughts?

MILES: No.

JOE: He's still a little traumatized.

MILES: I'm not traumatized.

JOE: Well *I* am.

SAM: I'm really sorry if my sister did anything—

MILES: —She didn't do anything!

JOE: Depends on how you look at it.

MILES: Dad!

JOE: I'm just sayin' these things can get a little murky.

SAM: Did you by chance find a pocket watch?

JOE: Here we go with the goddammed watch.

MILES: I'm leaving.

> *Miles bolts. Joe chases him*

JOE: Hey! Wait! Get back here!

> *Miles is gone.*
> *Sam is alone with Joe.*

JOE: *(re: Miles)* Still waters.

> *Sam smiles—unsure.*

JOE: Gets it from his mother. Who is very much alive contrary to what you may have heard.

SAM: I didn't hear anything.

> *Joe walks back in the apartment. His body language suggests that the 'colon blow' is starting to take affect.*
> *A jet flies over.*

JOE: Anything else?

SAM: Um . . . well, yeah, I was wondering . . . did you know our father?

JOE: Saw him a couple of times at the bar but that's about it.

SAM: What was he doing? When you saw him?

JOE: How the hell would I know?

SAM: Was he alone?

JOE: What—is this about the red head?

SAM: Did you see them together?

JOE: Once or twice. Look, I'm not gonna call the cops on your sister. No one was hurt. Just keep her away from my kid and we'll call it even.

SAM: Yeah. Of course.

> *Beat.*

SAM: I'm sorry, this will . . . can you just tell me what they were doing . . . when you saw them?

JOE: They *were at a bar.* They were *drinking.*

SAM: Did they look happy?

JOE: Are you asking me if they were fucking?

SAM: No!

JOE: It sounds like you're asking me if they were fucking.

SAM: I'm not!

JOE: What do you got against your old man enjoying the pleasures— (suddenly gets it)—oh . . . okay . . . I get it . . . this is about *you* and the redhead.

> *Sam crumbles a little.*

JOE: Jesus. So I'm not the only one gettin' cock blocked by my own flesh and blood, huh?

SAM: I don't—yeah.

> *Joe slaps Sam on the back.*

JOE: That is a son of a bitch, my friend, I don't know what to tell you. I thought I had this shit figured out but the more I think about it, the more I realize it's a minor miracle I can get from A to B without blowing my brains out . . . (realizes what he's said) I mean—I didn't mean—*shit* . . . you want a beer or something?

SAM: No thanks.

JOE: 'Course not, it's ten in the morning . . . I got a kind of health shake thing goin' over here if you want, got close to a pound of kale in it.

Sam actually smiles a little.
They both reflect for a moment.

JOE: You know your dad was . . . a good guy. I mean I didn't know him
    but I think he was . . . well liked over there . . . at the bar, so . . .

SAM: Thanks.

JOE: Yeah . . . you'll excuse me then, I gotta use the john.
    Sam steps back. Joe shuts the door.

SCENE 8

Graceland—later. Sara watches the Blue Angels.
She begins to walk in circles, slowly, methodically.
Miles appears—she walks away.

MILES: *(quiet)* Sorry.
    He backs away.

MILES: You were doing the breathing thing, weren't you?
    She pulls her cell out of her purse, starts randomly pressing
    numbers.

MILES: Sara?

SARA: *(to phone)* Fucker.
    She glares at him—stonefaced.

MILES: Hi . . .
    She goes back to her phone.
    A jet blasts overhead.

MILES: Imagine if one crashed. They do, you know, every few years.
    Are you not going to talk to me at all?
    Still nothing.

MILES: That's cool.
    She looks at him again.
    He walks toward her.

SARA: Don't.

MILES: Can I just say something?

SARA: You lied.

MILES: You didn't do anything wrong.

SARA: You and your dad do this a lot?

MILES: Do what?

SARA: Fuck with people.

MILES: No.

SARA: Part of the father/son training?

MILES: He didn't have anything to do with anything. I liked you—when I met you the other morning. You aren't like the other—okay, sorry, I guess I just related to you or something. I mean you're not like the happiest person on the planet, right? And like . . . neither am I. Neither is anyone as far as I'm concerned but everyone goes around faking it and saying how 'great' they are and it's all total bullshit. And I could tell you weren't one of the them, you know, like even though you're always saying you're fine I know that you're not, and that's okay, that's normal, right? But like, what is normal? Okay, now I sound like a fucking teenager which is whatever, it's fine—see, now *I'm* saying 'fine'. What I mean is, you made me feel like . . . maybe I was . . .

> *Out of nowhere—*
> *Anna, the redhead appears.*

MILES: Oh, shit.

> *Sara turns—sees her.*

ANNA: Hey.

SARA: Hey.

ANNA: I was hoping I might find you here. I wanted to give you this.

> *Anna takes an envelope from her bag, hands it to Sara—*
> *who refuses to take it.*

SARA: What is that?

ANNA: It's from your dad.

SARA: Where did you get it?

ANNA: It was on the dash of his car. 'S and S'—Sam and Sara.

> *Beat.*

SARA: I don't want that.

ANNA: You don't know what it is.

SARA: I don't care what it is, I don't want it.

> *Anna is lost.*

ANNA: Is . . . Sam . . . I mean, how is he?

SARA: Let's see . . . well, he's no longer attending classes, he smokes pot like he's going to the electric chair and he's delivering flower arrangements made of fruit so yeah, he's fucking stellar.

ANNA: He quit school?

SARA: I guess he kind of lost the ability to give a shit. Seems to be a theme in our family. Quit school, sleep with a teenager, shoot yourself in the head, what's the difference? Life's short, might as well fuck it up, right Miles?

MILES: I—what?

ANNA: Who are you?

MILES: No one. We didn't sleep together.

SARA: Shut up.

ANNA: Maybe I should go.

SARA: Why? You just got here. Let's catch up! You know what I found out? Men kill themselves more than women. I looked it up, Googled it! Suicide: men, women. Apparently women worry too much about people they'd be leaving behind, you know, 'loved ones'. Loved ones! I jumped off the roof of our garage when I was six but all I did was knock the wind out of myself. That's the other thing—women suck at killing themselves, they fuck it up. We just can't do anything right can we? What about you, you ever give it a shot?

ANNA: . . . No.

SARA: Well, there's always time. What are you doing sleeping with an old man who does crosswords anyway? Is that some kind of daddy thing?

ANNA: Look, Sara—

SARA: Cause he's *my* dad. He was my dad. I know he was just a fuck to you—

ANNA: That's not true.

SARA: But he was my dad.

ANNA: I know he was your dad. Look, I didn't plan on any of this happening. I didn't plan on it. I can't control who I care about . . . it's not something you can choose—it just happened, I don't know, I'm sorry, I never—

SARA: Sorry? Why? For fucking your boyfriend's father? Come on, who gives a shit!? How was it, by the way? Were father and son, you know, comparable? Or was one better than the other? My money's on Dad, I don't know, is that creepy?

    Beat.

ANNA: He missed you.

SARA: Bullshit.

ANNA: 'Sara's the only one who gets me.' That's what he'd say, over
and over,'Sara's the only one.'

Anna throws the envelope on the ground.

ANNA: I didn't have to tell you that.

Anna exits.

SARA: *(somewhere else)* Miles, give me your lighter.

MILES: Why?

SARA: Because I need to burn something.

MILES: I . . . quit smoking.

SARA: Give me your lighter Miles, and I'll forgive you.

MILES: For what?

SARA: Give it to me.

Pause.

MILES: No.

He takes the pocket watch out of his jeans, hands it to her.

MILES: I found it before you came over yesterday. I didn't tell you because I wanted you to stay.

Beat.

MILES: So, forgive me for giving a shit. I wanted you to stay.

*Miles takes the note from the ground and leaves. Sara con-
tinues to stare at the watch.*

Lights.

SCENE 9

Graceland. Later. Sara paces. She is on her cell.
Sam enters.
She closes the phone.

SAM: What happened?

SARA: *(holds up her cell)* Know where I was when Dad left this message?

SAM: No.

SARA: Getting my nails done. I had a date with the guy with the tattoos so you know, French manicure, important . . . Dad's about
to blow his head off and I'm getting white tips because some
twenty-two year old thinks it's hot.

SAM: What happened with Anna?

SARA: I was an asshole. What else.

SAM: Did you hurt her?

SARA: No I didn't hurt her—do I look like someone who's going to hurt people?

> *No response.*

SARA: Sam?

SAM: What?

SARA: Do I look like someone who's going to hurt people?

SAM: I don't think there's a look.

SARA: But if you didn't know me, what would you think?

SAM: I do know you Sara.

SARA: Come on, you know what I mean. If you saw me what would you think?

SAM: Can we not play this game?

SARA: It's not a game. What do you see when you look at me? I just want to know.

SAM: Where's this note? You said she had a note.

SARA: Fuck the note, it's not here.

SAM: Where is it?

SARA: Miles took it. Tell me what you see.

SAM: What do you mean he took it, why?

SARA: For his fucking collection, I don't know!

SAM: What are you talking about!?

SARA: TELL ME WHAT YOU FUCKING SEE!

SAM: DAD!

> *Beat.*
> *Absolute stillness.*

SAM: I see Dad.

> *She is stunned.*

SAM: You push people. You don't know when to stop. You drive people away and then want them back. You can't fathom why anyone would love you but when someone does it's never enough. You're so angry you don't even know it. You make horrific romantic choices again and again . . . And your jokes suck.

> *A long beat. Sara takes this in.*

SARA: Wow.

SAM: Sorry.

SARA: It's never enough, you're right.
>
> *Beat.*
>
> *Sam reaches in his pocket, pulls out a vial.*

SARA: What are those?

SAM: Doggie Valium.
>
> *He pops one in his mouth.*

SARA: Jesus.
>
> *She pulls out the pocket watch—hands it to Sam.*

SARA: Miles had it.

SAM: What is he—some kind of klepto or something?

SARA: No. He just liked talking to me. I'm big with the fifteen year olds.

SAM: I'll say.
>
> *Beat.*

SARA: Hey, I got a joke for you: What do ghosts drink?

SAM: I don't know—what?

SARA: Spirits!

SAM: Good one.

SARA: If I were a ghost I'd want a Harvey Wallbanger.

SAM: What is that?

SARA: I don't know but I want one. Maybe I'm dead.
>
> *She is starting to unravel—does her best to keep it together.*

SAM: No, you'd want a gimlet.

SARA: Of course, a gimlet. How dumb of me.

SAM: 'Light on the Roses'.

SARA: Light on the Roses . . . sounds like a country song.
>
> *Beat.*
>
> *It looks as though she might completely fall apart.*

SARA: Aw fuck . . .
>
> *She keeps it together.*

SAM: Sare?

SARA: No . . .

SAM: It's okay.

SARA: I think . . . he was lonely . . . I am . . . lonely.
>
> *Sara dissolves into quiet tears, crumbles to the ground. Sam goes to her—sits next to her.*
>
> *Lights.*

SCENE 10

> *Joe's apartment. Later. Joe stands at the window, holds a glass of white wine. The evening sun shines on his face. The intro to Nina Simone's 'Feelin' Good' plays on his stereo.*
> *The buzzer buzzes—he goes to the intercom.*

JOE: Yeah?

SARA'S VOICE: It's Sara Caruso.

> *Joe waits a beat. Buzzes her in. Cracks the door open. The music hits a raunchy bridge—Joe rushes to the stereo— turns it off. Goes to the kitchen counter and peels carrots. A few moments Sara stands at the door.*

SARA: Hi.

JOE: How are ya?

> *He stops peeling carrots.*

SARA: Um. You know.

> *He walks to her.*

JOE: Yeah.

SARA: Can I talk to you for a minute?

JOE: I can probably handle that. Come on in.

> *She walks in—unsure.*

SARA: The light's so pretty in here right now.

JOE: Yeah, think they call it dusk. Best time of day to take a picture . . . or make love.

> *Beat.*

SARA: Last night, it wasn't—I didn't—the thing is, I haven't been doing so well lately. Obviously.

JOE: Your dad died.

SARA: Yeah, my dad died. But this started a long time ago.

JOE: What's that?

SARA: Self—you know—destructive—but it's no excuse for—what I mean is, your son, Miles, I, I'm just very sorry about what happened, which was nothing, really, but it was still, Jesus Christ I suck at apologizing.

> *Beat.*

JOE: You're a beautiful woman.

SARA: Actually, I think I'm a sad woman.

JOE: A sad and beautiful woman. I think we have a foreign film on our hands.

    She smiles.

JOE: Hey, that was a good time the other night, huh? Me and you? Nina Simone?

SARA: Yeah. It was.

JOE: I thought so.

    A moment.

SARA: Is . . . Miles here?

JOE: He's on the roof. Watching the end of the airshow.

    Beat.

SARA: Do you mind if I go up there and talk to him?

    Beat.

JOE: I think I'll survive.

    Joe heads back to his carrots. Starts peeling.

SARA: You know, I think you're . . . a really good dad.

JOE: Elevator to the thirty-fifth, door to your right has stairs to the roof.

    She exits.
    Joe sets down the carrots—real sadness.
    Lights dim . . . except for a small corner downstage. Miles sits on the edge of the stage—(or something representing)—the rooftop.
    He's listening to his iPod.
    Sara approaches, watches him for a moment. He senses something, turns around, takes his earbuds out.

SARA: Hey.

MILES: What are you doing?

SARA: Looking for you.

    Beat.

SARA: You know, you sit on the edge of tall buildings people get the wrong idea.

    He looks down.

SARA: What are you listening to?

MILES: Hymns.

SARA: Really?

MILES: 'Devotional Radio pod-cast.' I found it on the internet.

SARA: How is it?

MILES: Not bad.

> *Beat.*
> *She moves to sit next to him.*

SARA: Can I?

MILES: I don't care.

> *She sits.*
> *She looks down—gets dizzy—grabs his arm.*

SARA: Remind me not to do that again.

MILES: Don't do that again.

> *She lets go of his arm.*
> *Beat.*

MILES: Did you really jump off your garage when you were a kid?

SARA: Yeah.

MILES: Did it hurt?

SARA: A lot. For some reason I thought I was going to fly or something.

> *They sit in silence for a moment.*

SARA: My dad . . . he was always singing. I mean especially if he'd had a few but . . . and it was always these obscure Texan, Southern hymns that no one on earth has ever heard of.

> *Beat.*

SARA: And once, on Christmas eve—there was this huge blizzard coming—and he and I drove downtown to do Christmas shopping, I was nine or something. And he parked the car and when we got out there was a fifty dollar bill lying in the snow. And he picked it up, told me to get back in the car and then he just stood there in the snow, smoking Pall Malls, waiting for whoever had lost the money to come back. It was a couple of hours. I listened to the radio—AM country. It was cold.

> *Beat.*

MILES: Did anyone ever show up?

SARA: No.

> *Beat.*

MILES: He sounds like a nice guy.

SARA: Yeah . . .

> *Beat.*

MILES: That was my first kiss. Last night.

SARA: I am so sorry.

MILES: No, it's good. I'm glad. I won't forget it you know?

SARA: Neither will I.

> *They sit. Quiet.*

MILES: Nose-Dive Starburst is next.

SARA: What?

MILES: The finale. They go up as high as they can—like straight up—
then they shut the engines down—it's called a stall—and they
turn everything around and head strait back towards the earth.
Full speed. And right when they're about to hit the ground they
pull up and splay out in a starburst pattern.

SARA: Sounds cool.

MILES: It is.

> *Pause.*

MILES: I suppose you're looking for this.

> *He hands her the note.*

SARA: Thanks.

> *Beat.*

SARA: So you're just up here watching the planes?

> *Beat.*

MILES: Pretty much.

> *They are quiet again. The distant sound of jets can be heard.*
> *After a moment Sara opens the envelope—pulls out the*
> *note—looks at it.*
> *A beat.*

MILES: What's it say?

> *Small pause.*

SARA: *(to no one in particular)* I love you . . .

> *She looks at him.*

> *Music cue: 'Led Zepellin's 'That's the Way'.*
> *Jet engines begin to roar.*
> *Lights dim.*
> *A group of jets rip towards the heavens.*
> *They look up—awestruck.*
> *The jets turn and hurtle back towards the earth—the sound*
> *is unmistakable, exhilarating.*

> *Blackout. End Play.*

Next Fall

Geoffrey Nauffts

PLAYWRIGHT'S BIOGRAPHY

Geoffrey Nauffts has worked as an actor both on and off Broadway, regionally and extensively in film and television. He's directed short plays by Kenneth Lonergan, Frank Pugliese, David Marshall Grant, Theresa Rebeck and Suzan-Lori Parks, as well as Naked Angels' critically acclaimed production of Steven Belber's *Tape* in New York, Los Angeles and London. As a writer, his credits include: *Baby Steps*, an award-winning short film starring Kathy Bates; *Jenifer*, a CBS movie of the week; and two seasons on ABC's hit series *Brothers and Sisters*. He is currently collaborating with Elton John on a score for *Showstopper*, a screenplay he co-wrote with Anthony Barrile for Ben Stiller's company, Red Hour, and is also writing a movie for HBO based on an NPR *This American Life* segment. His critically acclaimed play *Next Fall* opened on Broadway in March 2010, where it received the Outer Circle Critics' John Gassner Award for Best New American Play, and was nominated for a Drama League, Outer Circle Critics Award, Drama Desk, and Tony Award for best play. He recently concluded a four-year term as artistic director of Naken Angels where he's been a proud member for over twenty-five years.

ORIGINAL PRODUCTIONS

Next Fall had its world premiere in a Naked Angels production on June 3, 2009 at the Peter Jay Sharp Theater. The production then transferred to Broadway's Helen Hayes Theatre and opened there on March 11, 2010.

Next Fall was produced on Broadway by Elton John and David Furnish, Barbara Manocherian, Richard Willis, Tom Smedes, Carole L. Haber/Chase Mishkin Ostar, Anthony Barrile, Michael Palitz, Bob Boyett, James Spry/Catherine Schreiber, Probo Productions, Roy Furman in association with Naked Angels (Geoffrey Nauffts, Artistic Director; John Alexander, Managing Director; Andy Donald, Associate Artistic Director; Brittany O'Neill, Producer). Susan Mindell is the Executive Producer.

The production was directed by Sheryl Kaller, with scenic design by Wilson Chin, costume design by Jess Goldstein, lighting design by Jeff Croiter and sound design by John Gromada. The production stage manager was Charles Means and the stage manager was Elizabeth Moloney. The cast was as follows:

Holly . . . . Maddie Corman
Brandon . . . . Sean Dugan
Arlene . . . . Connie Ray
Butch . . . . Cotter Smith
Adam . . . . Patrick Breen
Luke . . . . Patrick Heusinger

CHARACTERS

Adam, 45, a substitute teacher
Luke, 30, an aspiring actor
Holly, 35, a candle shop owner
Brandon, 30, a property developer
Arlene, 50, a divorcee
Butch, 55, a businessman

SETTING

The action takes place in the present, as well as the five year period leading up to it. The place is Manhattan.

> *In a moment, in the twinkling of an eye, at the last trumpet, for the trumpet shall sound, and the dead shall be raised incorruptible, and we shall be changed.*
> —I CORINTHIANS 15:52

> *No one's the devil, here. We're all just trying to get along.*
> —ANONYMOUS

Next Fall

Act I

In darkness we hear brakes squeal to a crashing halt, followed by a car horn stuck in a plaintive wail. The horn begins to sound like a trumpet's call before fading out.

SCENE ONE

The small waiting area of an ICU at Jewish hospital. Mint green. Sterile. The low buzz of fluorescent lighting. There's a couch, two armchairs, a TV and a small coffee table, holding a box of Kleenex and some magazines. A pair of doors upstage lead to a hallway that appears to go on forever.

Brandon, 30, sits contemplatively thumbing the pages of an old book. Holly, 35, peruses a magazine next to him. She tosses it down with a sigh, and their eyes meet.

HOLLY: Weird, huh?

BRANDON: Yeah.

HOLLY: How quickly that rug gets pulled out from underneath you?

BRANDON: What rug?

HOLLY: Any rug. The proverbial rug. It's like, one minute you're doing the morning crossword, next thing you know, you're, well . . . here.

BRANDON: Yeah.

> *This hangs in the air for a moment, until Arlene, 50, blows in like a tornado.*

ARLENE: Here you go, hon.

> *She hands Holly a cup of coffee.*

ARLENE: Black, right?

HOLLY: Perfect.

ARLENE: Wish I could drink it like that. I mean, I like my cream and sugar, don't get me wrong, but I like my thighs, too. Especially when they're not rubbing up against each other.

HOLLY: Thanks.

> *She plops down on the couch with her own coffee.*

ARLENE: My dog is gonna strangle me, I swear. She's just gonna wrap her little paws around my neck and wring it.

HOLLY: You have a dog?

ARLENE: *(nodding)* My neighbor said she'd keep an eye on her, but... She's Puerto Rican... My dog, not the... Well, my neighbor's Puerto Rican, too... Chihuahua... That's Puerto Rican, right? Or is it Mexican?

BRANDON: Um...

ARLENE: It's something Latin. She's got that temperament, you know? I've only had her a week, and already it's like we're in prison and I'm her bitch. Can't stand it when anyone comes near me. She gets all snarly and yappy. It's made us real popular at the dog park, let me tell you.

HOLLY: It's always the little ones.

ARLENE: Oh, she's a pain in my butt, but I love her, I do. Like a biscuit sandwich. Luke's dad thinks I've turned into one of those scary dog people. He threatened to call my shrink the other day when he found out how much I've been spending on chewy toys.

HOLLY: Is he hanging in there?

ARLENE: Who?

HOLLY: Mr. ...

ARLENE: Honeycut... You can call him Butch. He's fine. He's off spraying his spray somewhere. Makes him feel better.

HOLLY: I only know Luke by his stage name.

ARLENE: The stage name, right. I wouldn't bring that up around Butch. It's kind of a sore subject.

HOLLY: I think it was a union thing if that makes him feel any better.

ARLENE: Not really.

> *She picks up her coffee and blows.*

ARLENE: Now, Brandon, why do you look so familiar?

BRANDON: Luke's Our Town opening?

ARLENE: That's right. Lord, my mind's going. I can't remember a thing anymore.

BRANDON: At that sushi restaurant?

ARLENE: It's not so much the long term memory. That's pretty good. My short term's not bad either. It's everything in between that's getting a little fuzzy. Was I flapping my gums the whole night? Holding court?

BRANDON: You seemed to be enjoying yourself.

ARLENE: Of course, I was. You should've stuffed a nori roll in my mouth, Brandon. That's what you have to do, you know, or I'll go on for days.

BRANDON: I remember your turban being quite the topic of conversation.

ARLENE: *(mortified)* With the nuts?

BRANDON: There were lots of squirrel jokes.

ARLENE: My friend Spike makes those. Uses raisins, too. Wheat Chex. M&Ms. Anything you can find in a bag of Trail Mix, Spike uses it. It's called "outsider art." Because that's where it ought to be hung—outside—where no one has to look at it. We're not speaking anymore, Spike and me. I mean, what the heck was I thinking?

HOLLY: I wore a do-rag my last two years of high school.

ARLENE: A do what?

HOLLY: Rag? It holds your jerry curl in place?

ARLENE: Shut up.

HOLLY: It's true. I have the prom pictures to prove it.

ARLENE: Good God, woman.

HOLLY: I wore a snood, too. One of those big yarn ones.

ARLENE: What the heck's a snood?

HOLLY: It's like a sweater for your hair?

ARLENE: No sir! How about you, Brandon? Any skeletons hanging in your closet?

BRANDON: Ties, I guess? I only wore red, white and blue ones when I worked in DC.

ARLENE: Now, is that how you and Luke know each other, hon? DC?

BRANDON: Luke's the one who convinced me to move up here.

ARLENE: Well, that's Luke, isn't it? Like Tom Sawyer with a can of white wash. His daddy's the same way.

HOLLY: Brandon works for a big property developer now. He's making more money than all of us.

ARLENE: Stop it.

BRANDON: I know. It's hard to believe, but it's been a good couple of years, so . . .

ARLENE: What about you two? How do you kids know each other?

Holly and Brandon exchange a glance.

HOLLY: We don't really. We've met like, what, once or twice, Brandon?

BRANDON: Through Luke, yeah.

HOLLY: Luke works at my shop.

ARLENE: The candle store? That's yours?

HOLLY: Well, candles and cards and tchochkes and things, yeah. We're expanding.

ARLENE: Chachis?

HOLLY: Tchochkes.

ARLENE: Is that like bagels . . . Something Jewish?

HOLLY: It's basically all the little, crappy things that clutter up your house. Knickknacks, I guess.

ARLENE: Okay, now you're speaking my language. My condo's like a chachi warehouse.

HOLLY: Tchochke.

ARLENE: Huh?

HOLLY: Never mind.

Holly sips her coffee.

ARLENE: From Capitol Hill to candles. No wonder his daddy's got high blood pressure.

HOLLY: Actually, candles are really in now.

ARLENE: Oh, I know, hon. I'm teasing. I love candles. Luke sends me a different flavor for every holiday. Just the other day, I got my pumpkin spice.

HOLLY: That's our best seller.

Laughter erupts down the hallway. It seems inappropriate somehow.

ARLENE: Someone's having a good time . . .

They listen for a moment. Arlene shifts gears.

ARLENE: And, so Luke likes it up here? He's having a nice life in New York?

HOLLY: He loves it.

ARLENE: I keep waiting to see his face on TV again. There was that commercial he did. For computers, was it? Or cell phones?

BRANDON: DSL.

ARLENE: Okay, see, now I have no idea what that is either. You two must think I'm some kind of hillbilly, twankin' my banjo down there in the boonies somewhere.

HOLLY: I don't know what it is either . . . and I have it.

ARLENE: I enjoyed that musical he was in a while back.

HOLLY: Who knew Luke could sing?

ARLENE: Like an angel . . . But my favorite still, Brandon, was that Our Town.

BRANDON: Yeah.

ARLENE: Luke was just terrific in that. Especially when the girl died. He was so believable.

HOLLY: Yeah, the acting thing's been going really well for him.

ARLENE: And he still has all that time to sell candles.

      Butch, 55, enters, with medical forms.

BUTCH: Idiots.

ARLENE: What now, Butch?

BUTCH: The taxi driver's uninsured.

ARLENE: Oh, for Pete sake.

BUTCH: No green card either.

ARLENE: Would you leave that poor man alone? He's traumatized enough as it is.

BUTCH: Who lets these jackasses across the border, that's what I want to know. He didn't just go through the red light. He ran right up on the sidewalk.

ARLENE: It was an accident.

BUTCH: And how come it takes an ambulance fifteen minutes to go ten blocks? That's just inexcusable.

ARLENE: Don't pay attention to him, you all. He hasn't been here an hour, and he's already tried to have two interns and a security guard fired.

BUTCH: Well, they were dumb, too.

ARLENE: It's called a Napolcon complex.

BUTCH: Napoleon was short.

ARLENE: We ought to see if we can't get you a shot for that while we're here, hon.

BUTCH: I'm keeping a list. That's all I'm saying.

ARLENE: Oh that's helpful, Butch. That's real constructive.

BUTCH: I'll sue the whole damn city if I have to.

ARLENE: Would you hush?!

> *Butch sits, frustrated.*

BUTCH: Knuckleheads.

ARLENE: Have you called Lynn yet?

BUTCH: I can't deal with Lynn right now.

ARLENE: Well, neither can I, and I'm the one she keeps speed dialing.

BUTCH: I told you not to give her your damn cell phone number.

ARLENE: *(to Holly)* Luke's stepmom.

HOLLY: Oh. I thought you were his . . .

ARLENE: Oh, no, hon. Lynn did a lot of the rearing, but I'm the real
deal. Poor thing had a brow lift and a tummy tuck yesterday,
can you imagine? And then this happens? She's been calling
every half hour in a complete Vicodin haze, bless her heart.
Can't understand a word she's saying.

> *(to Butch)*

Of course, she's got the housekeeper and the personal trainer
five times a week, so I can't feel too bad for her.

BUTCH: You coulda had that if you'd behaved yourself.

ARLENE: How about Ben? Have you reached Ben yet?

BUTCH: My phone's not getting any service.

ARLENE: Well, here, try mine.

> *Arlene fishes a cell phone out of her coat pocket and hands
> it over.*

ARLENE: Luke's brother. He's a sophomore at Georgia Tech.

BUTCH: An engineering major.

ARLENE: He's pledging a fraternity today.

BUTCH: Nuclear engineering. Got a 3.9 last semester.

ARLENE: Sweet kid.

BUTCH: He's gonna work for NASA someday. *(into the phone)* Ben,
it's your dad again. Give me a call as soon as you get this, son.
It's important.

> *He hands the phone back, the reality of the situation hitting
> them for a moment. Arlene sticks it in her coat pocket, and
> switches gears.*

ARLENE: That anesthesiologist seems nice, Holly. The one with the hook-nose and the beanie. And cute, too. Are you single?

HOLLY: Yes?

ARLENE: I'll introduce you later on. After Luke wakes up. So glad they brought him to a Jewish hospital.

BUTCH: Arlene . . .

ARLENE: What, we're lucky, that's all. They make great doctors. Accountants, too.

BUTCH: Christ on a Christmas tree.

ARLENE: If you clip those curly-Q things off the side of his head, he'd look just like George Clooney, wouldn't he, Holly?

BUTCH: Arlene, why don't you be still and muzzle it for a while.

  Adam, 45, enters, wet and exhausted. Holly is shocked to see him.

HOLLY: Adam?!

ADAM: There you are.

  He makes a beeline for the coat rack.

HOLLY: I thought your flight was canceled.

ADAM: You wouldn't believe the hoops I had to jump through to get here.

  Holly tries to cut him off at the pass.

HOLLY: This is Adam, everybody.

ADAM: We sat on the tarmac for like two hours.

HOLLY: I didn't think you were gonna make it in tonight.

ADAM: I'm starving. All I've had to eat today is like three Bloody Marys and a Cinnabon.

  *He hangs his wet coat up and turns, paralyzed when he sees
  Arlene and the rest of the gang staring at him.*

ARLENE: Hi, there.

HOLLY: This is Arlene, Adam. Luke's mom.

ARLENE: Nice to meet you.

HOLLY: And you know Brandon.

BRANDON: Hey . . .

HOLLY: Brandon was the first one to get here.

BRANDON: I only live a couple blocks away, so . . .

ADAM: You moved?

BRANDON: A few months ago . . . Yeah.

HOLLY: And Luke's dad.

ARLENE: Stand up, Butch. Have some manners.

The two men stare at each other.

ADAM: We've met.

BUTCH: We have?

> *Holly pushes Adam towards a chair.*

HOLLY: Why don't you have a seat, sweetie?

ADAM: Where is he?

HOLLY: Just out of surgery. He was in there for like five hours.

ADAM: Can I see him?

HOLLY: They want us to hold off for a while.

ADAM: Can't I just stick my head in?

HOLLY: He's still in the coma.

> *Adam sinks into a chair, the gravity of it all finally hitting him. Holly rubs his shoulders.*

HOLLY: Adam was just at his high school reunion. He must be feeling like we were when we first got here. It's a little overwhelming, isn't it, sweetie?

ADAM: He's gonna be okay though, right?

HOLLY: Of course, he is.

ADAM: I mean, that's what they're saying, isn't it?

ARLENE: Well, now, Butch, you were the last one to speak to the surgeon. What did he have to say, hon?

BUTCH: He said my boy's got fight in him.

ARLENE: He certainly does. We were just talking about that, weren't we, Brandon? "Pluck." That's what we called it growing up.

BUTCH: Pluck?

ARLENE: Yes, pluck, Butch. That's what we called it. And Luke's got a ton of it. What else did he say?

> *A beat.*

BUTCH: He's gonna need it.

SCENE TWO

> *Lights up on a rooftop. Five years earlier. Adam, pale and sweaty, is trying to catch his breath.*
>
> *Luke, 25, wearing a white shirt and black pants, steps out onto the roof and hands over a glass of water.*

LUKE: Here you go.

Adam takes a huge gulp.

ADAM: Thanks.

LUKE: Sorry about the Heimlich.

ADAM: Don't worry about it.

LUKE: I thought you were choking.

ADAM: I think it was more of an arrythmia thing.

    He downs the rest of the water and hands the glass back.

ADAM: Is the roof spinning or is it just me?

LUKE: Maybe you should try sticking your arms in the air?

    Adam looks at him, skeptically.

LUKE: I saw it on TV once. Some doctor show.

    Adam sticks his arms in the air.

LUKE: How's that feel?

ADAM: Like I'm under arrest.

LUKE: Might have been a cop show.

    He lowers his arms and sinks to the floor.

ADAM: I think maybe if I just sit here for a minute.

LUKE: Some party, huh?

ADAM: Fabulous.

LUKE: Who's anniversary is it anyway?

ADAM: My friend Holly's.

LUKE: The large woman?

ADAM: She's fat. You can say it . . . No, not her. That's a friend of hers.

LUKE: Oh, sorry. Didn't mean to . . .

ADAM: That's okay. She wasn't always like that, apparently.

LUKE: Who?

ADAM: The friend.

LUKE: You can tell. Some people just seem like they've been fat their whole lives, you know? Like they're used to it. But she looks like it kinda snuck up on her out of nowhere. And suddenly, there she was. This fat fatty.

ADAM: What happened to large?

LUKE: Like she woke up one morning in someone else's skin.

ADAM: Yeah, well, she's on the road to recovery now, so . . .

LUKE: What do you mean?

ADAM: It's not a real anniversary down there. It's a twelve step thing.

LUKE: Twelve step? You mean, like, AA?

ADAM: Yeah, only it's OA.

LUKE: OA?

ADAM: Overeaters Anonymous.

LUKE: Oh . . . Okay.

> *Adam wants to be alone now.*

ADAM: Listen, thanks for the water. I think I can take it from here.

> *Luke reaches out his hand.*

LUKE: We haven't officially met yet. I'm Luke.

ADAM: You gotta be kidding, I practically threw up on you.

LUKE: And you're . . .

ADAM: Adam.

> *Adam shakes it, tentatively.*

LUKE: Nice to meet you, Adam. So what do you do?

ADAM: *(off guard)* What do I do?

LUKE: Yeah.

ADAM: Like in life?

LUKE: Is that a trick question?

ADAM: You wouldn't think so.

LUKE: Like, me? I'm an actor.

ADAM: No kidding?

LUKE: Is it that obvious?

ADAM: The white shirt. The black pants . . . The serving tray.

LUKE: Okay, I'm an aspiring actor. I'm not really making any money
at it yet, so I guess, technically, I'm a cater waiter.

ADAM: I see.

LUKE: Not for long though.

> *Luke digs a postcard out of his pocket and hands it over.*

ADAM: What's this?

LUKE: A show I'm working on. We open next week.

ADAM: Oh . . . Well, break a leg.

LUKE: I wanted the part of George, but I'm the stage manager.

ADAM: Well, we all have to start somewhere.

> *Adam sticks it in his pocket.*

LUKE: What about you?

ADAM: Me? We're back to me again?

LUKE: Are you like a wall street guy? An accountant, maybe?

ADAM: An accountant? I look like an accountant?

LUKE: An ad exec? I don't know. A Sous chef?

ADAM: No, none of those.

LUKE: Come on help me out here.

ADAM: *(hitting a nerve)* I'm not so sure anymore.

> *Luke recognized this and joins him on the floor.*

LUKE: Well, what would you like to do?

ADAM: What would I like to do?

LUKE: You're a vamper.

ADAM: A what?

LUKE: You keep repeating the question. That's what I always do when I'm not sure how to answer.

ADAM: *(considering)* What would I like to do?

LUKE: See? You did it again.

ADAM: I'm thinking. Give me a sec.

> *Adam leans his head back and gazes up at the sky.*

ADAM: I read about this experiment once, they took a newborn, and stuck it in a room with no light, no love, no stimuli, and just left it. They'd come in, every so often, and feed it through some kind of tube, you know, but it basically had no human contact whatsoever.

LUKE: That's criminal.

ADAM: Maybe I'm getting it wrong. Maybe it wasn't a newborn. Maybe it was a mouse. Yeah, I think that's what it was. A baby mouse.

LUKE: Still.

ADAM: Anyway, that's how they raised the little rodent. And sure enough, he grew up to be, like, a complete vegetable. When they finally threw him into a tank with some other mice, he couldn't even move.

LUKE: Sad.

ADAM: Just sat in the corner and shook.

LUKE: And your point is . . .

ADAM: You tell someone "no" long enough, they start believing it. Does that answer your question?

LUKE: Not really. But we can move on to the next topic.

ADAM: I guess I'm a candle salesman.

LUKE: There you go.

ADAM: That's what I do.

LUKE: That wasn't so hard.

ADAM: Jesus, how did I wind up being that?

LUKE: You can change your mind if you like.

ADAM: No, I'm a candle salesman.

LUKE: Good for you.

ADAM: Yup, I sell candles.

LUKE: Okay, easy now.

ADAM: It's just the first time I've ever really admitted it out loud.

LUKE: And how does it feel?

ADAM: Terrible. I don't care if I ever sell another pumpkin scented anything for as long as I live.

LUKE: I hate pumpkin.

HOLLY: *(O.S.)* Adam!

> *Holly appears from the party below. Adam's immediately guilty.*

ADAM: Sorry.

HOLLY: It was quirky for like ten minutes, now it's just rude.

ADAM: I said, I was sorry.

HOLLY: Well, get back down there. It's my anniversary.

ADAM: I can't, Holly.

HOLLY: What do you mean you can't?

ADAM: The air. There's like a pall down there.

HOLLY: A pall?

ADAM: A heaviness, yeah. I don't know. Everyone just seems so . . . hungry.

HOLLY: You done, Shecky?

ADAM: What happened to all those past life regression weirdos you used to hang out with? At least those people knew how to party.

> *Holly sits, as it all comes clear.*

HOLLY: It's Belinda, isn't it?

ADAM: Who?

HOLLY: That's what this is all about.

ADAM: Absolutely not.

HOLLY: It's just a book, sweetie.

ADAM: A best selling book. She's making a fortune.

HOLLY: Well, good for her. We should all be so lucky.

ADAM: They're making a movie of it, too.

HOLLY: That's ridiculous.

ADAM: No, it's not. There's a huge bidding war, apparently.

HOLLY: It's a book on breast feeding, Adam.

ADAM: I'd pay to see that.

HOLLY: Okay, I'm leaving now.

> *She starts off.*

ADAM: I'm a candle salesman, Holly.

> *She stops and turns.*

HOLLY: What?

ADAM: I'm a forty year-old candle salesman.

HOLLY: What are you talking about?

ADAM: When you hired me, it was to help you get through the holiday season.

HOLLY: So?

ADAM: That was six years ago.

> *A beat.*

ADAM: I don't want to end up like that friend of yours downstairs.

HOLLY: What friend?

ADAM: The middle aged fat one who sells bongs in the smoke shop around the corner.

HOLLY: Rachel?

ADAM: The one who looks like she cries in her closet.

HOLLY: She's nicc.

ADAM: That's not what I want.

> *Another beat.*

HOLLY: Well, I sell candles, too.

ADAM: You own the shop, Holly. You're a shop owner. There's a big difference. Plus, you're not forty.

HOLLY: Neither are you.

ADAM: Yes, I am.

HOLLY: You're forty?

ADAM: Uh-huh.

HOLLY: You've been lying about your age the whole time I've known you?

ADAM: Yes.

HOLLY: *(processing for a moment)* Well, you're not fat.

ADAM: My body may not be, but my soul is.

HOLLY: Okay, now I'm really leaving.

> *Adam stands.*

ADAM: I want more, Holly.

HOLLY: There is more, Adam. There's cake. And we want to watch you eat it.

ADAM: I'm serious! I'll give you a couple more weeks.

HOLLY: *(realizing he's serious)* So, what, you're quitting? Great. Who's gonna help me unload that huge crate of Dyptiques we just got? You're the only one who knows how to pronounce those freakin' things.

ADAM: You'll find someone else.

> *She notices Luke for the first time.*

HOLLY: Hey, handsome, wanna sell candles?

LUKE: Is that better than cater-waitering?

HOLLY: Way better. Talk to me on your way out. I'll hook you up.

LUKE: Cool.

HOLLY: *(back to Adam)* You feel better?

ADAM: A little . . . You?

HOLLY: Fuck, no. I'm starving.

ADAM: Then have a piece of cake, Holly. Have two. You don't have an eating disorder.

HOLLY: You don't get it, do you?

ADAM: Get what?

> *She shakes her head and starts off.*

HOLLY: Okay, five minutes, and then I'm calling the guys with the straight jacket.

ADAM: Love you.

HOLLY: Yeah, yeah, yeah.

> *And she's gone. Adam blots his forehead.*

LUKE: Wow . . .

ADAM: Sorry about that.

LUKE: Was that like a mid-life crisis, or something?

ADAM: *(offended)* Mid-life crisis? No . . . What makes you say that?

LUKE: You quit your job and you're forty.

ADAM: Oh ... Well ... Maybe ...

LUKE: That was awesome.

> *Adam clutches his heart and starts pacing.*

ADAM: I think it's happening again.

LUKE: Maybe you should try sticking your head between your legs?

ADAM: How about I stick it back up my ass? Where it's been for the past six years.

> *He wanders over to the ledge and looks at the street below.*

ADAM: She went to school with me. Belinda. The girl with the book.

LUKE: Oh.

ADAM: We were in the same writing program.

LUKE: I get it.

ADAM: I was the one with all the promise, and she was the one destined to ...

LUKE: ... write books on breast feeding?

ADAM: I guess ...

> *Luke sidles up next to him.*

LUKE: I have a confession to make.

ADAM: What's that?

LUKE: I didn't really think you were choking when I gave you the Heimlich.

ADAM: You didn't?

LUKE: I just wanted to get my arms around you.

ADAM: Oh ...

LUKE: You looked so cute all doubled over like that.

ADAM: You should see me when I think I'm passing a kidney stone.

LUKE: I'd like that.

> *Luke moves a little closer. Adam gets nervous.*

ADAM: We better get back down there.

LUKE: How about grabbing a drink later?

ADAM: I don't thnk so.

LUKE: Why not?

ADAM: Well, I could be your grandfather, for one.

LUKE: Okay, now you're really making me horny.

> *Luke flashes him a killer grin, then exits. Adam takes out the postcard, stares at it for a minute, and then fans himself.*

SCENE THREE

The waiting room. Holly peruses a Newsweek magazine. Brandon talks on his cell phone.

BRANDON: No, the 220 Rivington offer is way too low . . . Look, I'm gonna be able to give this my full attention tomorrow. Could you please deal with it for now? . . . It's e-mail, just pretend you're me. Thanks.
      He hangs up and looks at Holly.
HOLLY: They found a new missing link.
BRANDON: Huh?
HOLLY: In Ethiopia. This one's 60,000 years older than the last one . . . That's encouraging.
      She tosses the Newsweek down. Adam enters with a cup of coffee.
ADAM: Well, my luggage arrived safely.
HOLLY: Thank God.
ADAM: In Pittsburgh.
HOLLY: Pittsburgh?
ADAM: Don't ask.
      He plops down on the couch, exhausted.
ADAM: God, that was awkward.
HOLLY: I thought you handled it pretty well.
ADAM: Are you kidding, it was a train wreck.
HOLLY: You're right.
ADAM: And you were the conductor.
HOLLY: Butch sure is a pistol.
ADAM: Yeah, and I'm sure he owns several, too.
HOLLY: He's way sexier than I imagined.
ADAM: Ew . . .
HOLLY: Not as straight-laced, I guess. I expected him to look more like one of those TV preacher guys.
ADAM: Yeah, well, you don't see me in a thong on a float, but I'm still a fag.
HOLLY: True.
ADAM: God, I hate hospitals. It'll be a miracle if one of us doesn't leave here with a staph infection. Where are they, anyway?

> *Holly and Brandon exchange a glance.*

BRANDON: With Luke.

ADAM: What?

HOLLY: The surgeon said it was okay, sweetie.

ADAM: When?

HOLLY: Like ten, fifteen minutes ago.

ADAM: Why didn't anyone come get me?

> *Adam rises, a little miffed, and starts off.*

BRANDON: Family only, Adam.

> *He stops in his tracks.*

ADAM: What?

BRANDON: They asked that it be family only.

ADAM: Who did?

BRANDON: The surgeon.

HOLLY: For now, sweetie. He seemed pretty adamant.

ADAM: Family only?

HOLLY: I don't think they can have too many people in the room. He just went through major surgery.

ADAM: Yeah, well, I'm not people, Holly.

HOLLY: I know.

ADAM: Who do you think he's been living with for the past four years?

HOLLY: I know, Adam. I know.

BRANDON: But it's not like they're strangers.

ADAM: Excuse me?

BRANDON: They said family only for now, so his parents went in. I mean . . .

ADAM: Okay, got it, Brandon. We know whose side you're on.

BRANDON: I'm not on anyone's side.

HOLLY: He's not, Adam. He really isn't.

BRANDON: I just don't think this is the time to be getting all bent out of shape about it.

ADAM: I'm not getting . . . (to Holly) Am I bent out of shape, Holly?

BRANDON: It's not about you right now. That's all I'm saying. It's not about any of us.

ADAM: What are you talking about?

HOLLY: Guys—

BRANDON: Luke needs us, Adam. He needs all of us together.

ADAM: You don't think I know that?

BRANDON: I'm not gonna argue with you.

ADAM: I am family, Brandon! I don't care what anyone says. I'm going in there!

> *He starts off again. Holly chases after him.*

HOLLY: But they don't know about you, sweetie.

ADAM: Oh, believe me, I'm well aware of that.

HOLLY: For a reason.

> *He stops and turns.*

HOLLY: There's a reason Luke's never told them.

ADAM: Yeah, because he's a wimp. He's a scared little coward who should've told them a long time ago.

HOLLY: That may be, but—

ADAM: What, Holly? What?

HOLLY: I'm not sure it's your place to tell.

ADAM: Oh, and whose place would it be?

HOLLY: Luke's.

> *A beat.*

HOLLY: Just think about it for a minute, sweetie, that's all I'm asking. When Luke wakes up. Is that really what he needs to deal with? On top of everything else?

> *Butch enters, sensing the tension.*

BUTCH: Everything okay in here?

HOLLY: We're fine, aren't we, guys?

BRANDON: I am.

HOLLY: How's Luke doing?

BUTCH: Alright, I guess. They had to clear us out of the room for a while.

HOLLY: What for?

BUTCH: More tests.

HOLLY: Okay.

BUTCH: They've got some monitor thing bolted to his head. Specialists marching in and out every five minutes. It's hard to keep track of what all's going on in there.

HOLLY: I'm sure.

> *Butch sits on the couch and pulls out his cell phone.*

BUTCH: They had to remove a piece of his skull.

HOLLY: His . . .

BUTCH: It's common, I guess. Because of the swelling. Epidural Hematoma. That's what they're calling it.

HOLLY: Okay...

BUTCH: Something about his fall. The timing of it all. The way his head hit the pavement. You wouldn't have known anything was wrong when they first brought him in. That's what the nurse told us. It was just like he was sleeping.

HOLLY: Is there anything we can do?

BUTCH: Just sit tight. Like the surgeon said. He doesn't seem quite as inept as the rest of the folks around here.

Butch starts dialing.

ADAM: *(trying to stay calm)* And so this... um... The family only request... How long do you think that will, you know, be in effect?

BUTCH: Not sure.

ADAM: Hours? Minutes? Days? What?

HOLLY: Adam...

ADAM: I'm just... We'd like to see him, right, guys? Even for a second.

HOLLY: We're just feeling a little out of the loop, is all.

BUTCH: Well, they can't have us clogging up the room. They need to be able to get in and out of there and do whatever it is they do. *(snapping phone shut)* Shoot, still no service.

Butch grabs Arlene's purse and starts digging through it.

ADAM: So, what's next then? Assuming all goes smoothly.

BUTCH: Next? I don't know. Physical therapy, I suppose. Rehabilitation.

ADAM: How much of that do they think he'll need?

BUTCH: They, who?

ADAM: The surgeons, they? I don't know. Whoever's in charge?

HOLLY: Sweetie...

ADAM: Months? A year, maybe? Longer?

BUTCH: Nobody's saying much of anything, right now, son. We probably won't know what's what for sure until we get him back home.

HOLLY: Home?

BUTCH: We've got a brand new facility just outside Tallahassee. State of the art from what I hear, and booked up like a five star hotel. I've got some strings I can pull. See if we can't get him in there.

Butch moves on to Arlene's coat. Adam's getting a little frustrated.

ADAM: Is that wise though?

BUTCH: Wise?

ADAM: Transporting him like that? I mean, he just went through major surgery.

BUTCH: I'm not sure if it's wise or not, but that's what I'm gonna do.

ADAM: It's just . . . Head trauma can be pretty serious from what I understand. Has anyone determined if there's been any . . .

BUTCH: No one's determined anything yet, son.

> *He pulls out a bottle of pills and examines the label.*

BUTCH: We all just have to sit tight.

> *A look of disappointment crosses his face as he pockets them again.*

BUTCH: And try not to worry.

SCENE FOUR

> *Adam's apartment. Five years earlier. Luke, in his boxers, prepares breakfast.*

LUKE: Wait til you taste these tomatoes. They're fierce.

DAM: *(O.S.)* Fierce? Tomatoes aren't fierce. Lions are. Whitney Houston is. Tomatoes are just . . . tomatoes.

LUKE: Where you been, Grandpa? Whitney Houston hasn't been fierce in years. She's a crackhead.

> *Adam enters in his boxers with a big smile on his face.*

ADAM: I know I said it already, but you were really amazing last night.

LUKE: Really?

ADAM: When you told me you were the stage manager, I didn't realize it was an actual part.

LUKE: The lead part.

ADAM: You were brilliant. The whole production was. I cried.

LUKE: I know, I heard you . . . Everyone in the audience heard you.

ADAM: I'm having a mid-life crisis. It was cathartic.

> *Adam sits in front of a plate of eggs, ogling them*

ADAM: Oh, my God.

LUKE: It's the best I could do with what you had in your fridge.

ADAM: I didn't even know I had a fridge.

LUKE: Dig in before it gets cold, mister.

ADAM: I think the only one who cried more than me was that weird lady in the turban.

LUKE: That was my mother.

ADAM: Did I say weird? I meant eccentric.

LUKE: Turbans are her thing right now. Last year it was track suits. The year before it was chunky jewelry.

> *Adam starts eating.*

ADAM: And your dad?

LUKE: He was a no show. Still mad I dropped out of law school, I guess. It's just as well. He gets kind of cranky whenever he and my mom are in the same room together. The "Arlene Show" can be a little exhausting after twenty years.

ADAM: How long have they been divorced?

LUKE: Twenty years. He kind of turned his life around after they split up. It was just me and him for a while there. I was like his little security blanket. He dragged me everywhere.

ADAM: So, that must have been challenging. Your folks divorcing when you were so young.

LUKE: I was just glad the craziness was over.

ADAM: Like, what kind of crazy?

LUKE: Like waking up in the middle of the night to a house full of pot smoke, Pink Floyd on the stereo, the front door wide open, and nobody in sight.

ADAM: Sounds like my entire four years of college.

LUKE: Well, it's no fun when you're in kindergarten, trust me. To this day, the smell of patchouli oil makes me weep.

> *Adam watches, curiously, as Luke closes his eyes, prays for a moment, then opens them again and digs in.*

ADAM: What was that?

LUKE: What was what?

ADAM: Where'd you go just then?

LUKE: I was praying.

ADAM: You mean, crystals and chalkras? Like a Deepak Chopra kind of thing?

LUKE: Not really.

ADAM: Then, who were you praying to?

LUKE: God.

ADAM: Oh.

Adam looks completely bewildered as Luke continues eating.

LUKE: Yum.

ADAM: Is that an every day occurrence?

LUKE: Pretty much.

ADAM: So, you're what, then . . . You're . . .

LUKE: A Christian.

ADAM: Okay.

He tries to proceed with breakfast as usual.

LUKE: Does that freak you out?

ADAM: Does it freak me out?

LUKE: Yeah.

ADAM: Why would it freak me out?

LUKE: No reason . . . Why? What are you?

ADAM: What am I?

LUKE: Besides a vamper.

ADAM: Nothing . . . I don't know. I didn't really grow up with a religion.

Luke stabs a tomato and pops it in his mouth.

LUKE: These tomatoes are fierce. I don't care what you say.

Adam looks at him like he's an alien all of a sudden.

ADAM: You're gay though, right?

LUKE: Uh . . . whose dick do you think you were sucking on all night?

ADAM: I know, but don't Christians consider that a sin?

LUKE: Uh-huh.

ADAM: So, how does that work, then?

LUKE: How does what work?

ADAM: Being gay and.. you know . . .

LUKE: This is gonna be a problem, isn't it?

ADAM: No . . . I'm . . . I just . . .

LUKE: We're all sinners, Adam. We all struggle with one thing or another. This one just happens to be mine.

ADAM: Do you atone then? Is that what you do?

LUKE: You really want to talk about this?

ADAM: Sure.

LUKE: You accept Christ as the son of God. That he died on the cross
for all your sins.

ADAM: That's it?

LUKE: Pretty much.

ADAM: And you'll go to heaven?

LUKE: If you believe. If you truly believe.

ADAM: And you do?

LUKE: Uh-huh.

> *Luke refills Adam's coffee.*

ADAM: Then how come you continue to sin? I mean, and don't get me wrong, that was some amazing sinning we just did, I look forward to more, but you sinned a lot. You sinned more than I did.

LUKE: I was hoping we could sin again after breakfast.

ADAM: You didn't answer my question.

LUKE: It's human nature, Adam. We can't escape it. But as long as you've accepted Christ...

> *A beat.*

ADAM: Is that why you didn't introduce me to your mom last night?

LUKE: I didn't?

ADAM: Nope.

LUKE: Might have had a little something to do with it.

> *Luke rises and starts clearing the table. Adam's fascinated.*

ADAM: So, let me see if I got this right. I'm assuming sin is sin. And if your sin is having sex with men, and my sin is, say, killing men who have sex with men, then as long as I've accepted Christ as my Savior, I'll go to heaven with you?

LUKE: Killing men who have sex with men? You mean, like Jeffrey Dahmer?

ADAM: Yeah... Well, no. Because he killed them, then he ate them. Plus, he had sex with them too, so no, not him.

LUKE: Like who then?

ADAM: The guys who killed Matthew Shepard.

> *A beat.*

LUKE: *(difficult to answer)* Technically, yes.

ADAM: Not only that, but I can continue to kill men who have sex with men, much as you continue to have sex with men, everyday for the rest of my life, and still go to heaven?

LUKE: Well...

ADAM: It's just a hypothesis.

LUKE: I know it sounds terrible, but... yes.

ADAM: Huh.

> *Another beat.*

ADAM: So then, if Matthew Shepard hadn't accepted Christ before he
      died, he's in hell, and his killers who, say, have, are going to
      heaven? Is that what you're saying?

      Luke stands there with his arms full.

LUKE: Can we change the subject?

SCENE FIVE

*Adam and Luke's new apartment. A year later. Holly, Chinese food
and a housewarming gift in hand, stands amid a stack of unopened
boxes as Luke tries to pry something off the door frame.*

HOLLY: And I thought my place was small.

ADAM: *(O.S.)* I told you.

LUKE: Please don't get him started.

HOLLY: I just don't know where you're gonna put everything, that's
       all.

ADAM: *(O.S.)* I like my old place better.

LUKE: Would you relax.

      Adam enters with a bottle of wine and two glasses.

ADAM: That kitchen is miniscule.

LUKE: Wait til I unpack everything and put it in its place. It'll look
      like a palace.

ADAM: What are you doing?

LUKE: Trying to get this thing off.

ADAM: What thing?

HOLLY: The mezuzah.

LUKE: Ma-wha-wha?

ADAM: Mezuzah. It keeps evil spirits out of New York apartments.

HOLLY: Actually, I think it protects your first born from being
       slaughtered.

LUKE: We don't have a first born.

ADAM: It's good luck.

LUKE: It's ugly.

ADAM: Babe!

LUKE: Alright, already... Jeez.

      Luke rolls his eyes and pockets the screwdriver.

LUKE: I don't see how a little metal thing's gonna ward off evil spirits anyway.

ADAM: Yeah, well I don't see how a golden trumpet's gonna signal the end of the world, so we're even.

    Luke disappears into the kitchen. Adam pours the wine.

ADAM: He literally believes that, you know. That people are gonna just start floating up to heaven.

LUKE: *(O.S.)* I didn't say "float."

ADAM: That, like, Doc Severinsen, or some other dead trumpeter, is gonna blow his horn three times—

LUKE: Gabriel.

ADAM: Yeah, him. And in the blink of an eye—

LUKE: *(O.S.)* Twinkling.

ADAM: Whatever.

LUKE: *(O.S.)* Get it right, sister.

ADAM: All believers will just disappear.

LUKE: *(O.S.)* It's true.

HOLLY: *(processing)* Doc Severinsen is dead?

    Luke reenters.

ADAM: You should have heard him on the phone this morning. Giggling with his friend Jill.

HOLLY: Who's Jill, the beard?

LUKE: She's more like a soul patch.

ADAM: Hysterically laughing about all the wacky things people will be in the middle of when it happens. Tickled to death at the thought of me being on a plane with a Christian pilot, because the plane will crash and I'll go down with it.

    He takes a sip of Adam's wine and giggles.

ADAM: See? This is funny to him.

LUKE: This is the thirty-nine dollar bottle of merlot we just bought?

ADAM: It was running low, so I mixed in a little of our ten dollar bottle.

LUKE: So, it's a twenty-nine dollar bottle, now.

ADAM: It's woody . . . muddy . . . shitty. Just drink it.

    Holly raises her glass.

HOLLY: Cheers, guys. To your new place.

ADAM: Salut.

    The clink glasses. Holly points to the gift bag.

HOLLY: And a little something . . .

> *Luke pulls an orange candle out.*

LUKE: Look, babe, it's pumpkin.

HOLLY: Didn't wanna come empty handed.

> *Luke gives Holly a kiss and gets back to work.*

HOLLY: So, you really think this thing's gonna happen, Luke?

LUKE: Uh-huh.

HOLLY: Like, in our lifetime?

LUKE: Maybe.

ADAM: And he and all his cohorts will float, or fly, or "beam" or whatever, up to heaven while the rest of us go to hell.

LUKE: That's not exactly how it works.

ADAM: All the Agnostics and Atheists. The Muslims and the Buddhists. The Hindus. The Jews. Three quarters of the world's population, all going to hell.

HOLLY: You mean, I'll finally get a decent apartment?

ADAM: No, you're going too, missy.

HOLLY: What about David?

> *Holly checks out the kitchen.*

ADAM: That asshole? You're still obsessing over him?

HOLLY: *(O.S.)* He's a Scientologist.

ADAM: Especially him.

> *She reenters.*

ADAM: Anyone who doesn't truly believe.

HOLLY: Even the Mongolian goatherder?

LUKE: Mongolian what?

ADAM: *(singing)* "High on a hill lived a Mongolian goatherd . . . "

HOLLY: You know, the guy who's been nothing but saintly to his family and fellow villagers his whole life, toiling in the fields, tending his flock, who's never even heard of Jesus. Is he going, too? Or his infant son, who can't even crawl yet? Or Rachel?

LUKE: The bong lady?

HOLLY: Her last name's Rosenberg. They're all gonna burn?

LUKE: Not the goat herder and his son.

HOLLY: Why not?

LUKE: Infants and retarded people are exempt.

ADAM: She said Mongolian, not mongoloid.

LUKE: Oh... Then, yeah. He'll burn with Rachel... Unless, of course, you know...

HOLLY: But what if you have your own set of beliefs? Beliefs that are equally as valid?

LUKE: I just know it's going to happen, you guys. It's kind of hard to explain.

ADAM: Try us.

LUKE: It's like... Imagine if you were a cancer patient, and they discovered a cure, but you were so pissed off you got sick in the first place, you refused to take it and you died.

ADAM: I have no idea what he's talking about.

HOLLY: Going to hell is cancer, bozo. And Jesus is the pill.

LUKE: Like that, yeah.

ADAM: But I don't believe in hell, so why should I care whether I burn in it?

LUKE: *(testy)* Because I do!
> *Luke tears a box open.*

ADAM: Don't get defensive, babe.

LUKE: Whatever.

ADAM: Tell her about the seven years.

LUKE: I'm not talking about this anymore.

HOLLY: What seven years?

ADAM: Apparently, there's a seven year period when we'll all get a chance to, you know, swallow the pill.

HOLLY: I thought everything happens in the twinkling of an eye.

ADAM: That's how long it'll take them to disappear, but the rest of us get seven more years before you-know-who arrives.

HOLLY: Mel Gibson?

ADAM: Close enough.

HOLLY: Well, I tell you what, Luke. If a third of the world's population suddenly disappears, I guarantee you, we'll accept Jesus. And it won't take seven years, it'll take more like seven seconds.

ADAM: Amen to that.
> *Adam and Holly clink glasses.*

LUKE: But what if you die before it happens?
> *A beat.*

HOLLY: Wait a minute. What?

ADAM: He's afraid I'll die before I get a chance to, you know, "accept Christ," and then we won't be able to be in the afterlife together.

> *Another beat.*

HOLLY: That's so sad.

ADAM: Not really. We're not allowed to be gay there, so what difference does it make?

HOLLY: That's true.

ADAM: No pets either.

HOLLY: Sounds like my last co-op meeting.

> *Luke slams a box down on the floor.*

LUKE: Why are you mocking me?

ADAM: I'm not mocking you.

LUKE: Yes, you are. You're being a jackass.

ADAM: We're joking, babe. Lighten up.

LUKE: Is it so wrong that I want you to go to heaven? I mean, what's the big fucking deal?

ADAM: Yes, because I don't believe in it, Luke. Not your version. It's too exclusive. Too many rules.

LUKE: Fine. Then I'll believe. For both of us.

> *He continues unpacking. Adam goes in for the kiss.*

ADAM: If you can believe so strongly, then how come you don't want me telling anyone you do?

LUKE: Because it's nobody's business! It's not something I go around shouting from rooftops.

ADAM: You're embarrassed, Luke. Admit it.

LUKE: I just don't like being judged, Adam. And that's what everyone does. Before they even get a chance to know who I am, they all have this predisposed disdain.

ADAM: Who does?

LUKE: You do! You never would've even considered dating me if you knew when we first met.

ADAM: The only reason we judge you, is because you guys go around judging everyone else. You people are all about judgment. You even have a whole day named after it.

LUKE: I don't judge anyone. It's not my place to do that. I'm just here to tell you there's a heaven. Whether you listen or not, that's up to you.

ADAM: Oh, I'm listening, babe. Believe me. And if you and all the other freaks are going to be the only ones up there, then no thanks, I'd rather burn.

Luke looks at Adam like he's a complete stranger all of a sudden. He gets up, and heads for the door, slamming it on his way out. Adam is fuming.

HOLLY: Awkward.

ADAM: The afterlife. Can you believe that shit?

HOLLY: Like you don't have enough problems in this one.

ADAM: I mean, the stories these people have been fed, the antiquated bullshit, it's mind boggling. I swear, if I hear one more parable about a flock of fucking sheep. It's like Shakespeare. Why are we still doing him after all these years?

HOLLY: Yeah, what a hack.

He sits on a box.

ADAM: Am I crazy? Does everyone think I'm nuts?

HOLLY: Not everyone.

ADAM: Martin and Bobby? Steven?

HOLLY: They do. Yes.

ADAM: Please, Steven's been dating abusive shits for years, and Martin and Bobby may as well be roommates.

HOLLY: They're just not sure what you're getting out of it. Besides the fact that he's young and hot. Bobby thinks maybe it's just you, once again, falling for someone who's unavailable. And if it is, this time, he thinks you've hit the jackpot.

ADAM: Yeah, well, I think Bobby might wanna stop blowing his trainer if he's gonna throw stones from that glass house Martin pays for.

HOLLY: They're offended, sweetie. Knowing how Luke feels. It's like an indictment of who they are.

ADAM: But he loves those guys!

HOLLY: Yeah, and he still thinks they're going to hell. It's self-loathing, Adam. And you're self loathing by association.

ADAM: But it's all he knows. It's what's kept the front door locked tight and the Pink Floyd off the stereo for all these years.

HOLLY: But at a certain point, you just have to break away from mommy and daddy and become your own person. I mean, I did. And my parents were big old Catholics.

ADAM: Not your dad.

HOLLY: Okay, but you can't get more Catholic than my mom. I mean, where did she take me for my sweet sixteen?

ADAM: The Vatican.

HOLLY: I'm just saying, there's a point when you gotta wake up and smell the coffee.

> *A beat.*

ADAM: What about Belinda? What does she think?

HOLLY: There are lots of gays in her church, and none of them think they're sinners. She doesn't get it either.

ADAM: Yeah, well, I don't get why she named her kid Mustard Seed.

HOLLY: Saffron.

ADAM: Parsley, Tarragon, Bullion Cube, whatever. It's weird.

HOLLY: I agree. She looks more like a root vegetable.

> *Another beat.*

ADAM: And you?

HOLLY: Me?

ADAM: Yeah. What do you think?

HOLLY: Truth?

ADAM: Yes, truth. No one calls me anymore.

> *Holly sits down next to him.*

HOLLY: What do you care what I think? Look within, sweetie. That's what my yoga teacher says.

ADAM: The one with the zero percent body fat?

HOLLY: He's a genius.

ADAM: Having a 29 inch waist and being able to breathe through your asshole does not a genius make.

HOLLY: Remember when you first started working at the shop? We'd hang out all the time. Couldn't get enough of each other. And at the end of the night, you'd walk me home. But only half way. Maybe a block or two further, if I begged. But as soon as we hit 74th and Columbus, you'd turn around and leave me there. It used to piss me off. I don't know why. I just felt like you should've walked me all the way. But you'd only go so far. And that would make me want you to even more.

ADAM: Yeah. So?

HOLLY: Well, a few weeks ago, after that weird benefit for Katrina victims or, no, kids with club feet—

ADAM: —Cleft palates.

HOLLY: —Cleft palates, right. And you were walking me home, telling me that story about how Luke dropped a fan on your face in the middle of the night—

ADAM: —I had Honeywell branded on my forehead for like—

HOLLY: —and there we were, suddenly, coming up to that same damn corner. I could just feel the dread rising in me. Old, stupid feelings, irrational ones, I know, but there they were again. Well, we hit 74th and you kept walking, past 75th and 76th, and before you know it, you'd walked me all the way to 82nd street, and you hadn't even noticed.

ADAM: I did?

She looks at her watch.

HOLLY: Shit, I gotta run.

ADAM: You can't leave me now.

HOLLY: I have to, sweetie. I'm late for my chanting group.

ADAM: Oh, Christ, what are you chanting for this week, a new boyfriend? A lot of good it's done you so far.

HOLLY: *(stung)* Thanks.

ADAM: I'm sorry. That was mean.

HOLLY: At least I'm trying. At least I'm open to it.

ADAM: I know. I'm a jerk.

HOLLY: You're always so good at figuring out exactly why something's not gonna work. This one's too this or that one's too that. These poor guys. It's like, they're all doomed from the get go.

ADAM: I'm usually right, though. I can't help it.

HOLLY: Did you ever think that maybe, in the end, you just don't have faith that any of them will stay?

Another beat.

ADAM: I'm still stuck on the whole walking you home analogy.

HOLLY: You're going places you've never been before, dummy. Who cares what the rest of us think. Just let yourself go.

She gives him a peck on the cheek and heads for the door, stopping before she exits.

HOLLY: Are fag hags allowed in heaven? Not that I care or anything. Just curious.

ADAM: I don't see why not. No crime in being a fag hag.

She breathes a sigh of relief, then adds before exiting.

HOLLY: Aiding and abetting?

ADAM: True.

>*Holly goes. Adam takes in the mess all around him.*

SCENE SIX

>*The waiting room. Adam and Butch sit on opposite sides of the room, flipping through magazines. Arlene paces on her cell phone.*

ARLENE: Oh, for Pete sake, how many did she eat? . . . The whole box? . . . Well, how the heck did that happen? Uh-huh . . . Uh-huh . . . Uh huh . . .

>*She exits down the hallway. Butch tosses his magazine down.*

BUTCH: Porn.

>*Adam looks up, completely confused.*

ADAM: What was that?

BUTCH: What was what?

ADAM: You said, "porn?"

BUTCH: Oh, I'm just goofing.

>*Holly enters, in her coat.*

HOLLY: You guys should really get outside for a bit. The air is gorgeous.

>*She hangs it up.*

HOLLY: They're still not letting anyone in?

ADAM: Nope.

BUTCH: How about a game of cards, Holly?

HOLLY: Me?

BUTCH: A little five card stud?

HOLLY: I'm not really big on cards.

BUTCH: No?

HOLLY: I've got this weird competitive streak.

BUTCH: Is that right?

HOLLY: It isn't pretty.

BUTCH: Come on. I'll go easy on you.

HOLLY: I don't think so.

BUTCH: You sure?

HOLLY: Pretty sure.

BUTCH: Some gin rummy, maybe?

HOLLY: Don't tempt me.

BUTCH: Nickel a point. Jokers are wild.

HOLLY: Okay, you're on, mister.

BUTCH: 'Atta girl.

>*Butch pulls out a deck of cards and starts shuffling. Holly takes a seat next to him.*

HOLLY: I'm a little rusty, so let's take it slow.

BUTCH: Don't worry. I'll be gentle. We'll play the seven card version.

>*Adam picks up the magazine Butch just tossed. It's the Newsweek. He points to the prehistoric man on the cover.*

ADAM: This guy, here?

BUTCH: What's that?

ADAM: The missing link?

BUTCH: Uh-huh?

ADAM: You find him pornographic?

BUTCH: I find it irresponsible, that's all. *(to Holly)* Don't forget now, jokers are wild.

HOLLY: Got it.

ADAM: Funny, I look at him and I see my fifth grade gym teacher.

BUTCH: Looks like an ape to me.

HOLLY: My fifth grade gym teacher was way hairier than that. Handsome woman. Looked just like a sheepdog.

>*Holly and Butch pick up their cards and arrange their hands.*

ADAM: But don't apes and humans have a very similar genetic make up?

BUTCH: I wouldn't know.

ADAM: We do. We're like one gene apart. I'm almost positive.

BUTCH: If you say so.

ADAM: You'd think there'd be some kind of correlation.

BUTCH: I'm feeling lucky, Holly.

ADAM: I mean, I'm not Einstein or anything. Just seems like a given.

BUTCH: Apes don't have souls, son. How can something without a soul morph into something with one?

>*Arlene reenters, snapping her cell phone closed.*

ARLENE: Well, Frieda shit all over the apartment.

HOLLY: Your housekeeper?

ARLENE: My dog. I don't have a housekeeper. That's Lynn, remember? Butch's new and improved wife.

BUTCH: The one who doesn't talk so much.

ARLENE: No, I never had that luxury, did I, Butch? You were broke when we were married, weren't you, hon?

>*She perches behind him and checks out his hand.*

BUTCH: I told you not to get that damn dog. You can't take care of yourself, let alone a four and a half pound Chihuahua.

ARLENE: Oh, would you hush. The neighbor's got it all under control. She's gnawing on a bull penis, right now. She'll be fine. She survived the streets of San Juan for eight months, she can crap on my Sisal for another couple nights.

HOLLY: I'm sorry . . . bull penis?

ARLENE: They advertise it as beef tendon, but the Oriental lady at the pet store gave me the real skinny.

BUTCH: Sounds like what they served on the plane.

ARLENE: *(re: cards)* I wouldn't play that if I were you.

BUTCH: Do you mind?

ARLENE: Okay, buster, but don't say I didn't warn you.

>*She scans the room for her purse.*

ADAM: What about bats?

ARLENE: Bats?

ADAM: Rats with wings, right? There's gotta be some morphing going on there, don't you think?

BUTCH: We're back on that, are we?

ADAM: Or Siegfried and Roy? They morphed two species and came up with a liger. How do you explain that?

ARLENE: How do you explain Siegfried and Roy?

BUTCH: Must have been on the ark at the same time, that's how. I don't believe one morphed into the other.

HOLLY: Aces are low, right?

BUTCH: Yup.

ADAM: The ark? See, now, there's a concept I've never quite been able to wrap my head around.

ARLENE: Anyone see my purse?

ADAM: All those animals on one little boat? I mean, does anyone else think that's a little over the top, or is it just me?

BUTCH: Says so right there in the Bible.

ADAM: I know, but the whole Bible sort of feels that way to me. With the parting of the seas and the walking on water.

HOLLY: Adam.

ADAM: I don't know. It all seems a little Vegas, for my taste.

BUTCH: I'm not the one who brought up Siegfried and Roy.

ARLENE: My purse, people. Who's got my . . . Oh.

Arlene finds her purse and starts rooting through it.

ADAM: Might just be me though. I mean, I didn't grow up with the Bible, so I've never really had any sort of connection to it.

BUTCH: *(re: cards)* You're killing me, here.

ADAM: In fact, I could probably wipe myself with it today, and wake up tomorrow, with a clean ass and a clear conscience.

The game, the conversation, everything comes to a crashing halt. All eyes fo to Adam.

ARLENE: I could have done without that visual.

ADAM: *(backpedaling)* I was just trying to, you know, illustrate my point.

ARLENE: Oh no, hon, we got it.

ADAM: I'm just saying. Give me an argument that means something. Give me science.

BUTCH: Science isn't all it's cracked up to be, son. They told us the world was flat for centuries. Sometimes it's just a tool used to disprove the word of God. Says so in the Bible. If you weren't so busy wiping your ass with it, maybe you'd know that.

Butch locks eyes with Adam. Holly lays her cards down, awkwardly.

HOLLY: Gin.

BUTCH: *(shaking it off)* Beginner's luck. Double or nothing.

Arlene gently tries to tug her coat out from underneath Butch.

BUTCH: Would you knock it off?

ARLENE: You're on my coat, Butch.

He grabs hold of it.

BUTCH: What do you need it for?

ARLENE: What do you mean, what do I need it for? I'm cold.

BUTCH: Don't snow me, Arlene.

ARLENE: I'm not snowing you.

BUTCH: Bullcrap.

ARLENE: Nobody's snowing anybody, Butch. Let go.

BUTCH: You want me to let go?

ARLENE: I mean it.

BUTCH: Oh, I know you do.

ARLENE: Butch!

> *Butch lets the coat go and Arlene falls backward landing on*
> *her ass. It's a startling moment. He pulls her bottle of pills out*
> *and holds them in the air.*

BUTCH: Is this what you were looking for?

> *He tosses them at her.*

BUTCH: It took you five years to get off that crap, and five hours to get
back on it.

ARLENE: Butch...

BUTCH: Don't Butch me. Our son's in a coma, sweetheart. Start dealing with it.

> *Butch storms out of the room. Adam and Holly look at each*
> *other uncomfortably as Arlene slowly picks herself up off the*
> *floor.*

ARLENE: *(trying to recover)* Boy, oh, boy. That was like Jerry Springer
time, wasn't it?

> *She pockets the pills and hangs her coat back up.*

ARLENE: Don't mind him. He's just... upset, is all.

> *She straightens her skirt.*

ARLENE: Better go see if I can... calm him down.

> *She starts off. Brandon enters, a concerned look on his face.*

ARLENE: Brandon?

BRANDON: It's Luke... They need you in there.

> *Arlene rushes off.*

HOLLY: What's going on, Brandon?

BRANDON: I'm not sure... He's... Something's changed.

> *End of Act One*

Act II

SCENE ONE

> *The waiting room. Brandon sits alone. Holly enters, in a daze.*

BRANDON: How's everyone holding up in there?

HOLLY: Okay, I guess. You going back in?

BRANDON: I think I'll stay out here for a while.

HOLLY: Me, too.

She sits next to him.

BRANDON: Has Adam talked to them yet?

HOLLY: There hasn't exactly been a good time. He spoke to the surgeon though.

BRANDON: And?

HOLLY: He thinks Adam should do whatever he can to persuade Butch and Arlene to, you know, do "the right thing." How do you make that call?

BRANDON: Yeah.

HOLLY: There's an organ transplant representative lurking around, smiling at everyone. Which is creepy.

A beat.

HOLLY: Would that be considered murder in their eyes, Brandon? I mean, what's the general consensus?

BRANDON: It's different for everyone. Butch and Arlene? Who knows where they stand?

HOLLY: Yeah, well, I know where I stand. Life's grand and all, but no thank you.

Another beat.

HOLLY: At least, that's where I think I stand. I mean, it's one thing to say it, but to actually have to . . . The whole thing is so confusing, all of a sudden.

BRANDON: Yeah.

Holly glances around the room.

HOLLY: Where's your . . . uh . . . Nevermind.

BRANDON: Bible?

She nods, sheepishly.

BRANDON: Arlene has it.

HOLLY: It's funny . . . Moments like this . . . How ingrained this stuff becomes . . . I mean, I sell candles for a living. I've been to fucking ashrams and silent meditation retreats. I've got like five yoga mats in my closet . . . But I haven't stopped crossing myself since I got here.

More sitting.

HOLLY: What about you, Brandon?

BRANDON: Me?

HOLLY: Yeah, where do you stand?

BRANDON: I think I probably feel the same way Adam does.

HOLLY: Really?

BRANDON: But for different reasons.

HOLLY: How so?

BRANDON: When it's your time, it's your time. That's what I believe. There's a plan for Luke. A perfect one. And I don't believe in getting in the way of that.

HOLLY: I guess.

BRANDON: But it's not really for me to say.

> *Holly thinks about this for a moment, then . . .*

HOLLY: Do you think it's for Adam to say?

SCENE TWO

> *Adam and Luke's apartment. Three years earlier. Adam enters through the front door.*

LUKE: *(O.S.)* Babe?

ADAM: Hi.

LUKE: *(O.S.)* You're home?

ADAM: My leg is bothering me. I hope I'm not getting a clot or something.

LUKE: A clot?

ADAM: Yeah, like what that cute reporter in Iraq died from? He had a wife and kids and everything, poor guy.

LUKE: *(O.S.)* Thrombosis? You don't have a thrombosis, Adam.

ADAM: I hope not.

> *Adam opens the closet door and a bunch of crap falls out. Unfazed, he hangs his coat up, stuffs the crap back in, and heads for the kitchen.*

ADAM: I'm making tea. Want some?

> *Luke rushes in from the bedroom.*

LUKE: Will you help me get rid of this thing in the bedroom?

ADAM: *(O.S.)* What thing?

LUKE: The ass photo.

ADAM: *(O.S.)* My Mapplethorpe knock off? It cost me a fortune. Why would I wanna get rid of it?

LUKE: Never mind.

> *On a mission, he starts plucking books off the bookshelf.*
> *Adam reenters, with his pants rolled up.*

ADAM: Does my left calf look bigger than my right?

LUKE: No.

ADAM: It feels bigger.

> *He sits, examining his calf.*

LUKE: How long does it take to get here from JFK?

ADAM: I don't know. Forty-five minutes, depending on traffic. Why?

LUKE: My dad just called.

ADAM: So?

LUKE: From JFK. He's on his way over.

> *Adam's jaw drops as Luke grabs the books and makes a bee-line for the closet.*

ADAM: Wait a minute. What?

LUKE: Hasn't thought about New York in thirty years and all of a sudden he's nostalgic.

ADAM: You mean I finally get to meet him?

LUKE: Not if I can help it.

> *Luke opens the closet door and the crap falls out again.*

LUKE: Would you mind giving me a hand here? We don't have much time.

ADAM: To what?

LUKE: Degay the apartment.

> *Luke shoves all the crap back in heads into the bedroom.*
> *Adam is freaking.*

ADAM: Your father's coming?

LUKE: *(O.S.)* Like any minute.

ADAM: What's he in town for?

LUKE: Some auction. I don't know. The whole thing was very last minute. Very spontaneous. Very, you know, psychotic.

> *He reenters with a Tinky Winky doll and tosses it into the closet.*

LUKE: He wants to check out my apartment while he's here.

ADAM: Our apartment.

LUKE: Yeah, well he doesn't know that. Are you gonna help me with the ass photo or what?

ADAM: I like that ass photo. It took me three years to pay for it.

LUKE: Well, I don't want it hanging over the bed when he gets here.

ADAM: How about I hang you over the bed?

LUKE: Is that a Capote book on the top shelf?

> *Luke snatches it off the bookshelf and tosses it onto the couch.*

ADAM: Why don't you grow some hair on your balls and just tell him already?

LUKE: *(O.S.)* Are you nuts? I told you what he said when I quit law school.

ADAM: No, you didn't.

LUKE: *(O.S.)* He said he'd never let me speak to my little brother again if he ever found out I was gay.

ADAM: And you don't think he knows?! All those years you were doing splits in your backyard in your little Richard Simmons shorts? Just tell him, already.

LUKE: *(O.S.)* I will. I promise.

> *Luke reenters with an armful of framed photos, and heads for the bookshelf.*

LUKE: Next Fall. When Ben's in college. I figure by then he'll be old enough to decide for himself.

ADAM: Now what?

LUKE: Photos.

ADAM: Luke!

LUKE: Just the lovey-dovey ones . . . I'm gonna put a few of my old ones up, just to, you know, sell the place a little more.

> *He takes some photos off the bookshelf, and replaces them with new ones. Adam grabs one and looks at it.*

ADAM: Who's that?

LUKE: My little brother.

ADAM: Looks like Adolf Hitler as a young girl.

LUKE: Give me that.

> *Luke snatches it back, cleaning it with his shirt sleeve.*

LUKE: I can't believe how filthy these got.

ADAM: You know, one of these days, it's all gonna come crashing down on you.

LUKE: Yeah, like today, if you don't start giving me a hand.

ADAM: And I ain't gonna be around to pick up the pieces.

LUKE: Windex. We need Windex. Would you mind running down to the deli?

ADAM: Absolutely not.

LUKE: Adam?!

ADAM: No, Luke. I refuse to participate in this homophobic bullshit.

LUKE: Then would you please start thinking of where you're gonna go, because I can't have you around when he gets here.

Luke selects a few photos, picks the box up and stands. The bottom of the box breaks, sending the photos everywhere.

LUKE: Fuck!

He gets on his hands and knees, desperately trying to collect them all.

LUKE: This would be so much easier if you'd just give me a fucking hand.

ADAM: Look at you.

LUKE: What, Adam? What?!

ADAM: You're like an animal in a trap trying to gnaw your own leg off.

This hits Luke for a moment, but then he quickly springs back into action.

LUKE: Fine. I'll get it myself.

He leaves the mess on the floor and bolts for the front door.

LUKE: But I want you out of here when I get back. I'm serious. Just for an hour or two. *(pleading)* Please.

He exits, leaving the door slightly ajar.

ADAM: I ain't going anywhere, sweet tits. You'll have to stuff me in the closet with the rest of the incriminating evidence.

Adam looks at the photos on the floor.

ADAM: Lovey-dovey ones?

He picks one up.

ADAM: I didn't even like you on this vacation.

He tosses it back into the box. Picks up another, and tosses it in. And before you know it, he's cleaned up the entire mess.

ADAM: Crazy.

Grabbing the Capote book, and placing it defiantly back up on the shelf, he picks up the box, and exits into the bedroom. There's a knock at the door.

BUTCH: *(O.S.)* Hello?

Butch pokes his head in, then enters, tentatively.

ADAM: *(O.S.)* I can't believe you took this thing down. What, the man's never seen a big black ass before?

Adam comes out of the bedroom, the ass photo in his hands. He stops short when he sees Butch standing there.

BUTCH: I'm sorry. I must have the wrong apartment.

ADAM: No... um... He's... He went to the deli.

BUTCH: I see.

ADAM: For Windex.

BUTCH: Okay.

ADAM: He should be back any second.

BUTCH: Terrific.

> *They stare at each other.*

ADAM: Excuse me, for a minute.

> *Adam exits back into the bedroom with the photo. Butch takes the place in again. He hears a loud crash.*

ADAM: *(O.S.)* Shit.

> *Adam returns, flustered.*

BUTCH: Everything okay in there?

ADAM: It's fine.

> *They stand there, awkwardly.*

BUTCH: I'm Luke's dad.

ADAM: From Florida.

BUTCH: Tallahassee, right.

ADAM: You're in for an auction?

BUTCH: I am.

ADAM: Cool.

> *Adam's teakettle whistles.*

ADAM: My water's boiling.

BUTCH: Do what you gotta do.

> *He starts off, then turns.*

ADAM: Would you like some?

BUTCH: Some?

ADAM: Tea?

BUTCH: Sure. What the heck.

> *Adam exits into the kitchen. Butch checks out the pad.*

BUTCH: Swanky place.

ADAM: *(O.S.)* Yeah, it's... you know... serviceable.

BUTCH: How long's he been living here?

ADAM: *(O.S.)* Who?

BUTCH: Luke.

ADAM: *(O.S.)* Oh... Yeah... Um... two years, I guess?

BUTCH: Two, really? How about that?

> *He wanders over to the window and stares out. Adam reenters with two cups of tea.*

ADAM: Here you go.

BUTCH: They're gone.

ADAM: Excuse me?

BUTCH: The towers. You can't help but notice on the way in from the airport.

ADAM: Oh, yeah. If you look down to your right there, you can see where they were.

BUTCH: I spent a semester here in college. The year they started construction on them. I used to go down, once or twice a month, to check out the progress. Watch them work their way into the sky. Made me feel proud to be here. New York. Like I was part of something.

ADAM: Honey?

> *Adam holds up a honey bear.*

BUTCH: Straight's fine.

> *He hands Butch his tea.*

BUTCH: Nice cups.

> *They blow on their tea.*

BUTCH: Dainty.

ADAM: So, you spent a semester here?

BUTCH: Working for Carl Randolph, yeah. They're auctioning off his entire estate this afternoon.

ADAM: You're going to the Carl Randolph auction?

BUTCH: Uh-huh.

ADAM: At Sotheby's?

BUTCH: He was sort of a mentor to me.

ADAM: That's like the hottest ticket in town.

BUTCH: I've got my eye on a set of books. Hardy Boys. First editions. Fifteen, maybe twenty volumes. All signed and in pristine condition. He kept them on display in his office. As a reminder, I guess. Of his childhood. His youthful aspirations. That always sort of stuck with me, and I thought I might like to have them.

ADAM: Carl Randolph? My God, he was like huge in the eighties. He made Donald Trump look like, well, Donald Trump. I used to see him on the subway, once in a while. No entourage. No bodyguards. Just him. I thought that was so cool. I mean, there he was, acting like he was one of us, when really he was, you know, Carl Randolph.

Butch smiles.

BUTCH: And who are you?

ADAM: Who am I?

That hangs in the air for a second, until Luke enters, instantly thrown.

LUKE: Dad!

BUTCH: Hello, son.

LUKE: That was quick.

BUTCH: Saheed was a yacker with a lead foot.

LUKE: And . . . So . . . You're having tea?

He sets the Windex down and quickly cases the joint.

BUTCH: Your friend here made it.

LUKE: Then you two have met?

BUTCH: We were just getting to that.

LUKE: This is Adam, Dad. We work together.

BUTCH: At the flower shop?

ADAM: Candles.

LUKE: Candles.

LUKE: Adam's been there longer than I have.

ADAM: Too long. I'm trying to move on.

LUKE: For two years, he's been saying that.

ADAM: Not two. Besides, I had a teaching interview today, and—

BUTCH: So, this is it, huh, kiddo?

Butch meanders around the place.

LUKE: This is what?

BUTCH: Your bachelor pad.

LUKE: Yup. This is it.

BUTCH: How about that?

Luke spots the Capote book, nabs it off the shelf, glaring at Adam as he heads into the bedroom.

LUKE: So, how was your flight?

BUTCH: Easy. Quick. Your mom thinks I've lost it.

LUKE: Well, it is a little out of the blue, Dad.

BUTCH: I know, but what the heck. Life's short and then you die.

ADAM: *(can't help himself)* And then what happens?

Butch turns from the bookshelf. Adam gives him a wink.

LUKE: *(O.S.)* Oh, no! What happened to the ass pho . . . the Mapplethorpe knock off.

ADAM: I broke it.

LUKE: *(O.S.)* Babe!

> *This hangs in the air, until Luke reenters, mortified. They all look at each other for a moment until Butch smiles.*

BUTCH: Where's the bathroom?

LUKE: In there.

BUTCH: Excuse me, men.

> *They watch him exit into the bathroom.*

LUKE: I can't believe I just said that.

ADAM: I don't think he heard.

LUKE: Are you crazy? Of course, he heard.

ADAM: And, so what if he did?

LUKE: This is unbelievable.

ADAM: Come on, babe. He knows. He called our cups dainty.

LUKE: Well, they are dainty.

ADAM: He thinks you work at a flower shop. He likes the Hardy Boys. He knows. He knows. And if he didn't before, he certainly does now.

LUKE: Somebody shoot me.

ADAM: He worked for Carl Randolph, Luke. The guy was his mentor.

LUKE: So?

ADAM: So? Carl Randolph was gay.

LUKE: No, he wasn't. He had a wife and he had kids.

ADAM: He was a big old leather queen. They wrote about it in Vanity Fair last month.

LUKE: Oh, God.

ADAM: Just tell him, already. I'll tell him with you. We'll hold hands and walk into the fire together.

LUKE: Or I could pretend the whole thing never happened. I'm good at that.

ADAM: Come on, babe. You don't want to end up like one of those people.

LUKE: What people?

ADAM: Who wake up in the middle of the night . . . Screaming.

They hear the toilet flush.

LUKE: Okay, but if I'm gonna walk into the fire, I'm gonna do it alone. Just me and him. Mano a mano.

ADAM: You want me to go?

LUKE: Yes. Please. Quick. Before I change my mind.

ADAM: I'm so proud of you.

> *They go to kiss, but quickly abort when they hear the door knob turn.*

ADAM: I'll be on my cell if you need me.

> *Adam scoots out the door. Luke takes a deep breath as Butch reenters from the bathroom.*

BUTCH: Tight squeeze in there.

LUKE: Yeah... you know... New York.

BUTCH: I like how you've got all those pictures on the wall. Gives you something to look at while you're on the crapper.

LUKE: *(bracing himself)* Dad?

> *Butch hands over a framed photo.*

BUTCH: This one must have fallen.

LUKE: Oh, thanks.

BUTCH: These are the folks you did that Huck Finn play with, right?

LUKE: Yeah.

BUTCH: You were good in that. *(pause)* You all were.

LUKE: Really?

BUTCH: Well, most of you... I mean, I'm no patron of the arts, but... this play... that was... something.

LUKE: You're kidding me.

BUTCH: Am I wrong?

LUKE: No, it's just... I'm just a little shocked, that's all.

BUTCH: Listen, I know I'm not the most supportive parent in the world. I thought it was a big mistake when you left law school, I'm not gonna lie to you. But that play... I don't know, I guess I kinda started to see how the acting thing might be something you could be proud of someday.

LUKE: Wow...

BUTCH: I mean, money isn't everything, right?

LUKE: Totally. I love it.

BUTCH: I remember some jerk was sitting in front of me. Yackin' the whole time, buggin' everyone, so I start shushing him, telling him to be quiet, and he turns around, like, what's your problem, and I say "That's my son up there, and if you don't start paying attention, I'm gonna bop you one." And boy, if that didn't shut him up.

> *The two men share a great laugh together, connecting finally, like old pals, then Luke switches gears.*

LUKE: Listen, Dad . . .

BUTCH: Let me ask you something though, kiddo. And this is something I was always curious about.

LUKE: Sure.

BUTCH: *(curious)* Was the nigger a fag?

LUKE: Excuse me?

BUTCH: That guy there. The one who played the slave. He was a fag, right?

> *Luke is completely sucker punched.*

BUTCH: He was kinda swishy, that's all. Like I said, I don't know my ass from my elbow when it comes to this stuff, I just thought it would have been nice to have someone a little more . . .

LUKE: *(stunned)* White?

BUTCH: Manly . . . In the part.

> *Butch gives him a wink.*

BUTCH: But what the heck do I know?

> *He rises.*

BUTCH: So, where'd your friend go?

LUKE: Oh, his leg hurt. Thrombosis or something.

BUTCH: Thrombosis?

LUKE: I don't know. There's always something going on with him.

BUTCH: Okay, well, come on then. Let's eat.

> *Butch grabs his bag. Luke just sits there, frozen.*

SCENE THREE

> *Adam's apartment. A year later. Adam, in his underwear, sits in front of his laptop. The glow of the screen illuminates his face.*

LUKE: *(O.S.)* Adam?

ADAM: Yeah?

LUKE: *(O.S.)* What are you doing?

ADAM: Nothing. Go back to sleep.
        Adam continues staring at the screen.
LUKE: *(O.S.)* Are you on that website again?
        He looks up, guilty.
ADAM: What website?
LUKE: *(O.S.)* The brain tumor website.
        He quickly snaps the laptop shut.
        Luke enters from the bedroom, half asleep.
LUKE: You promised.
ADAM: I know I did.
        Adam's in hell. Luke joins him on the couch.
LUKE: Tell me what the doctor said again.
ADAM: It could be a sinus infection, some kind of vertigo thing, a
        virus ... He doesn't know.
LUKE: He said it wasn't a brain tumor, Adam.
ADAM: He said he didn't think it was a brain tumor.
LUKE: You're still feeling dizzy?
ADAM: Not dizzy ... Fuzzy. Like my brain is swollen or something.
LUKE: What about the headache?
ADAM: It's more like my hair aches. Like my follicles are sore.
LUKE: Okay, you need therapy.
ADAM: And now the squishy noise is back.
LUKE: Electric shock therapy.
ADAM: It got so distracting I had to cancel all my classes this after-
        noon.
LUKE: Please, don't sabotage this teaching stuff. It took you so long
        to finally make the change.
ADAM: I can't help it! The fuzziness. The ringing. It's not normal.
LUKE: You're telling me?
ADAM: I'm serious!
        *Adam gets up and starts pacing. Luke sees that he's really
        spiraling this time.*
LUKE: Why don't you go get an MRI then? Come on, babe, I'll go
        with you. So we can know it's not a brain tumor, once and for
        all, and relax.
ADAM: But what if it is?
LUKE: You have to stop, Adam. Seriously. When there are so many
        people who really do have something to worry about?

ADAM: I know.

LUKE: You have so much to be thankful for.

ADAM: I know. I know.

LUKE: Then why do you keep trying to fuck it all up?

ADAM: It's not like I'm trying. It's not like I'm thinking, "Huh, life's pretty good right now. Maybe I should give myself a brain tumor."

LUKE: You're unhappy, Adam.

ADAM: I know I'm unhappy. My fucking head hurts! You'd be unhappy, too!

LUKE: In life ... It's like you don't feel you deserve to be, or something. Like the minute you actually do, it's all gonna be taken away from you. I mean, what are you so afraid of?
  A beat.

ADAM: Oh, God. We're gonna go there, aren't we?

LUKE: Where?

ADAM: To Jesus land. Go ahead. I know you want to.

LUKE: I didn't say anything.

ADAM: Why is it every time I reach out to you, every time there's some kind of crisis in my life, this is the only thing you have to offer?

LUKE: What are you talking about?

ADAM: It is, Luke. It fucking is.

LUKE: I don't know what you're talking about.

ADAM: Like when my dad died.

LUKE: I was there for you.

ADAM: Come on.

LUKE: I was fucking there for you, Adam! I flew half way across the country to be there for you. I held his ashes in my lap on the way home from the service. I mean, what more do you want?

ADAM: That's not what I mean.

LUKE: I sat in a different pew because you didn't want anyone to feel "uncomfortable." I took communion while you and the rest of your family just sat there like idiots. I practically wrote his whole fucking eulogy for you. Don't tell me I wasn't there, Adam. I was there.

ADAM: Before, Luke. I'm talking about the night he died. When we were lying in bed together. And you looked at me, all of a sudden, with this, it was almost smug, Luke, this holier than-thou look of pity on your face—

LUKE: —I was trying to comfort you!

ADAM: But it didn't mean anything! Don't you get it? You may as well have been speaking a foreign language! And for that to be the only thing you have to offer, at a time when I needed you the most. I'm sorry, but I've never felt so alone in all my life.

LUKE: Well, what did you want me to do?

ADAM: Hold me!

> *A beat.*

ADAM: I just wanted you to fucking hold me, Luke! Is that so hard to understand?

> *Another beat.*

LUKE: A little.

ADAM: Forget it.

LUKE: I'm sorry, but it is.

ADAM: I don't even know why I bothered to bring it up.

LUKE: Because I'm not afraid like you are, Adam. When the time comes . . . I welcome it. *(gentle)* You could, too.

ADAM: You're doing it again.

LUKE: I just hate to see you in pain like this.

ADAM: Listen, I would love that, believe me . . . It's like the one thing I envy you for . . . To know everything's gonna be alright . . . No matter what . . . To feel . . . safe like that? It would almost be worth it.

LUKE: It is worth it, Adam. It's so worth it.

ADAM: But I've never had that in my life, so how do I know for sure? I wasn't the one sitting in my dad's Chrysler Lebaron when the white light shined down—

LUKE: —It wasn't a white light.

ADAM: The warmth, the peace, whatever it was—

LUKE: Home, Adam. *(a pause)* I felt home. For the first time in my life. *(another pause)* It's there, babe. You just have to be open to it.

> *Adam, sits, completely lost.*

ADAM: This all started back in college. I had mono, and thought for sure it was AIDS. It was before there was even a test, remember?

LUKE: I was eight.

ADAM: Well, it was horrible, trust me. And I remember being convinced, at the time, that it was, like my punishment.

LUKE: Punishment?

ADAM: For being gay.

LUKE: Punishment from whom?

ADAM: Oh, I don't know . . . God, I guess.

> *A beat.*

ADAM: You don't have to believe in hell to walk around feeling like
you're gonna burn in it.

LUKE: What if He wasn't a punisher?

> *Luke moves closer.*

LUKE: You mentioned your soul the night we first met.

ADAM: I did?

LUKE: You said it was fat. That's how I knew we were meant to be.

> *He wraps his arms around Adam.*

LUKE: You believe, Adam. I know you do . . . And I knew that night
on the rooftop . . . whether you had or you hadn't yet . . . I knew
that one day you'd see.

> *He holds him closer.*

LUKE: Please, Adam . . . For me.

> *Adam, desperate for the pain to go away, closes his eyes and
> waits for something to happen. Nothing. So, he shuts them
> tighter, trying hard, to feel the warmth, something. Still
> nothing. He gives in finally, his face softening, and there's a
> peace that starts to wash over him. It's a little overwhelming,
> losing control, so he opens his eyes again, and finds himself
> back in his living room where he started.*

ADAM: I'm gonna get a sleeping pill.

> *He gets up and heads for the bathroom.*

LUKE: *(crestfallen)* Make it two.

ADAM: Can we wear our new sleeping masks?

LUKE: Sure . . . As long as it doesn't, you know, make your hair hurt.

> *Luke opens the laptop and stares at the brain tumor site.*

LUKE: Remember that huge fight we had a few years back?

ADAM: *(O.S.)* About the rapture?

LUKE: And I said that thing about the cancer patient, and the pill and
all that?

> *Adam reenters and hands over a sleeping pill.*

ADAM: Vaguely.

> *Luke holds the pill up for Adam to see, then pops it in his mouth and swallows.*

LUKE: See?

> *Adam considers this for a moment.*

ADAM: Yeah, but come on, babe. If it were that easy, who wouldn't swallow it?

> *He picks up his laptop and exits, leaving Luke there in limbo.*

SCENE FOUR

> *A small make-shift temple in Beth Israel. Arlene sits quietly, searching for answers.*
>
> *Adam enters, tentatively. Arlene sees him, then scoots over to make room. He braces himself and joins her.*

ARLENE: Quiet, isn't it?

ADAM: Yeah . . .

> *They take the place in. Torahs. A huge Star of David. Prayer shawls. A bowl of yarmulkes.*

ARLENE: They have this elevator here, some nice lady was telling me, it automatically stops on every floor. And I thought, now what on earth would you want that for? Turns out they're not supposed to use electricity on weekends. Jewish people. It's against their religion.

ADAM: I think it was about energy, originally. You weren't supposed to exert any on the Sabbath. Sort of like an "And on the seventh day He rested" kind of thing. But then, I guess, as time went on, and technology advanced, it included all the new and improved gadgets that made life easier.

ARLENE: I see . . . Well, I guess they're allowed to use all of that now, they're just not allowed to push any buttons.

> *They stare some more at their surroundings.*

ARLENE: So many things to consider.

ADAM: I'm sure.

ARLENE: And never having been in this position before.

ADAM: Of course.

ARLENE: Just need a little more time to . . .

ADAM: Sort things out?

ARLENE: Pray.

Adam notices Brandon's Bible in her lap.

ARLENE: I'm one, too. Does that surprise you?

ADAM: Me? No. I'm . . . No, not at all.

ARLENE: At least I think I am. Who knows anymore. But then I grab hold of this thing. So familiar. Like an old friend. I read a passage I've read a thousand times before . . . It gives me comfort somehow. Butch is a whole other story. He really clings to the damn thing for dear life, poor guy . . . I'm sure that's my fault, too. Just another victim of Lung Lady's evil ways.

ADAM: Lung Lady?

ARLENE: Oh, that's just something I started calling myself after we split.

ADAM: Were you a big smoker?

ARLENE: No. Well, yes. I was. But that's not why.

A beat.

ARLENE: I used to be a bit of a loose cannon. We both were. Butch and me. Couple of crazies. But at a certain point, Butch pulled himself together, and I just sank further into it all. I'd disappear for days at a time. Weeks even. Then six months in jail. For selling pot. Not even selling, really. Oh, it's a long stupid story, involving my ex-best friend, a one-armed beautician from Shreveport, I kid you not, and a couple of kilos of Maui Wowee, but I was just a fool. Mad at the world and no one was gonna tell me otherwise. Not even this sweet, little kid. When I got out, I was so determined to make it up to him, I scraped together some cash, and bought him a bicycle. It had the sparkly tassels, the wicker basket, and everything just like he wanted, and he wouldn't look at the damn thing. Just sat in his sandbox, ignoring me. I started stomping my foot and screaming at the little shit. "Now, you listen to me, young man." Like, all of a sudden, I'm gonna be a mother, right? Well, Luke wasn't having it, and he shouts back, "No, you listen to me, lung lady." And we just glared at each other for a minute, like a couple of mules, then I fell out laughing, and I thought, you know he's right. That's what I've become. One of those evil cartoon characters. Flames bursting out my metallic bustier. With dark and mysterious powers no one would ever understand.

ADAM: Lung Lady.

ARLENE: Of course, that's not what he meant, but the name sorta stuck. Eventually, I worked my way into the sandbox with him. He's sitting there all angry and defiant, just like his mama. And all of a sudden I can't speak. Afraid I might break him. Or lose him. He wiggles his little toes up against mine, and asks if people can glue their feet together. And I say, "Well, now why would anyone wanna do that?" And he looks up at me with those big, blue eyes, and says, "So no one can ever separate us." Well, that just took my breath away. And I realized I had to leave again . . .

    Another beat.

ARLENE: So, Lung Lady crawled back into her hole for another ten years until she was ready to resurface. Butch met Lynn not long after, so Luke finally had some . . . stability. Of course, who can recognize her now with all the work she's had done, but she's a good mom, I guess. Gave him a little brother who adores him. And me . . .

    Arlene takes out a Kleenex and blows her nose.

ARLENE: Better see how Butch is doing.

    She rises.

ADAM: Um . . .

ARLENE: Yes?

ADAM: Luke and I . . . We're . . .

    Adam rises, not quite sure how to proceed.

ADAM: He means so much to me . . .

    A beat.

ADAM: All of us, really . . . But especially . . .

    Another beat.

ADAM: He's always loved his life . . . Just as it is, you know? And now . . . Well, I can't imagine he'd be happy any other way . . .

ARLENE: I suppose you're right.

ADAM: He just wouldn't . . . I know it.

    They stare at each other for a moment.

ARLENE: You know, I got a chance to speak to the EMT guy when we first got here. A young, black man. Very nice. Apparently,

Luke went into shock right away, so there wasn't any pain, thank God.

ADAM: Yes.

ARLENE: But he kept asking for someone, just before he lost consciousness. It was faint, I guess, a little difficult to decipher, but the name, it sounded a lot like yours.

Brandon enters.

BRANDON: Your husband is asking for you.

ARLENE: Thank you, Brandon.

Arlene gives Adam's hand a squeeze.

ARLENE: I'll see what I can do.

She hands Brandon his Bible, and turns to Adam one last time.

ARLENE: Butch wasn't with me when the EMT guy told me all that, and I don't think I'll mention it to him. He's a good man, but he's not perfect.

She exits, leaving Adam sitting there.

BRANDON: They're getting a hotel room.

ADAM: Oh, yeah?

BRANDON: Butch says he'll think better if he lays down for a few hours.

ADAM: Probably a good idea.

A beat.

BRANDON: Adam . . .

ADAM: You were his emergency contact.

BRANDON: His . . .

ADAM: In his cell phone . . . You were the first one they called.

BRANDON: Oh . . . Yeah.

ADAM: *(searching)* I always thought he would change that, but . . . I guess . . .

Brandon joins him.

BRANDON: This might be a good time for you to be alone with him for awhile. I'll keep an eye out, you know. Just in case.

ADAM: *(wary)* Why are you doing this?

BRANDON: Don't ask why Adam. Just go . . . Go.

Adam looks at him for a moment longer, then exits.
Brandon takes the place in. He picks a yarmulke out of the bowl, and stares at it.

SCENE FIVE

> *Central Park. A year ago. Adam waits near a bench. Brandon joins him with two cups of coffee.*

ADAM: Is this okay?

BRANDON: Sure.

> *He hands one over.*

ADAM: This is like the fourth cup I've had today. What do I owe you?

BRANDON: Please. It's on me.

ADAM: Thanks.

> *They sit.*

ADAM: So... Long time, huh?

BRANDON: It has been.

ADAM: I read that article in the Times a few weeks ago. About the big merger. Congratulations.

BRANDON: Thanks. Things are... I just got promoted, too, so...

ADAM: Really? Should've gotten a Venti.

BRANDON: And you?

ADAM: I left the candle shop a while back. I think you knew that.

BRANDON: I think I did, yeah.

ADAM: It was time, you know?

BRANDON: Are you liking it? Teaching?

ADAM: Sure. You know, you get the summer off. The kids are great. It's all good.

BRANDON: Good.

> *They watch some cyclists ride by, feeling a little awkward.*

BRANDON: Hey listen, do you want your rug back?

ADAM: My rug?

BRANDON: The purple one with the frayed edges?

ADAM: Oh, God. No. Please.... We don't even have room for it. Consider it permanently on loan... For now.

BRANDON: Well, anytime you want it.

ADAM: I don't even like that rug.

BRANDON: Okay.

> *They smile at each other, tightly.*

BRANDON: How's Luke?

ADAM: Good. He's... That's actually why I called.

BRANDON: I figured.

ADAM: Right? I mean, it's not like we, you and I, it's not like we ever . . .

BRANDON: Yeah . . .

ADAM: And I feel bad about that. I do. I mean, I always hoped we'd be friends, but that never quite happened, did it?

BRANDON: Not really. No.

ADAM: And I never understood why. Or why you and Luke stopped hanging out, for that matter. I have an idea. I mean, we've all been in that position before, right?

BRANDON: What position is that?

ADAM: Oh, you know, having a friendship, a close friendship. Maybe there's an unrequited thing, maybe not. I don't know. Whatever. Then someone else enters the dynamic and fucks it all up.

BRANDON: Uh-huh.

ADAM: It's painful to be around. I get it. I'd do the same thing. But it's been like three years, Brandon.

BRANDON: Adam . . .

ADAM: I'm sorry.

BRANDON: It's just kind of between Luke and me.

ADAM: No, you're right.

> *A beat.*

ADAM: Then, I guess, you coming for Thanksgiving, I guess, that's not gonna . . .

BRANDON: I don't think so.

ADAM: It would mean so much to him. He's deep frying a turkey. He's making sweet potatoes and collard greens, and all this southern shit.

BRANDON: Um . . .

ADAM: Never mind.

> *Another beat.*

BRANDON: So is that all you wanted to talk about?

ADAM: I guess so . . . Yeah.

BRANDON: Because I've got an appointment I've got to—

ADAM: Actually, there is something else . . . Do you have a second?

BRANDON: Sure.

ADAM: God, this is awkward . . . Is it okay if I just dive in here?

BRANDON: Sure.

ADAM: Okay . . . So, Luke and I have been together a little over four years now—

BRANDON: Four? Wow!

ADAM: I know, who would have thunk it, right? And things are great, all things considered. More than great, really. I mean, we've got our issues, but who doesn't, right? Like, he's still not out to his parents, which is just sort of boring at this point, but frankly, they don't seem like the kind of folks I really want to spend a holiday with, so . . . Plus, he's out everywhere else in life, so it's mostly normal. It's a negotiation, like any relationship. He lets me watch CNN 24/7, I let him watch that show where people hop across the big, rubber balls and fall into the mud. He puts up with my tirades about the health care reform, I put up with his Martha Stewart magazines. He drops a fan on my face in the middle of the night, I—

BRANDON: Got it, Adam.

ADAM: We make compromises, that's all I'm saying. He's not even that extreme as far as all the Jesus stuff goes. He's pro choice. He believes in stem cell research. I think he may even vote for a democrat in the next election.

BRANDON: Someone you can bring home to mom, I get it.

ADAM: And I have. Many times. And she loves him. Oh, and we're talking about having a baby now, too. Well, I'm talking, but he's nodding his head a lot. So, it's mostly good.

BRANDON: Great. So, what's the problem?

  A beat.

ADAM: The praying after sex.

  Another beat.

ADAM: That's the one little quirk I'm still having a hard time with.

  Brandon's not sure how to respond.

ADAM: I know we've never talked about this kind of thing before, you and I. I mean, I don't even know if you're openly gay . . . Or un-openly gay, even. I assume you're gay . . . Or gayish. Gay friendly, at least. So, if you are . . . and you do . . . I mean, is that something you do, too? Pray after sex?

  Brandon shifts in his seat.

ADAM: You don't have to answer. I 'm sorry. It's just something that's really been bugging me lately. I mean, it's not like I see it. It's not like he's kneeling at the side of the bed flogging himself with a leather switch or anything. I wish, right? No, it's more like he feels dirty and silently asks for forgiveness. And it's not like it's all the time either. In fact, he hardly ever does it. But still, it's like, really? That's what you have to do? I mean, all the other stuff I can sort of deal with, but the praying after sex? It just sort of makes everything feel a little tainted somehow. I mean, how am I gonna feel loved for real with, you know, all that in the way?

Adam slugs back the rest of his cappuccino.

ADAM: Okay, I'll stop . . . You talk . . . If you want to. I know I'm sort of dumping this all out there, so . . . But, please. If you have any . . . pearls . . . I'd be glad for anything.

Brandon takes a moment to gather his thoughts, looks around to make sure no one's listening, then opens up.

BRANDON: I like black men.

ADAM: Excuse me?

BRANDON: Black men?

ADAM: Uh-huh.

BRANDON: I like them . . . That's all I've ever been attracted to . . . I don't know why, it just is.

ADAM: Men that are black.

BRANDON: Yes.

ADAM: And you're telling me this because . . .

BRANDON: Luke's not black.

ADAM: *(getting it)* I see.

BRANDON: I was never in love with him, Adam. Our friendship ended because we both chose for it to. There was nothing "unrequited" about it.

ADAM: Gotcha.

BRANDON: I've been struggling with this stuff my whole life. When I met Luke, it was like, finally someone who understood . . . But somewhere along the line things started to shift. When you two were just hooking up, it was one thing, but when it turned into something, well, more . . . Look, I understand the need to act on the urges, believe me, but to choose the lifestyle? To live like it was . . . right, I guess? Well, that's where we go our separate ways.

ADAM: So, you're saying there was a line and, at a certain point, Luke crossed it?

BRANDON: Moved it.

ADAM: So, it's okay to do ... whatever it is you do ... but when it comes to actually loving, that's where the line's drawn?

BRANDON: My line.

ADAM: At love? You draw your line at love, Brandon? Loving's too much of a sin?

BRANDON: *(gently)* If that's how you want to see it.

ADAM: That's not how I want to see it. That's not how I want anyone to see it. And I can't imagine it's how God wants us to see it either.

BRANDON: Well, it's how I see it. And Luke understands that.

> *A beat.*

ADAM: What about that guy in the chat room?

BRANDON: What guy?

ADAM: The married one ... Luke told me you really liked each other.

> *This stings.*

BRANDON: Oh, yeah? What else did he tell you?

ADAM: That he misses you.

> *This stings even more.*

BRANDON: Well, I miss him, too. And I'm sorry I can't support the two of you together. It just doesn't feel right.

> *Brandon stands.*

BRANDON: So, I don't think I can help with the whole praying-after-sex thing.

ADAM: I guess not.

BRANDON: Give him my love, will you?

ADAM: You sure that's allowed? Not gonna get struck by lightning or anything, are you?

BRANDON: *(genuine)* You're funny, Adam. I'll give you that. I wish we could've gotten to know each other better, too.

ADAM: Oh, well. Maybe in our next life. Oops. Sorry. Guess not.

BRANDON: I don't know if this helps any, but ... he chose you, Adam. When he moved the line. That's got to have cost him, you know? And maybe praying after sex is the price he has to pay.

ADAM: Maybe.

BRANDON: Still ... He chose you ... Isn't that enough?

SCENE SIX

Luke's hospital room. The fluorescent lights are off. Adam's asleep, curled up against Luke. All is quiet except for the eerie sound of a machine that breathes.

After a few moments, the door opens. Adam wakes with a start, sitting bolt upright as Butch flips the lights on.

BUTCH: What's going on in here?

ADAM: Oh...I...uh...

BUTCH: That's a hospital bed, son.

ADAM: Must have...

BUTCH: I know you're jetlagged, but...
> *Adam hops off the bed, a little disoriented.*

ADAM: What time is it?

BUTCH: A little after three.

ADAM: Brandon said you were getting a hotel room?

BUTCH: Couldn't sleep.
> *Butch walks over and examines the machinery.*

BUTCH: Didn't mess anything up over here, did you? These things are...

ADAM: I don't think so.

BUTCH: You sure? One flip of the switch and the whole thing can just...
> *Realizing he has no idea what he's talking about, Butch sits on the edge of the bed. He looks like an old man suddenly.*

BUTCH: There's a mother of three in Pennsylvania. Won't make it through the next twenty-four hours without a heart.
> *He smooths his son's covers.*

BUTCH: A pair of eyes to Albany. A kidney to White Plains. Everyone needs something.

ADAM: Yeah...
> *The machine breathes.*

BUTCH: You wanna make sure you're doing the right thing... You look for some kind of sign... Something to let you know... And then... Just like that...
> *Butch looks up at Adam.*

BUTCH: New Hope.

ADAM: Excuse me?

BUTCH: That's where she's from... The mother... Ironic, isn't it?

ADAM: Yeah.

> *Butch looks back down at his son.*

BUTCH: If you don't mind, I'd like to be alone with him.

> *Adam can't move.*

ADAM: Um . . .

BUTCH: Yes?

ADAM: I'm not quite done yet.

BUTCH: What's that?

ADAM: I'd like a little more time if that's alright.

BUTCH: Time?

ADAM: If that's alright, yeah.

> *Arlene enters, sensing trouble.*

ARLENE: What's going on, fellas?

BUTCH: He wants time, Arlene. This guy here. He wants more of it.

ADAM: It's not . . . under the circumstances . . . I don't think that's a
    lot to ask.

> *Butch slowly rises.*

BUTCH: Is that right?

ADAM: Look, I don't wanna play this game anymore.

BUTCH: What game?

ADAM: You know what I'm talking about.

BUTCH: There's a game?

ADAM: Yes, and I'm not playing it.

ARLENE: Butch, maybe we should—

BUTCH: I wasn't aware of any game, Arlene, were you?

ADAM: Ten minutes . . . Just give me ten more minutes and I'll be out
    of here.

BUTCH: Ten minutes?

ARLENE: Come on, Butch. We can—

BUTCH: I'm not going anywhere, Arlene.

ADAM: *(exploding)* I WANT MORE TIME, ALRIGHT!? I'M NOT
    ASKING ANYMORE, I'M TELLING YOU.

> *Holly rushes in, trying to calm Adam, but he backs away.*

ADAM: Now, I've been trying to be decent about all of this, but none
    of you are making it easy.

BUTCH: Who the heck is this guy?

ARLENE: Butch, please.

BUTCH: Walking in here like he owns the place.

ARLENE: Let's just—

BUTCH: I don't even know who he is.

ADAM: You don't know who I am?

HOLLY: Okay, everybody—

BUTCH: I could have your ass thrown out of here if I wanted.

ADAM: I'm sure you could.

BUTCH: And there wouldn't be a damn thing you could do about it.

HOLLY: Sweetie, maybe we should—

BUTCH: Coming in here, disrupting my family.

ARLENE: Okay, now. Stop it, Butch.

BUTCH: You've got a lot of nerve, son.

ADAM: I'm not your son.

BUTCH: No, you're not, are you?

> *The two men look like they're about to strangle each other. Holly looks at Luke and gasps.*

HOLLY: Adam?!

> *His eyes are wide open and he's staring right at Adam. Everyone's stunned for a moment.*

ARLENE: Luke?

> *Arlene leans in and touches her son's face.*

ARLENE: Can you hear me? It's me, sweetheart. It's mama.

> *Then, just as quickly, Luke's eyes shut again.*

BUTCH: Someone get a doctor.

> *Arlene continues gently trying to communicate with her sone. Holly runs off, leaving Adam there, frozen.*

SCENE SEVEN

> *Adam's apartment. Yesterday. A weekend bag rests on the coffee table.*

ADAM: *(O.S.)* Is there anything I own that doesn't make me look like a lesbian from Scranton?

> *Adam enters with a pile of clothes, and starts sorting through them.*

ADAM: I mean seriously. Since when did I start dressing like Paula Poundstone?

> *Luke enters with a deli sandwich.*

LUKE: Where's my cat?

ADAM: I have no idea.

LUKE: She was in here a minute ago.

ADAM: The vet said we shouldn't get too close. He's radioactive.

LUKE: For the first few days. It's been over a week.

ADAM: I'm not taking any chances.

LUKE: Adam!

ADAM: He's in the bathroom.

LUKE: She's not a he, you animal!

> *Luke puts his sandwich down, calling for the cat as he heads for the bathroom.*

LUKE: Patches?

ADAM: Did I snore again last night?

LUKE: *(O.S.)* Like a buzz saw.

ADAM: God, I'm becoming my father. I always thought I'd become my mother.

LUKE: *(O.S.)* You got her hips.

> *Luke enters again.*

LUKE: You should see her. All curled up like a biscuit sandwich.

ADAM: You sure you can't come, babe? I've got a ton of miles I can cash in.

LUKE: Positive.

ADAM: It would just be so much more fun if you were there. I'm staying at my brother's and you—

> *Adam sees that Luke is dying to eat, but needs to pray first, so he waits for him to do so, and then continues, a sweet shorthand between them now.*

ADAM: I'm staying at my brother's, and you love my brother.

LUKE: Believe me, there's nothing I'd rather do than sit around with a bunch of old farts comparing salaries all weekend.

ADAM: And hairlines. And potbellies.

LUKE: I'd love that, really I would. But I've got a ton of auditions this week. I'll go to your next reunion, I promise. I'll push your wheelchair.

ADAM: Fine, then don't forget to recycle when I'm gone. I'm tired of seeing your Dr. Pepper cans in the trash.

LUKE: Alright, already. Jeez, what crawled up your ass?

ADAM: Sorry, I'm just a little testy about having to fly in a hurricane.

LUKE: What hurricane?

ADAM: I don't know. There must be some hurricane heading our way. Don't we get them once a week now, thanks to you and all your ozone-eating Republican friends?

LUKE: George Bush did more for the EPA than Bill Clinton.

ADAM: Says who?

LUKE: I don't know. I read it.

ADAM: Where, in the Bible?

> *Luke chuckles.*

ADAM: You've ruined air travel for me, you know? Ever since you told me about the rapture, I start flop sweating if the pilot wears a cross or speaks with a southern accent.

LUKE: Well, you know the solution.

ADAM: Yeah. Fly El Al.

LUKE: Okay, Buster, but don't say I didn't warn you.

> *Adam gives him a sweet kiss.*

ADAM: Why would I need Jesus to save me when you already did?

LUKE: *(seeing something)* What's that thing on your face?

ADAM: What thing?

LUKE: That line thing.

ADAM: It's still there?

> *Adam drops everything and runs to the mirror.*

LUKE: What is it?

ADAM: A bed crease. I woke up with the fucking thing like five hours ago.

LUKE: So?

ADAM: So?! That didn't happen in my thirties. I'd wake up, and an hour later my face would spring back to normal. I've had this damn thing on my face for half a day now.

> *Luke cracks up.*

ADAM: It's not funny. Someday, you'll look back, ten, fifteen years from now, when you've moved on to someone else—

LUKE: Someone more age appropriate.

ADAM: Yes . . . You'll get a crease that takes half a day to go away, and your heart will break for me.

LUKE: And where will you be when that happens?

ADAM: Dead.

> *Adam throws some more stuff into the bag.*

ADAM: Wrong. Wrong. Wrong.

> *Adam collapses dramatically on the couch.*

ADAM: Please submit me for one of those make-over shows. I am begging you.

> *Luke pulls the sweater we've seen Adam wearing in the waiting room scenes out of the pile.*

LUKE: Here, wear this. You always look so handsome in periwinkle.

ADAM: Thanks.

> *He helps Adam pull it on.*

LUKE: It's just a reunion, babe. What's the big deal?

ADAM: What's the big deal?

LUKE: Oh, my God. You just vamped. You haven't done that in ages. You must really be freaked out.

ADAM: It's just... This is the first time I'm going back as a teacher. Before, I was a writer. Not a very successful one, but still... It just feels like a bit of a disappointment, that's all... Like I've let the home team down.

LUKE: You're gonna look ten years younger than all of them.

ADAM: My body maybe, but not the rest of me. I've got lines and creases. My hair's dry. It doesn't shine anymore. It's like someone cut an old man's head off and stuck it on a young man's torso. It's unnatural.

LUKE: Would you stop.

ADAM: I should either stop with the treadmill, and let myself go completely, or cash in my IRA and get a face, brow and a neck lift.

LUKE: You don't need a neck lift.

> *Adam glares at him playfully as he zips up his bag.*

ADAM: Okay, I'm outta here.

LUKE: Will you crack my back before you go?

ADAM: I don't like cracking.

LUKE: I bet the cute, new stock boy at the candle shop does.

ADAM: You want it cracked or broken?

> *Adam pushes Luke down on the couch. Luke puts his head in Adam's lap, and Adam starts cracking.*

LUKE: No, not like that... Yeah... A little higher.

ADAM: Is that a gray hair?

LUKE: Where?

ADAM: It is! Oh, my God! Thank you, Jesus!

> *Luke tries to break free, but Adam starts tickling him. The playful wrestling becomes more loving, until soon they're lying on top of each other, out of breath and happier than we've ever seen them.*

ADAM: I don't want to go.

> *Luke wraps his arms around Adam.*

LUKE: I love you.

ADAM: I know you do.

LUKE: *(sensing hesitation)* But?

ADAM: *(can't help himself)* I want you to love me more than Him.

> *Luke grins.*

ADAM: I'm serious.

> *The grin disappears.*

LUKE: I know you are.

> *Luke pushes Adam off. The mood instantly shifts. They both sit up, on opposite sides of the couch. A whole world between them suddenly, as they sit there in silence. It all seems so futile suddenly.*

ADAM: Did you ever think that maybe you were the crazy one?

LUKE: Not really, no... Once, maybe... for a moment... but then, you know...

> *Some muffled music from the apartment above.*

ADAM: The NYU kids are back... From summer.

LUKE: Yeah.

ADAM: How long's your brother been at Georgia Tech? He's a sophomore now, right?

LUKE: Uh-huh.

ADAM: It's never gonna change, is it?

> *A beat.*

LUKE: I'm not sure.

> *They sit there a minute longer, one looking more miserable than the other, until Adam rises, grabs his weekend bag, and walks to the door.*

ADAM: I don't think I can do this anymore.

> *And with that, he walks out the door, leaving Luke sitting there as the NYU kids grow louder.*

SCENE EIGHT

The waiting room. Brandon and Holly sit side by side. The mood is somber, reverent.

HOLLY: Have you ever sat Shiva, Brandon?

BRANDON: No.

HOLLY: Wonder if this is what it feels like.

BRANDON: I'm not even really sure what Shiva is.

HOLLY: Me neither.

> *They sit there for a moment until Arlene and Butch enter. Adam's not far behind. Arlene walks to the couch and sits next to Holly. She has a certain peace about her. Butch doesn't. Adam seems miles away.*

ARLENE: So... That's it. He's... It's... over.

> *Arlene takes hold of Holly's hand, remembering.*

ARLENE: I keep thinking about that play Luke was in, Brandon. That Our Town. Little images keep popping into my head. An ice cream parlor. Two giant step ladders. A cemetery made of chairs. I remember there wasn't much scenery to speak of, but somehow they made you see everything.

HOLLY: It was a beautiful production.

ARLENE: Yes, it was.

> *A long silence.*

ARLENE: But I can't quite remember what it was about.

> *Holly and Brandon exchange a glance.*

HOLLY: Well, there was this girl in a small New England town.

ARLENE: Back in the olden days, right. I remember that.

HOLLY: Uh-huh. And she dies. Gets consumption, or dies in childbirth or something, which happened a lot back in those days, I guess, and she just... dies. But she's allowed to go back and revisit one day of her life, and all the people she loved. And she's feeling so much for them. Because she's... But they don't know she is. And they take her for granted. And each other. And she sees how sad that is... and was... even before she died, and she wonders if anyone ever realizes how wonderful life is. How precious. Even as they're living it.

> *This resonates for a moment.*

ARLENE: That's right. Now, I remember.

Arlene looks to Butch.

ARLENE: Butch?

He stares out the window.

BUTCH: They take the organs out before they pull the plug . . . I never knew that.

ARLENE: Why don't you come sit with us?

BUTCH: Pack it all up in little coolers . . . Like they're off to a picnic or something.

ARLENE: Sweetheart?

BUTCH: I can't feel a thing, Arlene.

ARLENE: Come here, hon.

BUTCH: My fingers . . . My arm . . .

ARLENE: Butch . . .

BUTCH: They keep it so damn cold in here. How's anyone supposed to . . .

ARLENE: Do you want me to get the pastor?

BUTCH: The pastor? No, I don't think I want a pastor right now.

ARLENE: How about a walk then? Maybe we should go for a walk, hon. Just you and me. How about that?

Butch turns to the hallway where Luke once was.

BUTCH: Another blanket . . .

ARLENE: Sweetheart?

BUTCH: He needs another . . .

He starts towards Luke's room, stopping when he realizes what he's doing, then collapses out of nowhere. Adam is able to catch him before he hits the ground.

Everyone is stunned. Butch more so than anyone else. Together, he and Adam look like some sort of strange Pieta. Butch lays there, completely confused for a moment, then hides his face in Adam's chest and begins to weep. Adam looks at the others, unsure what to do, until, finally, he remembers something that might be of some comfort.

ADAM: Luke wasn't afraid. That's what he told me. He said the place he was going was gonna be so beautiful. He was certain of it. And he knew . . . that everyone he loved . . . most everyone . . . would, one day, be there with him.

Butch is somehow able to hear this. They all watch as he slowly pulls himself together, rises to his feet, and stares at Adam.

BUTCH: Carl Randolph.

ADAM: Excuse me?

BUTCH: The day I got my books. That's how I know you. Couldn't figure it out at first, but . . .

ARLENE: Why don't we get out of here for a little while, Butch? Go for a walk or something. We'll come back and deal with all the . . . with everything later.

BUTCH: A drink.

ARLENE: Whatever it takes.

BRANDON: There's a place around the corner.

ARLENE: Around the corner?

BRANDON: I'll show you.

ARLENE: Thank you, Brandon.

> *Arlene springs into action. Holly hands Brandon his jacket.*

BRANDON: I'll call you later.

HOLLY: Okay.

> *They hug. Arlene scribbles something on the back of a card as Butch wanders slowly out of the room.*

ARLENE: Would you go grab him, Brandon? I'll meet you at the elevator.

> *Brandon gives Adam's shoulder a squeeze on his way out. Arlene tears off a piece of the Newsweek and scribbles her number on it.*

ARLENE: This is my cell. Not sure where we'll be tonight, but please call. There's a lot to take care of, and I know I'm gonna need help.

> *She hands it to Holly, then moves on to Adam and hugs him for an uncomfortably long time.*

ARLENE: You, too.

> *She lets go of him and scoots out of the room. Adam and Holly just stand there. The buzz of the florescents is deafening. Holly's not sure how to comfort him.*

ADAM: He looked at me.

HOLLY: He did, sweetie.

ADAM: He opened his eyes and just . . . looked at me.

HOLLY: Adam, I'm . . . I'm so . . .

ADAM: It happens, I guess, that's what the nurse said . . . People wake up sometimes . . . for a minute or two just before they go . . . almost like they know.

A beat.

ADAM: And, you know, all the doubts, everything I've been question-
ing for the past five years, none of it meant anything, all of a
sudden. It was just us ... Me and Luke ... That's all that mat-
tered ...

Another beat.

ADAM: And it was like ... finally ... I believed.

Holly squeezes Adam's hand.

ADAM: I keep thinking about yesterday. Before I left for the airport. I
can't remember if we said goodbye.

He starts to crumble.

ADAM: I want to go.

HOLLY: With them?

ADAM: No. Home. Your place. Anywhere.

HOLLY: Okay. Let me just ... get our stuff.

Holly starts gathering their things.

HOLLY: Brandon left his Bible.

She picks up the Bible, and stuffs it into her bag.

HOLLY: God, this thing is so ... worn out.

*Adam keeps looking around the room like he's forgotten
something.*

HOLLY: Are you ready, sweetie?

ADAM: Am I ready?

*A phone rings. Confused, Holly follows the sound of the ring
over to the couch and holds up a cell phone.*

HOLLY: Must be Butch's.

She hands it over. Adam looks at the caller ID

ADAM: It's Ben ... Luke's brother.

Unsure what to do, he stares at the phone, then flips it open.

ADAM: Hello ... Oh ... uh ... No. This is ... um ...

He looks at Holly.

ADAM: My name's Adam.

Lights slowly fade to black.

End of play

Or,

Liz Duffy Adams

PLAYWRIGHT'S BIOGRAPHY

Liz Duffy Adams' play *Or,* premiered Off Broadway at the Women's Project's Julia Miles Theater, directed by Wendy McClellan. It had its second production at the Magic Theater in San Francisco, Loretta Greco directing. Adams is a New Dramatists alumna (2001–2008). She received a Lillian Hellman Award for Playwriting in 2010, the Lilly's inaugural year. Other honors include: New York Foundation for the Arts Fellowship, Will Glickman Award, Frederick Loewe Award in Music Theatre, Weston Playhouse Music Theater Award, and a commission from Children's Theater Company, Minneapolis. Plays include *Dog Act; Wet, or Isabella the Pirate Queen Enters the Horse Latitude; The Listener;* and *One Big Lie.* Residencies: MacDowell Colony, Djerassi Resident Artists Program, Millay Colony. Her work has been produced or developed at the Humana Festival, Portland Center Stage, Portland Stage Company, Syracuse Stage, Bay Area Playwrights Festival, New Georges, Shotgun Players, MOXIE Theater, Clubbed Thumb, and Crowded Fire Theater among others. Publications include *Poodle With Guitar And Dark Glasses* in Applause's "Best American Short Plays 2000–2001," numerous short plays and monologues in anthologies from Smith & Kraus and Heinemann, and several plays published in acting editions by Playscripts, Inc. and Dramatists Play Service. BFA: NYU's Experimental Theater Wing; MFA: Yale School of Drama. Adams has dual American and Irish citizenship and lives in New York City and Greenfield, MA.

ORIGINAL PRODUCTIONS

Or, was originally produced in New York City by The Women's Project. Julie Crosby, Producing Artistic Director. November 6–December 13, 2009

OR,

CAST:

Prologue, Jailor, Nell Gwynne, Maria } . . . . Kelly Hutchinson

Charles II of England, William Scott, and Lady Davenant } . . . . Andy Paris

Aphra Behn . . . . Maggie Siff

DIRECTOR:

Wendy McClellan

DESIGNERS:

Zane Pihlstrom (Set Design)
Andrea Lauer (Costume Design)
Deb Sullivan (Lighting Design)
Elizabeth Rhodes (Sound Design)

PLACE & TIME

London, 1666–1670. The first scene is set in a private cell of a debtors' prison. The rest of the play takes place in a rented parlor upstairs in a lodging house, from evening to dawn of one night.

The play is set in the Restoration period, but plays off the echoes between the late 1660s and the late 1960s.

CHARACTERS

Aphra Behn . . . . woman, late-20s to late-30s

Jailor
Charles II   } . . . . . . played by one male actor, Aphra's
William Scott   age or up to 10 years older

Nell Gwynne
Maria   } . . . . . played by one female actor,
Lady Davenant   early-to-late-20s

NOTE

In the premiere production, the male actor played Charles, William, and Lady Davenant, and the second female played Jailor, Nell, and Maria (and delivered the prologue). That breakdown is an option, depending on casting considerations. Additional dialogue to cover a costume change in the cross-gender version: Appendix One, page 236.

> *I will not purchase slavery*
> *At such a dangerous rate*
> *But glory in my liberty*
> *And laugh at love and fate.*
>
> —APHRA BEHN

> *Whore is scarce a more reproachful name*
> *Than Poetess.*
>
> —JOHN WILMOT, EARL OF ROCHESTER

> *We are stardust, we are golden*
> *And we've got to get ourselves back to the garden.*
>
> —JONI MITCHELL

Or,

Spoken by the actor who plays Aphra, in street clothes, intimately to the audience.

Or! Now that's a very little word
On which to hang an evening's worth of show
But I will now that little word enlarge
And show a vast unsettled world within
That open o and nosing thrust of r.
Our play will shortly ricochet between
A dense array of seeming opposites:
Spy or poetess, actress or whore
Male or female, straight or gay—or both
Wrong or righteous, treacherous or true
Lust or love, cheap hackney trash or art
Now or then, a distant fervent age
Or some more recent time of freedoms new.
And yet despite all seeming diff'rences
Those ors divide less than they subtly link
And what seem opposite and all at odds
Are in their deepest nature most the same.
We all embody opposites within
Or else we're frankly far too dull to live
And this our wilding world cannot be hemmed
Within a made-up symmetry of sense.
That being said, we'll open up the gate
Unhinge the R and step on through the O
To find our characters, from hist'ry fetched
Although they no doubt would not know themselves

If they were sudden brought into this room
To witness; O blame not our hapless scribe
For that; she pleads a playwright's hallowed right
To have her way with people and events
Too far long gone for most of you to know
Just as our heroine in her own time
Made free with truth where it might serve her will.
If Aphra could but be with us tonight
We hope she would forgive our trespasses,
While you we hope to solace and seduce
With all our most alluring stratagems.
O! Fire exits! There and there, all right?
Are all your cell phones off? Yes? Very good.
> Compose yourselves for pleasure, if you will.
> Cue the lights, let never time stand still.

Or

Aphra in a prison cell writing a letter, well dressed in her own clothes.

APHRA: And so I must, however I regret it
Now once more beg you, Sire, not to forget it
That here in debtor's prison I do lie
For lack of funds promised me as your spy.
To nag and scold my own adoréd king
Believe me, pains me more than anything.
But justice to myself demands no less
Than princely favor and full recompense.
And so—shit. Jailer! Jailer! Damn his eyes.
(Jailer enters)
Sweet kindly jailer mine, the ink's run dry.

JAILER: So? Ain't you writ enough?

APHRA: Not nearly, no

JAILER: And that to me is?

APHRA: Crucial, as you know.
For till I have an answer to my plea
I cannot pay my debts and be set free.

Nor can I, what's more to the point, you see
Reward you as I've promised faithfully.
So ink, tout suite, my greasy grasping friend
And soon I'll have another note to send.

JAILER: All right, all right, you'll get your fucking ink

APHRA: What charming words, into my soul they sink.

JAILER: See here, you, knock it off, I won't be rhymed.

APHRA: No no indeed, you're the prosaic kind.

JAILER: Damn right! I'll go and fetch your goddamned ink—

> *(Cutting her off with a look and a warning gesture before she can finish the couplet. He exits. Slight pause. She can't resist calling after him:)*

APHRA: Oh very well, you needn't make a stink!

> *(to herself, referring to his smell)*

Although in fact that's something he can't help
Though he stay silent yet his clothes will yelp.
Not to mention seethe with creatures creepin';
If I stay here o'er long I too'll be eaten.

> *(calling out to jailer:)*

And if you would, send me my woman, too!

> *(She looks out of a barred window, downstage.)*

Ah me, this is no very cheering view.

> *(A masked and cloaked black-haired man enters. Aphra speaks without turning, assuming it to be her servant.)*

O, Maria, see what ruin's here.
See where grass grows in the empty street.
Rome's fall no more melancholy looked
When once barbaric hoards had gone their way
Than this our plagued and battered city shows
Unnat'ral in its hushed and barren waste.
At night low moans of beggars substitute
For barks and howls of dogs and cats now gone.
They killed them all to slow the spread of plague
Though some I guess were eaten, such the need.
The rav'nous fire, so recently put down
Still smokes and smolders, darkening the sky.
Even here in our thick wallèd cell
The wind now shifts and brings a bitter scent.
Disease and fire have brought our city down

And war keeps it in poverty disguised.
I hardly knew it when we disembarked.
All our time abroad, O, how I longed
To quick sail back to our beloved town
To sail for London, our beloved town
The glittering and great phenomenon
The home of all that makes life bearable
Which I in my poor way fought to preserve
As here and there across the globe I flew.
But now that I at last have come to roost
What do I find but grandeur's sad decay
And my own state much like in disarray
Languishing unransomed and alone,
Abandoned by the great who late I served.
Maria, you've been faithful still, and true
      And I do swear your service to reward
      Can you be patient till we both are free?

CHARLES: As patient as a saint, so you with me.

APHRA: O! Who is this?

CHARLES: One who owes you much and means you well.

APHRA: I thought you were my woman.

CHARLES: No, I am your man.

APHRA: What do you mean? I have none.

CHARLES: I mean I would be a man for your turn, however you care to employ me.

APHRA: I see. You are some idle foolish rake, come to ogle and annoy a female prisoner. Well, it's dull enough here, you may as well entertain me.

CHARLES: Happy to return the favor, as you've entertained me with your private counsel. A spy, are you?

APHRA: And you're a knave and a rogue if you take advantage of your eavesdropping.

CHARLES: A knave and a rogue?

APHRA: A goddamned knave and a treasonous rogue!

CHARLES: Peace, peace, this is no way to keep me secret. Is this the honeyed tongue of the wily widow Behn?

APHRA: Do you know me?

CHARLES: We've met.

APHRA: Well, come on. Why do you remain masked? Reveal yourself to me and let me know who I have had the pleasure of abusing.

CHARLES: To be railed at by one of your wit and beauty is pleasure indeed. I am in no great hurry to forfeit the opportunity.

APHRA: Should I not rail then, if I knew you?

CHARLES: Possibly not.

APHRA: Then I shall enjoy it just a while longer too. Keep your disguise, charming fool. I'm somewhat disguised myself, after all.

CHARLES: In drink?

APHRA: Hah! If only I could afford drink. I gave my very last coins to keep myself out of the open prison and in the relative splendor of this private cell. No, disguised by misfortune, as you see.

CHARLES: If all were as disguised as you in your misfortune, the world would be a glorious place, however desperate. For all your poverty, you shine as the silvery moon piercing the envious murk of night.

APHRA: Now it's my turn to cry peace! Does it amuse you to mock a prisoner with elaborate flattery?

CHARLES: I promise you, I neither mock nor flatter. I find myself blown quite off course by your unsuspected . . . *luminescence*, all the more startling by contrast with your present grim setting. Our meeting before was brief and businesslike, and I too distracted with pressing cares. Now I can't help but see you more clearly. You mistook me for your servant, and that was no mistake: you may command me.

APHRA: Even masked, it's clear you are a pretty, witty man, and one I am beginning to be moved by. Will you be moved to remove your visor now and let me see who it is I am invited to command?

CHARLES: I will. And yet, one moment more before my revelation. Will you allow me to salute you properly, while you know me only by my voice?

APHRA: O, very well. Come, take your liberty.

CHARLES: Only for my sake?

APHRA: No, for my own, I confess. Your flattery has had its effect, so come, have your reward of it, and then reveal.

(They kiss. He unmasks.)

A good face, as I thought. With something familiar about it . . . .
O, god, the king! O! And I called you knave!

CHARLES: You didn't know me.

APHRA: Goddamned knave!

CHARLES: Yes, that's all right.

APHRA: And rogue. Treasonous rogue!

CHARLES: Really, I forgive you.

APHRA: And fool!

CHARLES: Yes! I beg you, let all that go by.

APHRA: Well, good Christ, you've changed.

CHARLES: I see you've recovered from the awful shock.

APHRA: Well, your majesty, the manner of the reintroduction has somewhat mitigated awe.

CHARLES: Quite.

APHRA: You have changed since my last and only audience, which was I must say a good deal more formal. It's been two years but you've aged . . . five.

CHARLES: It's been a rough couple of years. You despite your travails have not aged a day since you came to give me your report on Surinam. I believe you advised us not to lose it to the Dutch.

APHRA: Have we?

CHARLES: Pretty much. We have got New York off them.

APHRA: New York?

CHARLES: They called it New Amsterdam. A very good little town. No fabled rivers of gold, but oysters the size of dinner plates, so they tell me.

APHRA: I don't think much of this modern mania for naming places "New" something. An inherent contradiction, don't you think? If it's new it's not York and if it's York it's not new.

CHARLES: O, quite. You may as well call it Exactly Not Where I Want To Be Land.

APHRA: Please Don't Make Me Live in This Horrible Place Burg.

CHARLES: God I wish I Were Home Ville.

APHRA: You know a lot about that, don't you, majesty? Homesickness I mean.

CHARLES: Call me Charles when we're alone.

    And yes. I will confide to you, I was so many years longing for home that I hardly knew how to be glad once I was here; longing itself became such a habit of mind. I still sometimes wake up homesick, before I know where I am. You've been a rover, you know something about it too.

APHRA: I am desperately glad to be home again, except that I'm plainly desperate.

CHARLES: Yes, sorry about that. You must know, we haven't got nearly the money we need, what with one thing and another. You are far from the only spy left unpaid. But you are perhaps the most eloquent and persistent. Your debts have been paid. See, the door swings open. You are free.

APHRA: O, wonderful. Though perhaps the greatest wonder is that you came yourself.

CHARLES: I thought it would be fun. Look, I wasn't just toying with you before. You have drawn me onto a lee shore and wrecked me there, and I believe only you can draw me off again, to safety and sweet sailing, if you would.

APHRA: You do like your naval metaphors, don't you?

CHARLES: Yes, I do. I'd rather be on the sea than anywhere, except . . .

APHRA: Don't say it.

CHARLES: . . . your bed. Sorry. I hate a trailing off.

APHRA: This is very strange.

CHARLES: Not so strange.

APHRA: Not to you, I'm sure. You have a different woman for each day of the week, or so it's said.

CHARLES: An exaggeration, I assure you. I'm a one-woman man. At a time, and within reason.

APHRA: But I am not a professional mistress. I have greater ambitions.

CHARLES: I'm already married, you know.

APHRA: Yes, I know, god save her, and I mean greater even than to be queen. I will have an undying honor. I will know a godlike eternal fame. I will be a playwright.

CHARLES: A female poet? What, a new Sappho for the modern stage? Odd's fish, you're ambitious.

APHRA: Funny, I know. But I'm no kind of whore, the kind that marries or the other kind. I'll earn my own bread or go hungry. Thank you for paying what I was owed. Goodbye.

CHARLES: Wait, wait. Don't be so hasty.

APHRA: Well?

CHARLES: You still haven't called me by my name.

APHRA: Charles. Will that do?

CHARLES: Say it again.

APHRA: Charles. Charles. Beautiful Charles.

> *(They kiss again)*

Very nice. But a kiss won't transform me into a mistress nor you into a theatrical contract.

CHARLES: And that's all you want?

APHRA: Yes . . . yes.

CHARLES: You know, for a woman of the world you aren't terribly worldly. My favor is worth something.

APHRA: I don't need your favor, I've got my own contacts. Anyway I can't afford the cost.

CHARLES: The cost?

APHRA: A royal bastard and an end to my career.

CHARLES: Some would consider that a gain. Well, leave that for now. If you walk out of here with nothing but your still quite pretty clothes, where will you go? The city is devastated, the theaters not yet reopened.

APHRA: But they will be?

CHARLES: They will be. In the meantime, before you embark on your glorious career, let me continue to repay you for your service, agent one-six-oh.

APHRA: O, you know my number?

CHARLES: And your pseudonym, Astrea.

APHRA: Say that again.

CHARLES: Astrea.

APHRA: A lovely sound, from those lips. And from mine . . .

> *(They kiss. Very sexy.)*

O . . . . O, dear.

CHARLES: So bad? I'm told I'm not incapable of giving pleasure.

APHRA: O, yes, you are very much capable of undermining all my determinations. As low as my state is now, you might bring me very much lower if you bring me to fall in love with you. I've survived storms at sea, the malice of counter-agents, the assassination plots of enemy spies, near-starvation, and the maddening stupidity of a brief and necessary marriage. I've skirted plague, fire, and war. But the greatest danger for a woman, let me tell you, plague and fire and war in one, is all-consuming love for a man. As a nation under a tyrant, so a woman in love: all freedom lost for the sake of a specious security that only lasts as long as a sunny day in England; that is, as long as a man loves or a tyrant pleases to be kind.

CHARLES: Well, there it is. I'm no tyrant and you're no whore. But let me keep you for a while, not in return for services you may do, but for service already rendered. Just until you're on your feet in the theater and earning your third-day profits.

APHRA: O, but I'm not content to write for a third day only—I crave glory as much as if I'd been born a hero.

(As Charles speaks she stops, hearing herself, picks up her pen to make a note.)

CHARLES: I daresay I can help you there as well. A poet associated with a king is naturally—I beg your pardon, am I in the way?

APHRA: Sorry, just need to—that sounded rather well, I think I can use it—born a hero—I'm with you again, where were we?

CHARLES: I was making you a useful offer.

APHRA: You were humoring me.

CHARLES: Not at all. I wouldn't dare stand between you and anything you aspire to; I'm sure I'd be knocked aside like a bit of flotsam in a spring tide. Come, humor me. I believe it will be vastly amusing to harbor a playwright.

APHRA: I suppose it would only be fair. Did you see that Pindaric ode that's been going around, "On His Majesty's Heroism in the Great Fire"?

CHARLES: I've heard it quoted; modesty forbids my admitting to reading it myself. What, was that you?

APHRA: I can't risk signing my name yet, even in private circulation. The last female to dare set up openly as a poet was savaged almost to ruin, and she had an independent income and a country estate to retreat to. A popular hit in the theatre will give me some protection but until then I must be careful, especially with political poetry.

CHARLES: Why risk it then? Stick to pastoral themes. Hymn the joys of cookery. Bit safer.

APHRA: All your years of exile I was here, growing up under the Roundheads. A brutal, coercive, repressive regime, the rule of the mob disguised as democracy.

CHARLES: *(quoting Shakespeare)* "The blunt monster with uncounted heads,"

APHRA: "The still-discordant wav'ring multitude." Just so. I hated it for my country and I hated it for myself. I was a self-taught country girl longing for a wider world and the Puritans meant to keep me in a cage until I ate my heart out and died. The day of your Restoration it was dark and overcast, and then suddenly the sun broke through the clouds and made the crown on your dark head shine out like an answering sun—do you remember?

CHARLES: Yes. All the poets used it, it was custom-made for them.

APHRA: But that's how it was. The sun came out and I knew my life had just become possible. Freedom, especially for a woman, is only possible under an enlightened monarch. You're mine, and my pen, for what it's worth, is at your service.

CHARLES: It's a funny thing, bearing all that. Are you quite sure I'm enlightened enough to pull it off?

APHRA: You are. Enough to know that power needs poets, and poets need money.

CHARLES: Odd's fish, that's blunt enough. Well then, will you be my poet?

APHRA: And that's all?

CHARLES: I think you can trust my self-restraint, for all your beauty.

APHRA: Yes, I didn't mean to insult you or flatter myself. I meant, you won't ask me to continue my intelligence work? I long to leave behind one world of transformation and enter another.

CHARLES: No, you've done enough.

APHRA: Have I, by the way? I don't suppose you've read my reports yourself?

CHARLES: I've had summaries. But they tell me they were extremely well written.

APHRA: Did they tell you what I warned about the invasion? About burning our ships at anchor? They mean to sail up the Thames to the Medway—

CHARLES: Yes, yes, I'm not bothered about that. You must know we are quite safe from the sea.

APHRA: Surprise and treachery may bring the greatest down, as you have cause to know.

CHARLES: You are no longer Agent one-six-oh. Let us speak only of what really matters, of poetry, theater, and love.

APHRA: Ah, this would be that new life that I wanted.

CHARLES: May never by your old life you be haunted.

APHRA: Ah, this would be that new life I requested

CHARLES: I take you at your word, let mine be tested.

APHRA: Ah, this would be the new life that I asked for.

CHARLES: And this the truest Aphra I unmaked for.

(The scene changes; Charles exits; Aphra in her lodgings with Nell. Nell wears men's clothes, Aphra is writing. They're sharing a tobacco pipe.)

NELL: Good weed.

APHRA: Isn't it?

NELL: Damned good weed. Where do you get it? I haven't been able to afford it since they raised the tax.

APHRA: A friend is kind enough to get it for me.

NELL: A friend? Hmm, I wonder who is Aphra's friend. You're amazingly discreet, no one knows. All right, I know, I'm a nosy bitch.

APHRA: Not at all.

NELL: Not at all but mind your damned business, Nell. Never mind. I'm still so thrilled to meet you. I can't believe I had the nerve to come and bang on your door un-introduced like this. Everyone says you're the next big thing.

APHRA: Everyone?

NELL: That's the gossip. I swear, I thought I was climbing the stairs to fucking Olympus.

APHRA: Are you mad? I would have come to you weeks ago if I had dared, and thrown myself at the feet of the greatest actress of the new age! Your Florimell left me overcome with admiration.

NELL: Aw, don't be silly, I'm just an orange girl made good. You should have come backstage.

APHRA: Next time.

NELL: I'm not interrupting your work, am I?

APHRA: No, no, do forgive me the rudeness, but I've been promised an introduction to Lady Davenant of the Duke's Company and I need something new to show her; anyway I can write and chat at the same time.

NELL: That's a neat trick.

APHRA: O, I had to learn how. This is the first time in my life I've had a room of my own.

NELL: No family left, then?

APHRA: Finally managed to shrug them off; they're in the country.

NELL: Wasn't there a husband? A Dutchman?

APHRA: Plague.

NELL: Sorry.

APHRA: Don't be. What about you?

NELL: I'm on my own now; my last keeper had monstrous bad luck at gambling and had to retrench, but another one will come along soon. It's lucky that the aristos are all theater-mad, isn't it? I suppose yours is someone very grand indeed, to get such good tobacco.

APHRA: Not at all.

NELL: Not at all! Christ, you've got good manners, you must think I'm a wretched guttersnipe.

(Aphra stops writing and looks at her.)

APHRA: I think you're absolute heaven.

NELL: O. That's nice.

Are you writing a part for me? No, I know, I'm with King's and my son-of-a-bitch producer would never let me out of my contract to play with the rivals.

APHRA: It's a shame. I do have a part for you, you'd be perfect in it. A beautiful Amazon warrior who falls madly in love with her enemy and is utterly undone.

NELL: O, you're killing me, I'd die to play that! We own all the old revival rights you know, all I get to play are the goddamned classics, where Dukes gets all the new plays. It's so unfair. A breeches part, I suppose?

APHRA: Yes, until the end when she succumbs to love and changes to women's clothes.

NELL: Yeah, see? So right for me. They love me in the breeches parts, so they can look at my legs.

APHRA: I don't blame them.

NELL: Yes, they're nice, aren't they? On the way over here a man really took me for a rent boy; I had to run away! Wouldn't he have been disappointed!

APHRA: Not necessarily. Might have swung both ways.

NELL: Is that what your friend is like?

APHRA: I think that's what most people are like, if they only knew it.

NELL: I don't know. I grew up in a brothel and I can tell you, some people are astonishingly particular about what they like; only one very specific thing will rouse 'em and nothing else will do. We had one regular fella who would have his favorite girl take off her stockings and wriggle her big toe into his—but maybe I'd better wait until I know you better. Am I shocking you?

APHRA: I didn't grow up in a brothel, but I hope nothing in that realm can shock me. Nature endowed us with a glorious gift for pleasure and nothing is more natural than to take all honest advantage of it.

NELL: And by honest you mean?

APHRA: Willing. The only sensual sin is to take what isn't freely given. If I am lucky enough to attract the true affection of a lovely man or woman, and if together we can increase the sum total of happiness in the world for even an hour, I consider that an act of virtue, not vice.

NELL: You are persuasive. I can't think how to argue with that, even if I wanted to.

APHRA: But you don't want to?

NELL: I don't.

APHRA: Shall I read you a bit from the play?

NELL: Yes, please.

APHRA: "Even now I was in love with mere report, with words, with empty noise; and now that flame, like to the breath that blew it, is vanished into air, and in its room an object quite unknown, unfamed, unheard of, informs my soul; how easily 'tis conquered!"

NELL: Did you just write that, while I was here? Am I the object that informs your soul?

APHRA: Mm hm.

(Aphra kisses her.)

NELL: This is strange.

APHRA: Not so strange, is it?

NELL: Well, no. Just sudden.

APHRA: Sudden love is truest, undisguised.

NELL: And she who sudden loves will take the prize.

APHRA: Nice.

NELL: Thanks.

Sudden love steals sweet throughout my veins.

APHRA: And steals away what little wit remains.

NELL: Ha bloody ha. Your turn.

APHRA: By Cupid's sudden arrow I've been hit.

NELL: And suddenly your love is all I—shit.

APHRA: What?

NELL: Sorry, it wasn't going to rhyme!

APHRA: Idiot!

NELL: Critic!

> *(Another kiss)*

Who kisses better, me or your keeper?

APHRA: You bring him up so much, are you already jealous?

NELL: O, never jealous. He's just a man, I suppose. Where would any of us be without men to pay the rent?

APHRA: We can earn our own, I suppose?

NELL: Are you joking? I have to spend all my earnings on clothes and carriages, just to keep my reputation up.

APHRA: You could marry?

NELL: The fatherless daughter of a whorehouse keeper? Who do you think I could find to marry?

APHRA: I shudder to think.

NELL: Anyway, what's the difference, except you're selling yourself to just one man. No way around it, to be a woman is to be a whore and if god doesn't like it why did he make it that way? Though come to think of it, men are whores too.

APHRA: What, the men too?

NELL: That's right, every one of them, flirting and pandering and cocksucking their way all the way up the ladder! Any man that isn't a cocksucking trimming whore is probably dead; no way else to survive these slippery times. You laugh, but it's true, you know it is. Name me a man or woman in the kingdom can't be named whore.

APHRA: Well, but what about the king? Is he a cocksucking whore?

NELL: No, worse, a teasing whore! With one hand he tickles the balls of the Parliament while with the other he keeps his cousin Louis well fluffed, all to keep the money coming in. He dirty-talks the Catholics until they're hard and hopeful, then turns around and jilts them when his ministers hold up a sack of cash. It's true! I don't blame him, I adore him—where would I be without him to reopen the theaters and set the fashion? But just between us, let's call a spade a goddamned shovel.

APHRA: O, my god, I love you, foul mouth and all.

NELL: Is it so foul?

APHRA: It's delicious . . . But I have to come to the king's defense. He wants to help the Catholics, he really believes in religious toleration—

NELL: But he needs money for the war, so his hands are tied, I know, I know. But don't let's talk about war and politics; it's such a bore and you must have had enough of all that in your previous career.

APHRA: My previous career?

NELL: Don't go all mumchance, everyone knows you were a spy.

APHRA: Everyone knows..?

NELL: There are no secrets in the theatre, it's much too small a world and all anyone does is gossip. Anyway, your mask is off with me now, isn't it?

APHRA: All right, it's true. And yes, I've had enough of it. It's a nasty little world of lies, subterfuge, backstabbing and betrayal.

NELL: Wait, are we talking about spying or the theater?

APHRA: A man I was fond of was killed, not long after he was seen with me in Antwerp.

NELL: Was he a spy too?

APHRA: A double agent.

NELL: And you blame yourself for his death? I doubt it was your fault.

APHRA: You don't know anything about it.

NELL: I have some idea of what the life of a double agent must be like. Doubles your chances of someone wanting to slit your throat. Sorry; O, sorry, I'm a tactless cow.

APHRA: No, you're right, but it's an ugly world, isn't it. Don't you wish we could go far far away, back to a simpler time?

NELL: Was there ever a simple time, since there were people in the world?

APHRA: There was, long ago.
Before the wars of ministers and kings
Before the need to struggle for our bread
Before all strivings base and harsh there was
A golden age of happiness sublime
Where lovely nymphs—like you with fewer clothes—

In fragrant groves lay hidden from the sun
Which dappled through the leaves to gild their days
While night time 'neath the pearly moon there played
The gentle shepherdesses and their swains
Living all for music, poetry, love
Before the grim unnatural rule of law
Of gods and men, O sweet Arcadia!
Pure freedom was the natural state of man
And woman, human spirit sanctified
In harmony with all the natural world
    Unfettered, unrepressed, and unashamed
    A happier better time could not be named.

NELL: Sounds fucking fabulous. And guess what—it sounds like right now!

APHRA: What, now?

NELL: Well, or any minute. The puritans had their day, now it's our turn to make a new golden age.

APHRA: What about the war.

NELL: The war can't last forever.

APHRA: It feels as though it already has.

NELL: Come on, don't be such a nostalgia queen. Look around, it's already begun. We can love who we want, girls or boys; we can wear any clothes we want—

APHRA: Girl's or boy's.

NELL: Yeah! The world has changed. A woman can be an actress, a playwright, a poet, a libertine, a spy. A nobody like me is the it girl everyone loves; you can shed your murky past to become the toast of the theater; every day and night is a party and a happening and a grand fucking festival of art and love. We are lucky to be alive right now. This is our utopia, and it's never going to end.

APHRA: How lovely it would be to believe that.

NELL: O, just chose to believe it, that's what I do. Tune in and turn on, just like this.
    (Another kiss)

APHRA: You have a genius for living in the moment. I believe you could make the saddest man in the world smile.

NELL: I certainly could, and I would, if he could pay my landlord. I'll have to choose someone soon but I can't make up my mind;

plenty of rich admirers and each one as dull as a rainy day. Money's not enough, I have to have wit, don't you?

APHRA: Nell, I think I'm having a brilliant idea.

NELL: Are you?

APHRA: If I can get this play produced I'm sure it will be a success.

NELL: I like your confidence.

APHRA: Well, to be honest I swing back and forth between confidence and knowing for a fact that it will be the biggest bomb the London theater has ever seen and I'll be hounded by the shame into my grave. But let's assume it's a hit.

NELL: Yes, let's.

APHRA: Then I'll be able to keep myself. And I think you'd love my friend.

NELL: Thanks very much, but I don't need anyone's castoffs.

APHRA: O, you'd want this one.

NELL: Would I?

APHRA: Trust me.

NELL: Well, but wouldn't it cost you a pang, to pass him on to me?

APHRA: I'm never jealous. Possessive love is a sort of slavery, I abhor it. I love you both; if you loved each other my happiness would be multiplied, not diminished. Only still love me too; don't leave me; then I would believe in your new golden age, and we would all live there together.

NELL: Now I see why you haven't remarried. You're far too romantic.

APHRA: Yes. Though to be honest it's not pure altruism on my part. I can't make him happy and he'll soon find someone else anyway.

NELL: Who is he that a goddess like you can't make him happy? Fuck 'im, he's too fussy for me.

APHRA: No, it's fair enough. I won't . . . I don't care to . . . Well, to be blunt, I don't let him fuck me. We exchange every other pleasure but that.

NELL: Why not?

APHRA: For one thing, I don't want to get knocked up.

NELL: O, if that's all, there are ways.

APHRA: I know, and none of them can be counted on. Anyway, if we're really letting our hair down, I've never really cared that much about that part; it's all the rest that does it for me.

NELL: I love it, I could do it for hours. Did you see my Cleopatra last season? "O happy horse, to bear the weight of Antony!" I love that line, I know just what she means.

(A knocking at the street door below.)

Expecting someone?

APHRA: No, but—*(Listens at the door.)* Maria's letting him in. Damn. Ah, Nell, darling, would you mind terribly withdrawing for a bit into my bedroom?

NELL: Love to, but not alone.

APHRA: Please, Nell.

NELL: Why hide me, I thought you were going to give me to him wrapped in a bow.

APHRA: O, yes, but, not yet. You don't understand; he's a very private man and I myself don't want it known who he is.

NELL: Christ, either you don't trust me to keep my mouth shut or you're deranged with love for him—either way I think I'm jealous after all.

APHRA: Don't be, I promise I'll tell you everything when the time is right, but right now if you love me for pity's sake get in there and don't eavesdrop.

(The door closes behind Nell, Aphra turns around and the same moment a masked dirty-haired man rushes in.)

APHRA: O!

WILLIAM: Astrea!

(He rushes straight across and embraces her.)

APHRA: Stop! Who are you?

WILLIAM: Don't you know me?

APHRA: You're masked!

WILLIAM: And will stay that way for now if you don't mind, I don't know if I was followed—what's in there, are we alone?

APHRA: Just my woman below—and a cellar full of burly male servants. Tell me your name this instant or I'll have you turned out.

WILLIAM: Does this remind you?

(He kisses her.)

APHRA: William? I thought you were dead!

WILLIAM: I will be if you don't help me—god, you feel good.

APHRA: You don't, you're filthy, get off me.

WILLIAM: Sorry sorry, just such a relief to get here alive, thought any number of times I'd been recognized, look how my hands are shaking, nerves are fucking shot, excuse my language, I'm a wreck as you see, nervous as a cat—you're doing well, look at you.

APHRA: Pull yourself together and tell me what's going on. I thought you'd been seen leaving our last rendezvous, I was told you'd been killed.

WILLIAM: Who told you, that bugger Corney? Wishful thinking. But I had to lay low for a while.

APHRA: In a ditch?

WILLIAM: I know, I'm a mess, I know. Astrea, for the love of Christ what does a man have to do to get a goddamned drink?

APHRA: He has to tell me what he's doing in my rooms in London when he's in fear of his life and knows perfectly well he'll be hung for treason if he's discovered.

WILLIAM: Hung? Don't you think I rate the axe? My father did.

APHRA: Your father was a man of principle; you're an opportunistic coward.

WILLIAM: O. Not in love with me anymore, I take it? That's too bad.

APHRA: Don't worry; for the sake of the past at least I won't betray you. But stop trying to play me; I know you didn't risk your life for love.

WILLIAM: All right, yes, I've got information, and where else could I go? I had to get out of Holland, France is out of the question, and I loathe Scandinavia. You think England's bad, you've never spent a winter in Copenhagen.

APHRA: William.

WILLIAM: All right! But not a word of sense until you give me a drink.

APHRA: Sense first.

WILLIAM: Listen to you, lady ice queen; when did you become so cool? Last time I saw you, you were weeping hot tears while a fat Belgian landlord shook you down for the rent and look at you now.

APHRA: Bitch and stay thirsty or speak your piece.

WILLIAM: Right, all right, sorry, right. Well. In a nutshell. Here it is. I know of a plot to murder the king and put his Catholic brother on the throne. Now can I have a drink?

APHRA: O god. When?

WILLIAM: Tomorrow.

APHRA: Who?

WILLIAM: Who do you think? bastard Catholic terrorists—ah, ah, no names yet; if you don't mind, I'd like to hold a bit back.

APHRA: Until you're paid?

WILLIAM: All I want's a full pardon. And my father's lands back. A title would be nice. And that's my last word until you've slaked my thirst.

APHRA: Goddamn it, William. Fine, I'll fetch a bottle. Stay here. Right here! I'll be back in a moment and then you'll tell me everything you know if I have to beat it out of you.

WILLIAM: You and your cadre of burly manservants?

APHRA: Shut up. And don't move.

> *(She goes out. Instantly, Nell pops out of the other door.)*

NELL: Hello, you must be—eek!

> *(William, startled, has grabbed her and pulled out a pistol.)*

WILLIAM: What? Treachery? Who are you, boy?

NELL: *(grabbing his hand and putting it on her breast)* Not a boy, for starters, you fuckwit.

WILLIAM: O. No, you're not, are you? Who are you? Did you hear what we talked about?

NELL: I tried to but that door's a lot thicker than it looks. Why, what did I miss?

WILLIAM: Did you really hear nothing? Tell me the truth or I'll blow off your head.

NELL: I said I didn't. Put that away before it goes off; you're trembling like a virgin.

WILLIAM: *(lowers pistol)* Well, what were you doing, lurking and sneaking around like that? You scared me half into my grave.

NELL: I wasn't lurking and sneaking. I wanted to see what sort of man Aphra's friend was, and now it's clear he's a rude nasty strangely-high-strung raving lunatic. And not exactly a fanatic about bathing. I can't believe she loves you so madly, I wouldn't give rat's balls for three of you.

WILLIAM: How much did she give for *you*? I'm not fussy, I haven't had a girl *or* a boy in weeks.

NELL: You couldn't possibly afford me.

WILLIAM: I can if she can. Come on, how about some credit? I'm
   about to come into money.
   (Aphra enters.)
   O, you're back. Where's my bottle?

APHRA: Maria's decanting one. What's this?

NELL: I wanted to meet your friend and I'm sorry to say: unim-
   pressed. Really, darling, I think you could do better.

APHRA: O, no, he's not—Christ, he's not—

WILLIAM: What am I not, sweetheart?

APHRA: Not—at his best. He's been ill. Very ill. Not fully recovered.
   May be contagious. So really, Nell, you'd better go.

NELL: But there's a bottle coming. And we're just getting to know
   each other. I'm learning more about you and your peculiar
   tastes every moment.

WILLIAM: Really, why be hasty, there's plenty of time for what we have
   to talk about. Your little hermaphrodite and I were just coming
   to terms.
   (Knocking below again. William jumps.)
   For Christ's sake, Astrea, what sort of a bear garden are you
   running?

NELL: Astrea?

APHRA: Shh. *(Listens at door,)* O god. Nell—

NELL: No, I won't hide again, are you ashamed of me?

APHRA: I'll explain everything later I swear please for me.
   *(In one swift movement Aphra kisses her, whirls her into the
   inner room, shuts the door and wheels back to William, who
   has drawn his pistol.)*

WILLIAM: Who'd you tell I was here? *Lying bitch!

APHRA: *(*overlapping)* No one!

WILLIAM: *(continuous)* Just remember if I'm taken now the king will
   be killed—you're the only one in England who'd believe me.

APHRA: I didn't betray you, you idiot, it's—my lover! Quickly, hide!

WILLIAM: Is he so jealous?

APHRA: He isn't jealous at all—or, I mean, yes, ferociously jealous, he'll
   kill you if he finds you here—O, hell, *wanted man*, remember?

WILLIAM: Right. All right.
   *(He heads for the inner room; Aphra pushes him into a cup-
   board.)*

APHRA: Not with her! In there!

WILLIAM: Get rid of him quickly.

APHRA: Of course I will. Be silent!

> *(The instant he's hidden Maria enters.)*

APHRA: O, Maria.

MARIA: Oof, those stinkin' stairs, my knees are popping like corks. Here's your stinkin' bottle.

APHRA: Didn't I hear the door?

MARIA: She's cleaning her boots, it's filthy muddy out.

APHRA: She? Who is it?

MARIA: Did you think it was himself? No, it's a lady. Where's the actress?

APHRA: She's—tired, she's lying down. What lady?

MARIA: I don't know, do I, Dave something. And the other one? Have you turned conjurer? It's like a disappearing act up here.

APHRA: He's—resting too.

MARIA: Wear 'em out, don't you?

APHRA: *Dave?*

MARIA: No, that's not it. Something to do with furniture.

APHRA: Maria, for pity's sake—

MARIA: Davenport! That's it.

APHRA: Davenport . . . Davenant?

MARIA: That's what I said.

APHRA: Lady Davenant is here?

MARIA: I said so didn't I, she'll be right up.

APHRA: Did she say why she's come?

MARIA: Maybe she heard it's a good spot for a nap.

APHRA: All right, never mind, Maria, you may go. *(Maria doesn't move.)* Please.

> *(Maria starts to go.)*

MARIA: Some stinkin' manners, that's all I ask for. Didn't get dragged through stinkin' jungles and stinkin' vomitous sea voyages and stinkin' lousy Europe and how many stinkin' months of waiting to be paid—

> *(The cupboard door opens a crack and there's a pointed cough from William. Maria turns.)*

What's that cough? You coming down with something?

APHRA: No, no, just, smoke. Ahem.

(Maria turns to go again. Behind her back Aphra hastily slips the bottle into William's hiding place.)

MARIA: —and on top of that thrown into stinkin' prison and sticking by her every step of the way without a grumble without a word of complaint only to be told "you may go" without a please or a thank you which is the very least I think I'm stinkin' entitled to—
(She turns back at the door.)
How many—*(puzzled, where's the bottle?)* glasses you want?

APHRA: Never mind, Maria, that's all right, thank you so so much, what would I do without you, off you go please thank you.
(Maria exits. William pops out.)

WILLIAM: Do you expect me to drink this ghastly plonk?

APHRA: Drink piss if you please, just get back in there!

WILLIAM: Temper!

APHRA: Didn't you hear?

WILLIAM: All I could hear were footsteps going away; this thing is surprisingly solid. Bit of a quickie, wasn't it?

APHRA: That was just my woman but Lady Davenant is here.

WILLIAM: Who the devil is Lady Davenport?

APHRA: Davenant! Lord Davenant's widow, manager of the Duke's Company and the woman who holds my future in the palm of her hand!

WILLIAM: What are you frivoling on about, what about the plot?

APHRA: Damn the plot, a production's at stake! No, I know, I know, but just please be quiet and give me five minutes; if I can save the king's life, get you a pardon *and* launch my career it'll be damned good day's work.

WILLIAM: Are you mad? Now just—
(Aphra slams the cupboard door on William. She whirls to face the door—but after a split second she can't resist rushing to her desk and dashing off a line or two standing—then she drops the pen and curtsies deeply as Lady Davenant sweeps in already talking. She speaks not necessarily super-fast but relentlessly, never pausing even when asking a question; Aphra may try to speak but fail to get a word in, hastily nodding where required.)

LADY DAVENANT: Hello darling hello you must be Mrs. Behn, forgive me forgive me horribly ill-mannered I know I know my dear late Lord D used always to tell me but I thought I'd just pop in to

say but O of course you must think I'm a madwoman I haven't
introduced myself Lady Davenant, Duke's Company you
know—I won't unmask, just swooping in on my way to see what
King's has up and it won't do to have 'em see me in the house
taking notes—well but I've heard all about you, setting up for a
poet, love your nerve darling love your *guts*, sign of the new age
isn't it, sign of the times, women kicking over the traces and
damn the naysayers and why not, darling, why not, look at me,
my dear late Lord D passes on and everyone expects me to sell
the license but ho, I say, ho ho, why should I not carry on as before after all there's nothing much to it, choose the plays keep
the players sober within reason and hollah, the money rolls in;
after all Johnny does most of the work, Johnny Downes our
prompter, he bullies 'em through their paces with his bell and
whistle and what have I do to but count the gate? and I can
count I assure you though I wasn't raised for it but who could
be married all those years to my dear late Lord D without sharp-
ening her wits, a lovely man but O as practical as a spring hare I
assure you a mad *bunny* would have been more rational—you've
no view here do you well what does a poet want with a view, inward views no doubt inward views—mind you why should he be
practical, a great man, a great trainer of actors, a great man of
the theater, you know he was the natural son of the great man
himself, O yes, not much of a secret so I don't mind telling you,
the natural son of Mister Shakespeare himself so there it is,
blood will tell, but genius is rarely sensible so I learned to count
for sheer self-protection and I will tell you darling it is the most
useful skill I could have mastered and I recommend it to you
heartily if you haven't learned it so there it is I'm the queen of
Dukes as the joke goes and I need a play; that scatterwit sotted
dog Shadwell—I abuse him though I love him—promised me
one and sugar-talked me into booking it and all and what does
the fool do but get himself clapped by a Holborn drab, he's in
the country sweating it out of himself and swears he cannot finish the play so there it is, can't leave the playhouse empty it's a
hole in my pocket, rehearsals begin tomorrow, I can give you
Lizzie Barry for a lead and you won't find better, say what you
will of Nellie Gwynne, Lizzie is a honey and the wits adore her,
give her the prologue and you won't be hissed off at the start and

that's half-way there, I'll give you the usual third-day's profit and not a penny mislaid, I see to it myself, well? have you a play for me? is that it? nearly finished is it? finish it by morning? cutting it fine darling cutting it fine but there, I'm a soft touch, I'll take a flyer on you only don't be late, mustn't keep actors waiting around without the play they'll start to drink then it's quarrels and misbehaving behind the scenery and asking to go home early—utter utter chaos darling, never leave actors with nothing to do, remember that—get me the thing by let's say nine on the clock and if it's any good at all we'll have an agreement and O what sort of play is it, comi-tragedy, yes? that's good, beginning to go out of style but the people still love a comi-tragedy and if you'll take my advice you'll pad it out with a song or two, give everyone a chance to buy an orange and fondle their neighbor without fear of missing something important, you know the sort of thing *(goes right into singing without a pause, shockingly loud)*

> *Ho! The world goes round and round!*
> *Hi! Around and round it goes!*
> *Ha! The world goes round and round!*
> *Hey ninny! Ninny! Ninny!*

Well not *that* but you see what I mean, and O one other thing I won't have one of those "or" titles, you know what I mean, one of those greedy get-it-all-in titles, "the something something *OR* what you something," I don't care if the great man did it, they take up half the poster and the typesetter charges by the word, make up your mind and pick one, thank you; now understand me darling this is a rare opportunity, a lucky chance, if you can't deliver me the thing in time I'll be horribly vexed and I don't know when I'll have another chance for you and you know King's don't need you, Duke's is your only hope; mind you they clamor me *Who is she What sort of education Jumped-up nobody from nowhere* and I say well who was Mister Shakespeare hah! and that lays 'em by the heels so remember that darling and don't let 'em fright you; I've seen your poetry, you've got the spark all right, don't let anyone tell you otherwise but it don't do anyone any good if you can't write "the end" and get on with it; there that's what I came for lovely chatting I feel we're friends already must fly don't mind showing me out just write! Write! Write! Write! Write!

(Her last words are shouted off as she exits, her steps clomping back down the stairs. Aphra stands momentarily stunned, then rushes to her writing table, all else forgotten, and begin writing furiously—but almost immediately Charles comes in, tossing aside a mask he's just taken off.)

CHARLES: Sorry to be unannounced, your woman was just letting someone out. *(Embracing her.)* Ah, that's more like it. It's been a bitch of a day, you've no idea.

APHRA: O good but.

CHARLES: Yes, I came masked, I know you don't want anyone to know. You're a perverse creature, do you know that? Many women would like to be thought my mistress without the bother of it, and you only want the bother. So to speak.

APHRA: O god that feels nice but.

CHARLES: Have you fallen in love with me yet, by the way?

APHRA: Not a bit.

CHARLES: *(kissing her neck etc.)* No?

APHRA: No . . . I don't love you . . . except as much as . . . as I should. O.

CHARLES: Why is the sound of you telling me you don't love me the nicest thing I've heard all day? People are always complaining about my spaniels, but their barks are music compared to the yelping and yapping and howling of the parliament, never mind the court. A damned pack of needy dogs baying day and night. But here's balm for my abused ears: the sweet voice of not-my-mistress.

APHRA: Charles, do let me go. I can't ask you to stay, I've got a play to finish.

CHARLES: That's unkind. May I see what you've written so far?

APHRA: No, it's too soon, it's not ready to be seen. You'll be the first, I promise you, just give me the night.

CHARLES: No, that's too hard. How can you throw me back to the dogs like that, just when I need some peace and comfort? Let's go within and lie together for a bit—no, you know I never ask you for the final favor, as they say, rather vulgarly, but all the rest of it . . . *(nuzzling her again)* Don't you want to?

APHRA: Yes, mmm, yes.

(They're heading toward the bedroom when she comes to her senses again.)

O, no, we can't. Sorry, I do want to, I really truly do, Christ I do, but I can't. Not just now. I've got to finish the play.

CHARLES: I suppose I should admire your work ethic. I don't, quite, but I should.

APHRA: So you'll go?

CHARLES: Yes, but not just yet. You're forcing me to be businesslike, so I'll admit I had another purpose in coming to see you just now. A far lesser purpose, of course, and I meant to leave it for later. But there it is. It's William Scot.

APHRA: *(remembering for the first time since Lady D's visit, then covering.)* O my god William! I mean, what? William Scot?

CHARLES: Your old contact. He was thought to be dead, but he's been seen. He's here in London.

APHRA: Here in London?

CHARLES: I'm sorry, this must be a shock.

APHRA: No, no. Well, yes, it is a bit.

CHARLES: Look, I told you I wouldn't ask you to spy for me anymore. Your name is off the list of agents, and I didn't want to drag you back into it, officially. But unofficially, I'm asking you for a favor. He's bound to come to you. I want you to let me know.

APHRA: But, why? If he is alive, he's just a broken-down old spy. He never was any good, and he'd be utterly useless by now.

CHARLES: It seems he may be back in the game. We have information he's joined with the discontented Catholics in their latest assassination plot.

APHRA: What? No.

CHARLES: Does it surprise you? His father helped to kill my father; one regicide breeds another.

APHRA: But he doesn't care about all that. It was a disaster for his family.

CHARLES: Quite. *(Slight pause)* No, he's in it for the money. I imagine they've promised him his father's estate back, that's all his sort cares about. Well, it's what most people would care about.

APHRA: Are you sure? About Scot?

CHARLES: We aren't sure about anything.

APHRA: Perhaps he's still playing a double-game, for our side?

CHARLES: If he is, he hasn't told us. No, the man can't be trusted. We'll get him in the Tower and find out what he knows. Are you all right?

APHRA: Yes.

CHARLES: I know he was your lover too. Perhaps I'm asking too much of you, to betray him to me. Of course, I rather hoped you cared a bit for me, enough at least not to want me dead.

APHRA: Charles, don't. I'm as devoted a friend and subject as you've got. I'm just trying to think. If Scot is a traitor I'll turn him in without a second thought. But I know him, better than anyone does. If he has information, who better than me to find it out? I promise you, no torture the Tower can offer will expose his innermost thoughts more quickly and thoroughly than I can by gentler methods. Will you trust me? Will you give me a chance to find out the truth?

CHARLES: You're asking a great deal.

APHRA: I know. And please don't misunderstand me. I'm not asking it for his sake, but for yours.

(Pause)

CHARLES: Very well. I'll go, shall I? and leave the field clear.

(He starts to go toward her bedroom.)

APHRA: Where are you going?

CHARLES: To empty my bladder. No objections, I hope?

APHRA: Of course not, but—my bedroom's such a mess, I don't want you to see it like that, you'll think I'm such a lazy slattern. Would you mind using the downstairs closet?

(He looks suspicious, but goes. Aphra hesitates briefly between going back to her play and checking on William— maybe she writes a line—then goes to William's hiding place and reveals him dead asleep. [Note: this may be a stand-in wearing William's coat with his face hidden.] She picks up the bottle—empty.)

William? William!

(She hears Charles coming back and hides William again. Charles re-enters, picks up his mask.)

CHARLES: I don't think Maria thinks much of me.

APHRA: Why?

CHARLES: She just called me a stinkin' nuisance.

APHRA: She's rough around the edges. But you couldn't ask for a more loyal servant.

CHARLES: Loyalty is a virtue, to be sure. I wonder if you would do me a great favor.

APHRA: Anything.

CHARLES: I left a couple of cavaliers at the pub on the corner. It's part of a ruse I've been persuaded into, to go about with some like-dressed men, make me less of a target in case anyone penetrates my disguise. Great nonsense I suppose, but would you mind terribly fetching them for me? (*She hesitates.*) I'm sorry to put you out.

APHRA: No, not at all, of course it's no trouble at all. I'll be back in a moment.

CHARLES: Don't hurry, I'll be quite entertained on my own.

> (*She goes out, with some reluctance. He puts on his mask, goes straight to the inner door, opens it, and pulls Nell out.*)

CHARLES: Hah!

NELL: Hey!

CHARLES: What's this?

NELL: Who the hell is asking?

CHARLES: You're not Scot, at least, thank god. Too young.

NELL: Too young for what?

CHARLES: Not much, apparently. Tell me, boy, what did you hear?

NELL: Not a thing, what *is* that door made of?

CHARLES: Well. You're too well dressed for a servant and too confident; as insolent as a wilderness of monkeys.

NELL: Who are you to call me a monkey, you great ape! And where's Aphra?

CHARLES: She'll be back soon. Not very soon; my friends will insist on buying her a drink, if I know them. (*He relaxes, starts to see the funny side.*) Well, just when I thought I knew her. Keeping a boy.

NELL: Why shouldn't she?

CHARLES: Why indeed? I only wonder she didn't tell me. I hope I'm generous enough not to mind her using my coin to buy herself pleasure in my absence.

NELL: O. *You're* her keeper, not—Hmm. Well, come on, it's your turn to say who the hell are you. Interrogating each other will pass the time until she comes back.

CHARLES: Very amusing, but who the hell *are* you?

NELL: Who's asking? And who's your tailor?

CHARLES: Why do you ask about my tailor?

NELL: I just thought we might want to expand our repertoire. And it's a nice coat. Why don't you take it off, since we're chatting? (*She helps him off with it and tries it on herself; regarding the rest of his clothes:)* Those are nice too. Did you ever think of donating your castoffs to the theater? Costumes cost the earth.

CHARLES: Are you an actor? That would explain a lot.

NELL: What would it explain?

CHARLES: The insouciance, the wit, the being so much at home in other people's bedrooms—

NELL: Beast.

CHARLES: No, no, I love actors. They're so kind, generally speaking.

NELL: I know I am.

CHARLES: Are you?

NELL: Very, very kind.

CHARLES: Expensively so?

NELL: Damn, why does everyone think I'm a whore?

CHARLES: I didn't use the word, but aren't you?

NELL: Can you pay? *(He nods.)* Then give us a kiss.
        (They kiss.)

CHARLES: You're not a boy.

NELL: You can tell by a kiss?

CHARLES: The kiss, no; boys and girls kiss just the same. I felt your breasts. Small but perfect.

NELL: Now who's insolent?

CHARLES: Do you mind?

NELL: Are you kidding? I fucking love it.

CHARLES: Odd's fish, I have it! You're Nell Gwynne.

NELL: How'd you know?

CHARLES: I saw your Florimell, of course. You're even more beautiful up close; how often can that be said?
        (He begins to carry her into the bedroom.)

NELL: Wait. I'd better know who you are first.

CHARLES: Are you sure you want to know? It might be fun to keep the mask on.

NELL: Kinky. But yes, I need a name to cry out at the proper moment.

CHARLES: Very well.
        (He removes his mask. Pause.)

NELL: O.

CHARLES: Yes.

NELL: You're just as beautiful up close too.

CHARLES: Thanks.

NELL: Charles the Second, good for Aphra. Well, I've already had two
lovers called Charles, so you'll be my Charles the Third.

*(He roars with laughter and carries her within. Happy
shrieks off from Nell, then the door is slammed shut. Instantly
it opens again and Nell comes back on.)*

NELL: Wait a moment—

*(She looks around, then picks up Charles' mask from where
he tossed it.)*

Ah, there it is.

*(She goes back the bedroom door, opens it looking in, holds the
mask up to her face and poses. Imitating Charles playfully:)*

Odd's fish!

*(Then she slips in, closing the door behind her. William stag-
gers out of the cupboard.)*

WILLIAM: The fuck'd everyone go?

*(He opens the bedroom door. Looks for a moment. Closes the
door.)*

Well. Don't I feel left out.

*(He hears a noise on the stairs, hides. Aphra enters, stops,
confused not to see Charles. Heads toward inner door.
William re-emerges.)*

I wouldn't.

APHRA: William! Where's—I thought you were passed out.

WILLIAM: *(indignant)* I wasn't, I could drink twice that much and
shoot the eye out of a trout at a hundred paces.

APHRA: Why a trout?

WILLIAM: I'm just bloody tired, haven't slept in a bed in weeks.
Speaking of bed, did you know there are two people having at it
in there as we speak?

APHRA: What? Who?

WILLIAM: I don't know, couldn't see their faces, I'm just glad one of
them's not you. We do have business to discuss, if you can spare
me a moment.

(Aphra is stricken, staring at the bedroom door.)

Astrea? *(pause)* Here, do you want to borrow my pistol, commit
a crime of passion?

APHRA: What? No!

WILLIAM: Then tear yourself away from your messy personal life and pay attention to something far more important: me.

APHRA: You. Yes, you. What's the plot?

WILLIAM: Just like that?

APHRA: I don't have all night for this, I've got a deadline!

WILLIAM: Right! Well, it's simple enough. Charles goes for his usual morning constitutional with his dogs and the rest of his entourage in St James Park—

APHRA: Tomorrow morning?

WILLIAM: —that's right, and their man shoots him.

APHRA: That simple?

WILLIAM: It's the simple plots that succeed.

APHRA: He'll never get away.

WILLIAM: No, they know that, it's a suicide mission. He's been promised the best room in heaven if he does the Pope's bidding on earth. And if he survives long enough to be questioned he can't tell anything—the men were masked who instructed him.

APHRA: Are you in on it?

WILLIAM: Am I—

APHRA: Are you one of the conspirators?

WILLIAM: Well, of course they think I am, otherwise I wouldn't know the plan.

APHRA: You're not a Catholic. What do they think is in it for you?

WILLIAM: That James will reward me with my father's lands back, once he's king.

APHRA: Do they think you're that stupid? James reward the men who kill his brother?

WILLIAM: Don't you think he'd love to be king?

APHRA: Of course he would, that doesn't mean he'd turn on Charles. All those years in exile together, they're as close as brothers can be, religious differences aside. No, this is a very stupid plot. It won't play.

WILLIAM: Stop thinking like a scribbler, Astrea; what does it matter if it's a stupid, simple plot, it's no less dangerous. Take it to your control, get me a guarantee, I'll give them the big names, take my reward and go. They can take their time after that getting the details out of them in the Tower.

APHRA: See, it's the Catholic part that I'm not quite buying.

WILLIAM: Not buying?

APHRA: It's too easy, it's too pat. There's so much anti-Catholic feeling now, rumors of Popish plots in every coffee house, all hideously exaggerated, but they make a very handy scapegoat when people are grumpy about the war dragging on and the economy going to shit. See what I mean? Too obvious.

WILLIAM: Don't believe me then, I'll be off, let the king be shot.

APHRA: *(ignoring him)* So if it's not actually the Catholics, who would it be? Not the French, they want Charles right where he is. The Dutch don't want a Catholic on the throne. Disgruntled old Cromwellians? They wouldn't trust you for a minute. It's a snarled-up Gordian Knot of questions and I don't have time to sort it out. O, that gives me an idea. May I see that pistol of yours?

WILLIAM: Here you are, why?

APHRA: *(Pointing it at him)* Tell me the truth or I'll kill you.

WILLIAM: What? No you won't.

APHRA: What do you mean, of course I will.

WILLIAM: Don't be ridiculous. You're an intelligence operative, not an assassin. Remember that time in Surinam when a rat got into the room? You wouldn't let me kill it, you made me catch the damned thing and let it go outside.

APHRA: It was a sweet rat. And it was so frightened. O, all right, here's your pistol back.

WILLIAM: That's better. Stop all this nonsense and believe what I'm telling you.

APHRA: I'd love to, William. I would love for you and me to save the king's life and for you to be rewarded and for everyone to live happily ever after. It would be a wonderful story and a wonderful happy ending. It just doesn't ring true. If I don't trust my instincts as a spy I have to trust them as a playwright. There's something wrong, and if you won't tell me the truth soon it'll be too late; they know you're in London so it's only a matter of time before they look for you here, no matter what I do.

WILLIAM: What? What was that last bit? I've been seen?

APHRA: Yes. I'm supposed to turn you in.

WILLIAM: That's bad news.

(The inner door begins to open. William starts violently and bolts into hiding, Aphra whirls around.)

CHARLES: *(off, low)* Aphra?

APHRA: Yes?

(Charles sticks his head out.)

CHARLES: Did I hear voices?

APHRA: No, no, I'm just working, acting out the parts as I write, you know.

CHARLES: O. Wait a moment.

(He disappears back inside. William pokes his head out of the cupboard.)

WILLIAM: Hsst, damn you, what are you playing at? Get rid of him or I'll shoot both your damned whores just to get your undivided attention.

(He vanishes again. Aphra picks up a page of her play and begins reading aloud, to cover her lie to Charles [see Appendix 2]. Almost immediately Charles comes into the doorway, holding a blanket around himself.)

CHARLES: I've, em, met your friend Nell.

APHRA: So I gathered.

CHARLES: Extraordinary girl. I was quite carried away.

APHRA: She has that effect.

CHARLES: But I've become distracted thinking of how I'm abusing your hospitality. Do I go too far? I wouldn't wound your feelings for the world, you do know that?

APHRA: I do and it's quite all right.

CHARLES: Is it?

APHRA: *(hurriedly)* My dear, believe me, all's well, I adore you but tonight I can think of nothing but the play, you have my blessing to be happy, honestly.

CHARLES: Very well. I can see it's a matter of indifference to you.

APHRA: Charles—

CHARLES: I won't disturb you further. Good luck with it.

APHRA: Charles . . .

(He's gone back within.)

Damn.

(Turns, see the play, picks up her pen irresistibly and begins writing again. William re-enters slowly.)

WILLIAM: Charles?

APHRA: *(absently)* What?

WILLIAM: Charles.

APHRA: *(all attention on him now)* It's a common enough name.

WILLIAM: I knew you were an ambitious creature but pandering for the king? What, giving him an all-round evening, a tumble with a slut and the betrayal of an ex-lover into the bargain?

APHRA: It's not him!

> *(Nell pops out of the inner door, too suddenly for William to hide.)*

WILLIAM: *(starting violently)* Christ!

NELL: *(seeing William)* O, still here? *(to Aphra)* Who is it, anyway?

APHRA: No one, a cousin, just visiting.

NELL: *(for William's benefit)* Let him out of Bedlam, did they? Not sure that's wise. *(To Aphra:)* Never mind, I only came out to say, *thanks!* You're right, he's utter bliss. Don't laugh but I think I may be in love. And how convenient that it should be with him, the bloody king of bloody England!

APHRA: Nell—

NELL: I mean, jackpot!

APHRA: Nell—

NELL: I won't forget you when I'm a Duchess, I promise.

APHRA: Nell—

NELL: *(kissing her and exiting)* Must get back, we'll chat it all over later, so much to talk about, love you madly, bye.

> *(She's gone. William shakily points his pistol at the bedroom door.)*

WILLIAM: To think that door is all that separates me from the man who ruined me and killed my father.

APHRA: After your father helped to kill his father.

WILLIAM: Strange thing to have in common, isn't it, both our fathers having had their heads chopped off with a big official axe, ought to give us a sense of kinship. Shall we see what he thinks?

APHRA: You're not after revenge, after all?

WILLIAM: No. Sod that. Just survival. If you think I'll trust mine to the king's mercy you don't know me at all.

APHRA: Put the pistol down. You aren't an assassin either.

WILLIAM: Are you sure?

APHRA: William, what good would it do you? This isn't why you came
here. Come back to your senses. Let me help you. I swear, his
being here is a coincidence. You're safe if you trust me.
*(She has walked steadily up close to him. She puts her arms
around his neck and kisses him. He slowly lowers the pistol.)*
That's right. That's right. Believe me, I'll help you if I can.

WILLIAM: Why should you? You don't love me anymore, you said so.

APHRA: It's not quite that simple. I never did know how to stop loving,
I only know how not to let it stop me. Look, you don't have
much choice. Trust me or keep running, but I don't think you'll
make it this time. Come on, my sweet frightened rat. Tell me.
There isn't a plot, is there?

WILLIAM: Not that I know of.

APHRA: So what's the game?

WILLIAM: I can't stay in exile another day. I'll die of homesickness, if
I don't starve or get my throat slit.

APHRA: So you thought you could cry up a Catholic plot and be believed.

WILLIAM: Most people would believe it. And you know a real plot is
coming; those religious fanatics are out there, scheming away.

APHRA: But this plot isn't real. And you would have given real names.

WILLIAM: That's the genius of it. Many birds with one stone. Me with
my pardon and lands, and several right bastards who've be-
trayed me in the past thrown into the Tower. They may not have
been planning to have the king shot in the morning, but there's
plenty of tar to stick to them, once anyone starts looking. It will
work, Astrea. Help me and I'll cut you in. Don't look like that,
it's brilliant. Back me up, be my witness and my guarantee. We'll
both have titles before it's over, you can stop staining those
pretty hands with ink and live a life of ease.

APHRA: You would have innocent men sent to the Tower. Ruined,
tortured, perhaps executed. For nothing more than your personal gain.

WILLIAM: Don't tell me you're shocked. It's the way of the world.

APHRA: It's the way of your world.

WILLIAM: I've been out there, Astrea. I've been out there for years.
I've seen it. I was just in Terschelling when we burnt the town,
the Great Bonfire, as the English papers so cheerfully called it.

APHRA: They evacuated it first.

WILLIAM: Of course that's what they say. I was there. I heard the screams of the old people burnt alive in their beds. I saw a girl gang-raped to death by soldiers. O, most people got out; as the sack of an enemy town goes it was a May fair. But tell that to all the people who came creeping back the next day to find their home a pile of smoldering rubble. I can still smell it. You have no idea.

APHRA: I have no idea? Where do you think I've been all these years? Remember Surinam? I watched a good man hung, cut down still conscious and cut apart piece by piece, all because he wanted simple freedom for himself and his family. We can trade horrors until the sun comes up. The difference is the horrors have gotten into you; I've chosen to leave all that.

WILLIAM: You've chosen to forget, you've chosen willful naivety for the sake of an easy life, you've left me out there doing the dirty work while you whore yourself and write fucking poetry!

APHRA: What's happened to you? You weren't always like this, were you, or did I just not see?

WILLIAM: You're the one who's changed; when you were a spy you were still a woman, you had a tender heart. Now you're a writer I don't know what you are; you've hardened, Astrea.

APHRA: Call me Aphra.

WILLIAM: Why don't I call you Miss Johnson?

APHRA: What do you mean? My married name is Behn.

WILLIAM: Your married name is crap. Hah, you didn't think I knew, did you? I thought it might come in handy one day, if you ever turned on me.

APHRA: What do you think you know?

WILLIAM: That Mister Behn never existed, that you were never married, that you made him up and killed him off just like the ruthless playwright you've become, that you wanted a widow's freedom and didn't want to earn it.

APHRA: My god, you've got an overheated imagination. Johan Behn was my husband, he died in the plague.

WILLIAM: You didn't waste time mourning him, did you?

APHRA: It wasn't a love match.

WILLIAM: O, knock it off. You're an outrage and a scandal, an unmarried woman carrying on over three continents, an infamous lying whore. Well, that's what they'll say. Even if I can't prove it, it doesn't take much mud to smear a woman past redemption. No theater will dare have anything to do with you, no man of quality will have you even for a mistress, you'll be lucky to stay out of prison. How long do you think you'll survive? Starve in the street or take refuge in the lowest cathouse till the pox takes you. In a year no one will recognize you. Your name will vanish as though you were never born.

APHRA: *(very still)* The frightened rat has teeth.

WILLIAM: Yes, he has. Help me and we'll both survive, and thrive. Betray me and I'll take you down with me. Pretty simple, isn't it?

APHRA: It is.

WILLIAM: Yes? *(She nods. He looks at her, not sure she means it. She takes a breath.)*

APHRA: Yes. Yes, I do see. I don't have any choice, do I?

WILLIAM: Not much.

APHRA: Why should I fight it? Why should I betray who I truly am— who we are?

> *(She turns and embraces him, both arms around his neck.)*

WILLIAM: You're still my Astrea?

APHRA: And you will always be my Celadon.

WILLIAM: Long time since I've heard that name.

APHRA: I gave you that name. You were my first love. Did you think I could ever truly forget?

> *(He studies her face, and believes her. They kiss.)*

WILLIAM: All right. All right then. Thank god that's settled, I hate to quarrel. Shall we have a drink on it?

APHRA: Go down to Maria, tell her I said to give you a bottle. I'm all right, I just need a moment.

WILLIAM: That's right, take a breath, collect yourself. I'm sorry I had to play a bit rough. It'll all be for the best, you'll see.

APHRA: Yes.

WILLIAM: Right. Back in a moment with the drink and then we'll get into the details.

> *(He exits. She looks after him.)*

APHRA: I'm sorry, William. But you're right, it is perfectly simple.

> *(She starts toward the bedroom door. She gets right up to it, ready to knock. Then stops, and turns, takes a breath, steeling*

herself for the hard task. Her gaze falls on her manuscript.
She hesitates, then she rushes over, picks up the pen and
scribbles standing. Murmurs:)

Just . . . a quick . . . line . . . or two . . . and then I'll turn him in,
come what may.

(The sound of a muffled pistol shot from downstairs. What
was that?!)

Maria?

(She hesitates for a second, torn—can't resist scribbling for
another moment or two—then tears herself away and goes
toward the door.)

Maria!

(Maria enters.)

MARIA: Yeah?

APHRA: What was that? It sounded like a pistol shot.

MARIA: That's right. I shot the stinkin' bastard.

APHRA: What? You shot William?

MARIA: Yeah. Well, except I missed.

APHRA: O.

MARIA: So I stuck him like a pig.

APHRA: You . . .

MARIA: Took the carving knife and *pht*, that's right.

APHRA: He's dead?

MARIA: Think he's going to get away with stinkin' blackmail? Not if I
have anything to say about it.

APHRA: My god, Maria. You were listening?

MARIA: Good thing I was. We're all right now. Those two wastrels you
left cooling their heels on the steps, they're lugging the body to
the river. Let the fish have him, he'll do them more good than
he ever did anyone on dry land. Speaking of which, the land-
lady's got a nice eel pie in. Shall I bring some up for you and
your friends? Sun'll be up soon; you'll want breakfast.

APHRA: That . . . would be very nice.

MARIA: *(exiting)* All right, then.

APHRA: Maria.

MARIA: Don't thank me. I didn't follow you through stinkin' junglcs
and stinkin' ships and stinkin' Europe and stinkin' prison and
stinkin' all to have some stinkin' bastard blackmailing son of a

poxy whore ruin us just when we're on the brink of theatrical success. Write me one of those clever-servant parts and we're even.

APHRA: You want to act?

MARIA: Wouldn't be acting, I could do it in my sleep.

> *(Maria exits. Aphra stands, still stunned, absorbing William's
> death. Then she takes in the silence. She's alone for the first
> time all night. And there is her manuscript. She sits, picks up
> her pen. . . and then she is utterly absorbed in writing. After
> all the frantic action, it's a quiet, peaceful scene. Time passes.
> Perhaps a distant clock tolls. Perhaps there's music.*
>
> *The inner door opens, and Nell and Charles enter quietly,
> both in a lovely state of semi-undress. They stand for a mo-
> ment and watch Aphra write. A glint of sun begins to climb
> through the windows, gilding them all. Aphra stops writing,
> puts her pen down. They come to either side of her, a quiet,
> intimate tableau of three.)*

NELL: Have you been writing all this time?

APHRA: It's done.

CHARLES: Is it?

NELL: Are you pleased?

APHRA: I think so. I had to kill a character off. But on the whole, a
happy ending.

CHARLES: Shall we read it now? We can take parts.

APHRA: Aren't you tired? Look, the sun's coming up.

CHARLES: I feel strangely wakeful. Perhaps I only don't wish to lose a
moment sleeping when I may be talking with the two of you.

> *(Charles picks up the manuscript and moves a little away
> into the light to read.)*

NELL: You sure it's all right?

APHRA: Surprisingly painful after all, for a moment. Tell me I've lost
nothing.

NELL: Not an atom of my love, nor his.

CHARLES: This is good.

APHRA: I know. I mean—no, I can't help it, it is. And in—what?—
three hours—Lady Davenant will have it in her hands, and then
the actors will have their parts, and then rehearsals will begin—
and then—O Lord.

CHARLES: *(still reading)* This is very, very good. This will be the hit of
the season.

APHRA: Will it?

CHARLES: The first of many. You'll have your glory. I prophesize.

NELL: Damn right.

APHRA: *(to nell)* You haven't even read it yet.

NELL: Doesn't matter, I know it—you'll be one of the fucking immortals! The name of Aphra Behn will never be forgotten.

APHRA: And nor will that of Nell Gwynne.

NELL: *(re: Charles)* He's got a lock on it, kings are always in the books.

CHARLES: *(looking up from the manuscript)* Not quite sure I see what you're doing at the end.

APHRA: Playing with ambiguity. I hope.

Maybe the sun is coming out at last

CHARLES: And gilding all with its all-hopeful blast.

Or maybe it's a false dawn all too brief

NELL: That storm clouds soon will pocket like a thief.

Or maybe a new golden age we herald

APHRA: Where love and peace no longer are imperiled.

Or maybe we may work to make it so

NELL: And love each other whether yes or no.

A thousand years of peace this day begins

CHARLES: A vision that may vanish, for our sins.

But I'll embrace it, for this glitt'ring day

APHRA: And what will happen next, no one can say.

The world spins round and everything is new

For now I'll be content to spin with you.

(Brief pause.)

NELL: Back to bed?

CHARLES: Excellent thought.

APHRA: Love to.

(All three exit to the bedroom. Almost immediately Aphra runs back in, picks up the pen, crosses out a line and scribbles another. As she writes:)

Coming! I'll be just . . . a . . . moment . . . .

End of play

Appendix One

*Additional dialogue **in bold** to cover the male actor's costume change,
if he is playing Lady Davenant. Page 217.*

APHRA: Damn the plot, a production's at stake! No, I know, I know,
but just please be quiet and give me five minutes; if I can save
the king's life, get you a pardon and launch my career it'll be
damned good day's work.

WILLIAM: Are you mad? Now just—

> *(Aphra slams the cupboard door on William.* **Instantly
> Nell pops her head out the bedroom door.***)*

NELL: **Can't I come out yet?**

APHRA: *(whirling round to her)* **O, Nell, Lady Davenant!**

NELL: *(instantly getting it)* **What, here?**

APHRA: **Yes!**

NELL: **O my god!**

APHRA: **I know!**

> *(****They embrace passionately for an instant, then
> Aphra thrusts her back in and slams the door.*** She
> whirls to face the door—but after a split second she can't re-
> sist rushing to her desk and dashing off a line or two stand-
> ing—****great clomping steps are heard climbing the
> stairs****—she writes faster, speaking lines aloud—
> the steps grow closer—**then she drops the pen and curt-
> sies deeply as Lady Davenant sweeps in already talking. She
> talks not necessarily super-fast but relentlessly, never pausing
> even when asking a question; Aphra may try to speak but
> fail to get a word in, hastily nodding where required.)*

Appendix Two

*Excerpt from Behn's The Young King. The recommended part of the excerpt is **in bold**; the rest of it for context. Part of this text is used on page 49 to help cover the male actor's costume change from William to Charles-in-a-blanket, and other lines from it—including stage directions—may be used any time Aphra's writing becomes so active that she thinks aloud.)*

Thersander is a Sythian prince and Cleomena a princess of Dacia. Their countries are at war. They fell in love while he was in Dacia in disguise, under the name Clemanthis. She mistakenly believes he was killed in the war by the prince of Sythia. She's here in disguise to take revenge, and fails to recognize him.

LYSANDER: *(Thersander's aide)* Sir, there's without a youth that desires admittance.

THERSANDER: From whom comes he?

LYSANDER: He would not tell me that, but has a letter, which he'll deliver only to your Highness.

THERSANDER: Bring him in, it may be from Amintas .
> *(Enter Cleomena dressed like a country shepherd; she gives him a note.)*

THERSANDER: *(reading)* **Guard thee well, Thersander; for thou shalt die by the hand that brings thee this.**

CLEOMENA: **Here's to thee, dear Clemanthis!**
> ***(She stabs him; he falls into Lysander's arms.)***

LYSANDER: **Help, treason, help!**

THERSANDER: **Ah, lovely youth, who taught thee so much cruelty? And why that language with that angry blow?**

CLEOMENA: **Behold this face, and then inform thyself.**
> ***(She reveals herself.)***

THERSANDER: **'Tis Cleomena ! Oh ye Gods, I thank ye! It is her hand that wounds me, and I'll receive my death with perfect joy, if I may be permitted but to kiss that blessed hand that sent it.**
> ***(Enter King and Guards.)***

Phoenix

Scott Organ

PLAYWRIGHT'S BIOGRAPHY

Scott Organ's play *Phoenix* had its world premiere at the 2010 Humana Festival and its New York premiere at The Barrow Group. As a playwright, Scott's work has been commissioned by The Atlantic Theater Company, developed by The New Group and The Barrow Group, and has been performed and work-shopped throughout the United States. His full length play *Fixed* premiered at the Hangar Theater in Ithaca, New York. His play *City* was produced at the Circle X Theater in Los Angeles where it won the LA Dramalogue Award for best new play. It was subsequently produced at the 1st New York International Fringe Festival, directed by Tony Award winner Michael Rupert, and at The Flea Theater in New York, directed by Kevin Moriarty.

His short plays *China* and *The Mulligan* were published in New American Short Plays 2005, edited by Craig Lucas and have been performed throughout the country. His one-act play and everybody else can be found in Best American Short Plays 2002–2003. His short play *Afraid. Yes. Of.* premiered Off-Broadway as a part of The Fear Project at The Barrow Group. Many other short plays have been performed at the Atlantic Theater Company's 453 New Works Series, which he helped create.

Scott's screenplay *Better Man* was a 2008 Scriptapalooza Screenwriting Competition Quarter Finalist. He is also the author of the screenplay *Ghostkeepers* and the original television pilots *The Powerball 7* and *The Pines*.

ORIGINAL PRODUCTION

Phoenix had its world premiere at the 2010 Humana Festival of New American Plays at Actors Theatre of Louisville (Marc Masterson, Artistic Director), directed by Aaron Posner.

CAST

Sue . . . . Suli Holum
Bruce . . . . Trey Lyford

CREATIVE TEAM

Dramaturg . . . . Sarah Lunnie
Set Designer . . . . Michael B. Raiford
Costume Designer . . . . Lorraine Venberg
Lighting Designer . . . . Jeff Nellis
Sound Designer . . . . Benjamin Marcum
Props Master . . . . Mark Walston
Stage Manager . . . . Kimberly J. First

Phoenix had its New York premiere at The Barrow Group, directed by Seth Barrish, April 3–May 3 2010.

CAST

Sue . . . . DeAnna Lenhart
Bruce . . . . Dusty Brown

CREATIVE TEAM

Production Stage Manager . Porter Pickard
Stage Manager . . . . Kate Erin Gibson

CHARACTERS

Sue: A woman in her 30s.
Bruce: A man in his 30s.

SETTING

New York, NY and Phoenix, AZ

TIME

The Present

❙ Phoenix

SCENE 1

Bruce and Sue, in a coffee shop.

SUE: Three things.

BRUCE: Oh, Okay.

SUE: Yeah.

BRUCE: We're diving right in.

SUE: There's three things I want to say.

BRUCE: Okay. Good things come in threes, right? Isn't that what they say?

SUE: Deaths.

BRUCE: Sorry?

SUE: And deaths. Come in threes. Is what they say. And good things too.

BRUCE: Okay. Well. Before you start, let me just be the first to say welcome back.

SUE: Thank you.

BRUCE: What did that mean "let me be the first to say?"

SUE: I don't know.

BRUCE: I'm the only one here.

SUE: No big deal.

BRUCE: How about this—welcome back.

SUE: Thanks again.

BRUCE: And how was it?

SUE: Uh, the trip? It was okay. It was business.

BRUCE: I wasn't sure I would hear from you.

SUE: You did. You are.

BRUCE: It's been a while. It's been ... what? A month?

SUE: Four weeks.

BRUCE: A month, right?

SUE: No. Four weeks isn't really ...

BRUCE: Okay, right. Four weeks.

SUE: I was away.

BRUCE: On business.

SUE: That's right.

BRUCE: Well. Welcome back.

SUE: Thank you.

BRUCE: A good trip?

SUE: I guess. Neither good nor bad.

BRUCE: Okay.

SUE: Yeah. No, it was fine.

BRUCE: All right. Number one.

SUE: What?

BRUCE: You had three things.

SUE: Oh. For a second I thought that was like a catch phrase or something ...

BRUCE: Which?

SUE: You said "number one." Like "number one."

BRUCE: Meaning?

SUE: No. Let's just ...

BRUCE: Right. The three. Let's hear it.

SUE: One.

BRUCE: (pretending it's his catch phrase-) Number One.

SUE: What?

BRUCE: No, it's a .... Go ahead.

SUE: The first thing I wanted to tell you. Before I left town.

BRUCE: Back then, yes ... Four weeks ago.

SUE: Is I had a great time with you that night.

BRUCE: Me too.

SUE: I did. On that ... you know, it didn't even qualify as a date ...

BRUCE: Drinks, or ...

SUE: Yeah.

BRUCE: Me too. I thought we really hit it off.

SUE: Yeah.

BRUCE: And the whole, crazy night, it was funny, it felt like we were stupid college kids or something.

SUE: We actually were kind of stupid.

BRUCE: But, yes, it was fun, the whole ... I was going to say date.

SUE: Hook up, I guess.

BRUCE: Better than that. Drinks.

SUE: Well.

BRUCE: Just the hanging out, you know? Talking, and ... as a team, you know, our silver medal performance in the trivia thing.

SUE: We were robbed.

BRUCE: My fault ...

SUE: No ...

BRUCE: It was ...

SUE: Absolutely not. To say no one is buried in Grant's Tomb ...

BRUCE: Yeah ...

SUE: That he's "entombed-"

BRUCE: "Entombed."

SUE: Not buried. Is ...

BRUCE: I agree.

SUE: We were robbed.

BRUCE: You are so good at trivia. You are. You're very trivial ... minded .... You're smart.

SUE: Well, it was fun.

BRUCE: And, you know, I hadn't planned on things going where they did. You know, later.

SUE: I thought they might.

BRUCE: And .... You did?

SUE: Yes.

BRUCE: Oh. Well. I wasn't going to presume, or hope that .... I just didn't really have a plan, per se, in my head.

SUE: I knew.

BRUCE: You did?

SUE: I know myself. And I liked you.

BRUCE: Liked me?

SUE: That night. You know, and still. You're a great guy.

BRUCE: Thanks.

SUE: You're a little weird.

BRUCE: Oh.

SUE: Yeah. You are.

BRUCE: Okay.

SUE: But I think that's okay. There's good weird and there's bad weird.

BRUCE: Right. Bad, like, come look at my homemade chain mail armor that I made with my own two hands . . .

SUE: You have chain mail armor?

BRUCE: No, I'm saying if . . .

SUE: Yes. And no. There's worse weird, believe me.

BRUCE: Or I'm in a barbershop quartet.

SUE: Depends. I feel like some guys could pull that off.

BRUCE: I'm not in one.

SUE: Depending on who you are.

BRUCE: I'm not in one.

SUE: That's fine.

BRUCE: Do you think that I should look into it?

SUE: A barbershop quartet?

BRUCE: Yes.

SUE: No.

BRUCE: Then we are agreed. See, I knew we get along.

SUE: Yeah. No, it was fun. That night.

BRUCE: Agreed once again.

SUE: Better than most.

BRUCE: Okay, I can live with that. "Better than most." I won't put it on my headstone, but . . .

SUE: Meaning. Meeting strangers. Your odds, you know. They suck.

BRUCE: Right.

SUE: Not better than most.

BRUCE: Okay.

SUE: As far as drinks with strangers go, that was my most enjoyable yet.

BRUCE: Number One!

SUE: I get it.

BRUCE: Sorry.

SUE: No, it's kind of funny, actually.

BRUCE: Most enjoyable yet for me too.

SUE: Okay.

BRUCE: Just handing out the superlatives now, aren't we?

SUE: Yes.

BRUCE: Bestest not-quite-date ever.

SUE: Yeah, and-

BRUCE: I'm just glad you called, and I'm glad to see you in person and it had been a while and I was holding out hope, but it had been a bit, so I was a little nervous I wouldn't hear from you, but here you are.

SUE: Here I am.

BRUCE: Yes. Time had passed. A month. Or, you know, nearly-

SUE: Right.

BRUCE: Which was enough time for me to think, "okay, I get the point..."

SUE: Yeah, well...

BRUCE: And think, "next time, Bruce, get the girl's number, too," you know?

SUE: Sure.

BRUCE: Don't just settle with handing yours over. It's fundamental. But, damn, that was fun, right, that night?

SUE: Yeah, it was.

BRUCE: Right? And here you are. You called.

SUE: Yeah.

BRUCE: Awesome.

SUE: And I should get to the second thing.

BRUCE: Let's do this.

SUE: Okay, then.

BRUCE: I like your style. It's very, you know...

SUE: Okay.

BRUCE: Hit me.

SUE: Bearing in mind all that I said...

BRUCE: (I'm) Bearing...

SUE: I can't see you anymore.

> *Pause. He begins waving in front of her face.*

BRUCE: I'm right here. Right here.

> *(pause.)*

I didn't expect that.

SUE: Are you bearing in mind still?

BRUCE: Is that supposed to take the sting out?

SUE: I guess it is.

BRUCE: What? That you like hanging out with me but you don't want to see me anymore so, what? It kind of evens out?

SUE: Yes?

>   *Pause.*

BRUCE: There's somebody else?

SUE: No.

BRUCE: You sure?

SUE: Yes.

BRUCE: Because then I would understand.

SUE: Then yes. Someone else. My husband, in fact.

BRUCE: No one else.

SUE: No.

BRUCE: You just prefer the company of say, no one, over, say, me.

SUE: I like you. I just don't want to be involved with anyone right now.

BRUCE: I hear you.

SUE: Good.

BRUCE: I mean, I hear you. Dinner for one, nothing like it.

SUE: Right . . .

BRUCE: You know. A can of soup is just the right size for . . . . And sprawling all across the bed. The great long late nights alone with not a fucking soul to talk to except your two cats . . .

SUE: You should probably get out more.

BRUCE: You know what, Sue? I probably should.

>   *Pause.*

SUE: How did you know I have two cats?

BRUCE: I didn't.

SUE: I do.

BRUCE: Congratulations.

SUE: Thank you.

BRUCE: Cats don't live forever, you know.

SUE: Yeah.

BRUCE: I'm sorry. That sounded mean.

SUE: It's just the truth.

BRUCE: Well. Just because it's the truth doesn't mean I have to spout it out all the time.

SUE: It's not a problem.

BRUCE: You know, "More than 25 million people have died of AIDS."

SUE: Really?

BRUCE: Just because it's true doesn't mean I have to spout it out.

SUE: Is anyone doing anything about AIDS, I mean, seriously...

BRUCE: Well. I won't lie to you...

SUE: Don't.

BRUCE: I am sorry you're not interested. I am.

SUE: It's not you. I just... it's not something I want to do right now. I was away and I was thinking about my life, about the world, and...

BRUCE: And what?

SUE: And I just thought...

BRUCE: What?

SUE: I don't know. I don't know.

BRUCE: You should figure that out.

SUE: Well, no, I don't really have to figure any fucking thing out.

BRUCE: Of course not. I'm sorry.

> *Pause.*

Yeah. Sorry.

SUE: Forget it.

BRUCE: Our first and last fight.

SUE: Yeah.

BRUCE: Not bad. Only one fight.

SUE: Not bad.

BRUCE: You keep the cats.

SUE: Thanks.

BRUCE: We'll split up the books later.

SUE: Yeah.

> *Pause.*

I should go. I need to go.

BRUCE: Okay.

SUE: I have to check in at work.

BRUCE: Okay.

SUE: Well, Bruce. It was nice to talk to you.

BRUCE: And you.

SUE: It was nice to see you and I wish you all the best.
>   *(pause.)*

In all your future endeavors. Whatever they may be.

BRUCE: Right back at you.
>   *She starts out.*

Sue.

SUE: Yeah?

BRUCE: Three.

SUE: What?

BRUCE: Number three?

SUE: Oh.

BRUCE: Yeah.

SUE: Right. I said three.

BRUCE: You did.

SUE: Forget it.

BRUCE: No, no.

SUE: Uh...

BRUCE: Let's hear it.

SUE: Yeah...

BRUCE: So far it's—one, I like you. Two, let's never see each other again. I'm really looking forward to three. What could it be?

SUE: It's, uhh...

BRUCE: Come on. You said three.

SUE: Remember, of all the myriad things we discussed that night, and you said you couldn't have kids...

BRUCE: Yeah.

SUE: Yeah, well...

BRUCE: Great first date material. Genius.

SUE: Well—we were talking about everything.

BRUCE: Oh, fuck.

SUE: What?

BRUCE: That's why.

SUE: What?

BRUCE: You want children.

SUE: No.

BRUCE: Of course.

SUE: I told you I didn't. That's why it came up.

BRUCE: Of course you would say that now.

SUE: No, I said it first, I said I don't want kids and then you told me . . .

BRUCE: Stupid stupid me.

SUE: No, that's not it. Seriously.

BRUCE: What then?

SUE: Well.

BRUCE: Go ahead.

SUE: You can.

BRUCE: I can what?

SUE: You can have kids.

BRUCE: Why?

SUE: I don't really know why.

BRUCE: Well, no. How do you know?

SUE: Because I'm pregnant.

BRUCE: Right, right, right.

SUE: Yeah.

Pause.

BRUCE: With whose?

SUE: Whose?

BRUCE: Uh-huh . . .

SUE: With you.

BRUCE: Me.

SUE: Yeah. That's what I'm trying to tell you.

BRUCE: With me.

SUE: Yes.

BRUCE: Me.

SUE: Yes.

BRUCE: But I can't.

SUE: You can. You can. I thought you should know.

Pause.

So, you know, now you know something new about yourself.

BRUCE: Okay. We were careful still.

SUE: Not careful enough.

BRUCE: Right.

SUE: I thought this was something you should know.

BRUCE: Right.

SUE: That you deserved to know.

BRUCE: And there's been no one else.

SUE: No one else.

BRUCE: Really?

SUE: I would remember. I remember those things. Sex. With people.

BRUCE: Wow. I was told I couldn't.

SUE: I know.

BRUCE: That's what they told me. That's what the doctors told me.

SUE: Well. They were wrong. And no worries—I am going to take care of it.

BRUCE: Take care of the baby?

SUE: Take care of the situation.

BRUCE: Oh. Oh.

SUE: Yes. I'll take care of it. I don't need any help is what I'm saying.

BRUCE: Oh.

SUE: Financial, or otherwise. No worries.

BRUCE: No worries.

SUE: Yeah.

BRUCE: Holy shit.

SUE: What?

BRUCE: Really?

SUE: Yeah. I thought you should know.

BRUCE: Yeah.

SUE: It seemed the right thing to do.

BRUCE: Thank you.

SUE: I have to go now.

BRUCE: What?

SUE: So. Once again. Thanks for a fun night.

BRUCE: Really?

SUE: What?

BRUCE: And now you're just walking out the door?

SUE: I have work. I have to check in with them.

BRUCE: I feel like you've chucked a grenade on me and now you're permanently walking out forever.

SUE: I have to check in with work. I just got back into town last night.

BRUCE: Isn't there more that we need to talk about?

SUE: I don't think so, no. It's pretty straightforward.

BRUCE: Is it?

SUE: Yeah. For me, at least.

BRUCE: But we're, you know, even if it's ... some weird .... I mean, this is something we've shared, or ... you've dropped this grenade on my lap. Because I was told that I couldn't.

SUE: Yes. They were wrong. And I really do apologize but I have to leave.

BRUCE: I feel-

SUE: I'm sorry.

BRUCE: I feel the least you could do is talk to me ...

SUE: I can't.

BRUCE: For a few moments at least.

SUE: I can't.

BRUCE: A few minutes out of your entire life you could loan some out to me to let me register this, to talk about this with you, for whom without this would never be happening. Can you not give me that?

SUE: No.

BRUCE: Not even that? Not even that?

SUE: No.

> *He looks shocked. Pause.*

At least not now. Not now. Later maybe I can find a little time.

BRUCE: That would be nice.

SUE: We'll see.

BRUCE: Beyond nice, it would be a tremendous act of charity ...

SUE: Can I call you later?

BRUCE: Will you?

SUE: I'll try.

BRUCE: If you try you will succeed.

SUE: Yeah.

BRUCE: Calling is easy. I can show you.

SUE: No.

BRUCE: I can even set you up so you press just one single number and it will call me.

SUE: Okay ...

BRUCE: It's called speed dial.

SUE: I'll call you.

BRUCE: Okay, then.

> *He sticks out his hand.*

SUE: What is that?

BRUCE: A handshake. A deal.

> *She hesitates.*

I know it's one huge hell of a commitment thing, this having to place a phone call to me, but . . .

> *She shakes his hand. Lights out.*

SCENE 2

> *A phone ringing. Bruce and Sue on their phones, apart..*

BRUCE: *(looking first at his phone)* If it isn't my old friend "restricted caller."

SUE: Keeps the stalkers at bay.

BRUCE: Am I a stalker?

SUE: You have potential . . .

BRUCE: Someone who finally believes in me.

SUE: But to the point.

BRUCE: Right. Okay.

SUE: I don't have a lot of time . . .

BRUCE: Okay. My turn for three things.

SUE: Okay.

BRUCE: Maybe three. Depending on what you say.

SUE: Okay.

BRUCE: Seriously. Thank you for taking the time to call.

SUE: No problem.

BRUCE: I really appreciate it . . .

SUE: It's fine. Let's just go ahead.

BRUCE: Oh. Okay.

SUE: Yeah.

BRUCE: One is—have you . . .

SUE: Have I?

BRUCE: You know . . .

SUE: No, I don't.

BRUCE: What is it they say—terminated . . . the pregnancy?

SUE: Abortion is another term you may have heard.

BRUCE: Yeah.

SUE: Have I done that yet?

BRUCE: Yes.

SUE: No, I have not.

BRUCE: Oh.

SUE: Not yet.

BRUCE: Okay. Then two: When are you doing that?

SUE: Why?

BRUCE: I just wanted to know.

SUE: In a week or so.

BRUCE: Oh.

SUE: Yeah.

BRUCE: You have to wait? I mean, I don't even know . . .

SUE: It's a scheduling thing.

BRUCE: Oh.

SUE: I'm going to a facility—a place I'm very familiar with.

BRUCE: Okay.

SUE: It's a clinic that I know and trust.

BRUCE: You're a nurse.

SUE: That's right.

BRUCE: So you know people.

SUE: I do.

BRUCE: You're a . . . what are you . . . you're a traveling nurse?

SUE: That's right.

BRUCE: And what is that?

SUE: Well. It's a nurse. Who travels.

> *Pause.*

BRUCE: Have I done something to piss you off?

SUE: You've impregnated me.

BRUCE: I didn't mean to.

SUE: I know.

BRUCE: Not only did I not mean to, I didn't think it was physically possible.

SUE: I know.

BRUCE: You were, as I recall, rather forthright in the removal of my pants.

SUE: On a side-note, you should, you know, consider rotating your stock . . .

BRUCE: What?

SUE: Your so-called "protection."

BRUCE: If you're implying that my condoms were somehow old as a result of a lack of sexual activity on my part in recent, what, years, then, you know, you're dead on.

SUE: I'm just saying, they have expiration dates.

BRUCE: Mine don't.

SUE: Because, I think, yours pre-date the modern practice of listing the expiration date.

BRUCE: Oh, man.

SUE: Look. It's just this whole thing is a bit of a pain in the ass, and I agreed to call and talk, briefly, with you, and you're not necessarily making anything easier with the . . . casual conversation . . . the "tell me about your job" blah blah blah . . .

> *Bruce looks a little like he's been punched. A pause.*

I signed up with an agency. I travel to different hospitals and facilities all over the country, sometimes outside the country, and I work for short periods of time, usually three months or so, and then I go somewhere else.

BRUCE: All the time.

SUE: Pretty much.

BRUCE: But you live here.

SUE: No. Not really.

BRUCE: Really?

SUE: Yeah.

BRUCE: You don't live here?

SUE: No.

BRUCE: This never came up that night.

SUE: I find it takes away from a first date, telling the other person you don't actually live here.

BRUCE: Wow.

SUE: My mother lives here. I come here a few times a year.

BRUCE: You didn't tell me this.

SUE: You know what, Bruce? Had I—we wouldn't have had such a good time.

BRUCE: And we wouldn't be pregnant.

SUE: We aren't pregnant.

BRUCE: Okay.

SUE: I'm sorry I didn't mention it that night.

BRUCE: So when you said you were going away on business, you weren't just going away on business?

SUE: No.

BRUCE: You were leaving for . . . what?

SUE: Three months.

BRUCE: So when you said you would call me when you got back?

SUE: I misrepresented when I would be getting back.

BRUCE: Misrepresented.

SUE: I lied.

BRUCE: So you did. And why are you back?

SUE: Nothing. Just coincidence. Job stuff.

BRUCE: Oh.

SUE: My job ran short and I'm being reassigned.

BRUCE: So I just got lucky then.

SUE: Depending on how you look at it.

BRUCE: That you happened to be back in town and happened to call.

SUE: I never would have even told you if you hadn't told me that you couldn't have kids.

BRUCE: I never would've heard from you.

SUE: Probably not.

BRUCE: No.

SUE: No. Definitely not.

BRUCE: Okay.

SUE: I don't want to be in a relationship.

BRUCE: I've gathered.

SUE: Yeah.

BRUCE: At least not with me.

SUE: No, that's not true. I liked you.

BRUCE: There you go again with the past tense . . .

SUE: Because, Bruce, and I am truly sorry if this sounds harsh, but you are past tense.

BRUCE: I already am.

SUE: I thought I made that clear. But you made me shake your hand. And here we are.

Pause.

So what's number three?
> *He says nothing.*

I've upset you.

BRUCE: No.

SUE: I've called you past tense.

BRUCE: You did do that.
> *A beat.*

SUE: Look. If I am short with you, it's because I have a whole army of brutal hormones fucking in a huge way with my body right now.

BRUCE: You do?

SUE: You know what? I knew we had conceived. I knew it when it happened.

BRUCE: How could you know something like that?

SUE: I felt it.

BRUCE: Really?

SUE: I know that seems crazy but it's true. And I ignored it because I thought we had been safe and remembered you telling me that you couldn't have kids. But I gotta tell you—the hormones kicked in right away. They're quite the tremendous force, let me tell you.

BRUCE: Thanks for telling me that.

SUE: I don't know what the fuck is going on, really. I don't recognize myself. I want to kill most people. I want to sleep. I want to eat all the time except when I want to throw up.

BRUCE: Sorry . . .

SUE: Would you like to know what I had for lunch?

BRUCE: Of course.

SUE: Two big disgusting bearclaws. For lunch.

BRUCE: Yum.

SUE: I'm a healthy eater.

BRUCE: I like a bearclaw.

SUE: Don't say that word.

BRUCE: Bearclaw?

SUE: Stop.

BRUCE: Sorry. You said it.

SUE: Do you want me to vomit?

BRUCE: No, I don't.

SUE: You see? This is what I've been reduced to. And to top it all off, I have another week of this.

BRUCE: I'm sorry.

SUE: It's not your fault.

BRUCE: Nonetheless.

SUE: Or it is your fault.

BRUCE: I am so sick of you bad-mouthing my condoms.

She smiles at this.

I didn't know you'd feel the pregnancy so soon.

SUE: You do. At least I do. Pretty damn soon. It's just a pain in the ass. And I am eager to have it done with. So if I seem to be . . .

BRUCE: No. It's okay.

SUE: You want to tell me your third thing?

BRUCE: Uh . . .

SUE: No, go ahead. The hormones have spiked or something. I won't snap at you. I promise.

BRUCE: You sure?

SUE: I promise.

BRUCE: Okay. The third thing—may I come with you.

SUE: Come with me where?

BRUCE: When you . . . terminate the pregnancy.

SUE: May you come with me?

BRUCE: Yes.

SUE: No.

BRUCE: No?

SUE: No. What the hell kind of question is that?

BRUCE: A stupid one, I guess.

SUE: Yes.

BRUCE: A stupid one.

Pause.

SUE: Why? Why would you want to do that?

BRUCE: Because. I'm not exactly sure. Because I'm involved . . .

SUE: Nominally.

BRUCE: Biologically.

(pause.)

Look. I'm not trying to insert my will into all of this. I realize that's not my place.

SUE: That's good.

BRUCE: And frankly it's not as if I want you to do anything different than what you want to.

SUE: Good. Because you would get nowhere with that.

BRUCE: No. I don't.... I don't want kids. I really don't.

SUE: Okay.

BRUCE: I just want to be party to this thing that has happened...

SUE: Nothing has really happened.

BRUCE: No?

SUE: No. Nothing of consequence.

BRUCE: To you, perhaps.

SUE: Yes, to me.

BRUCE: I didn't even know that I could have kids.

SUE: And now you know. But that is unrelated to this. It's of no consequence.

BRUCE: I want to come along.

SUE: Why?

BRUCE: I can't explain it. All I know is I feel very compelled to be there. To... participate in it. To... live it.

SUE: You realize your "participation" would be sitting on a shitty couch reading an old copy of Rolling Stone?

BRUCE: That's fine.

SUE: It's a procedure. A relatively simple one at that. It's fucking outpatient.

BRUCE: I understand that.

SUE: And you still want to be there?

BRUCE: I do.

SUE: Well, no.

BRUCE: I insist.

SUE: You can't insist. You have no right to insist.

BRUCE: Okay, it seems you got me there.

SUE: Yeah, well...

BRUCE: Look. I just want to be there. I do. And though I may have no rights, per se, I ask you to let me do this. That, and then I leave you alone. I'll just meet you there—I'll read the Rolling Stone—you'll come out, we'll say hi, and then that's that.

SUE: That's that?

BRUCE: Yeah.

SUE: Why?

BRUCE: I don't exactly know. I don't.

SUE: You supply your own transportation?

BRUCE: Of course.

SUE: And afterwards, that's that?

BRUCE: My word.

SUE: Okay, then.

BRUCE: Really?

SUE: Yes. You want to meet me there, I won't stop you.

BRUCE: So that's a yes?

SUE: That is a yes.

BRUCE: Thank you.

SUE: No problem.

BRUCE: So when are you doing it?

SUE: Next Wednesday.

BRUCE: Okay, great. Where?

SUE: Phoenix.

BRUCE: Phoenix . . . ? Is that the name of the facility?

SUE: That's the name of the city.

BRUCE: What city?

SUE: The city where the clinic is.

BRUCE: Phoenix, Arizona?

SUE: Yes.

BRUCE: Phoenix, Phoenix?

SUE: Yes. My next job. Phoenix.

BRUCE: Next Wednesday way the hell off in Phoenix. Arizona.

SUE: That's right.

     Long pause.

BRUCE: What time?

SUE: What?

BRUCE: What time is your appointment?

SUE: Oh, come on.

BRUCE: Come on what?

SUE: You're not coming to Phoenix.

BRUCE: Yes, I am.

SUE: Bruce . . .

BRUCE: I think so, yes. So, you know, where do I go? And what time?

SUE: I don't know. I haven't worked out all the details.

BRUCE: Okay. Well. Will you call me when you do?

>   *(beat.)*
>   You said yes.

SUE: Fine. I'll call you the night before.

BRUCE: That's the best you can do?

SUE: Do you want me to call?

BRUCE: Fine. Will you shake on that? Metaphorically speaking?

SUE: What's with you and shaking?

BRUCE: It used to mean something. It means something to me.

SUE: Okay, fine.

>   *Bruce does a shaking motion.*

BRUCE: Are you shaking?

>   *She isn't.*

SUE: Yes.

BRUCE: You promise?

SUE: Yes.

>   *They shake.*

BRUCE: Okay. See you Wednesday..

SUE: Right. Okay.

>   *Lights out.*

SCENE 3

Bruce has two coffees—he holds one out to Sue.

BRUCE: Cream, right?

SUE: Bruce.

BRUCE: No cream? I was sure it was cream. They were about to close so I had to make some executive decisions. Decaf, because of the hour, I hope that's okay.

SUE: Bruce.

BRUCE: They're closed. I thought we could walk or something.

SUE: What are you doing here? When I called you I fully expected to catch you at home . . .

BRUCE: I told you I would come.

SUE: I thought you might have a modicum of what some people call "common sense."

BRUCE: And thanks for meeting up with me tonight. I know we didn't phone-shake on that part.

SUE: You drove for like three days all the way out here. What was I supposed to do?

BRUCE: I wasn't expecting anything.

SUE: That's good.

BRUCE: I told you that. My arm is starting to hurt.

> *She takes the coffee.*

SUE: Bruce. It's certifiable. Really. Think about it. And yes, I take cream.

BRUCE: I have a backlog of vacation. Use it or lose it, you know? And I've always wanted to go to the Grand Canyon State.

SUE: They have flights, you know. They actually fly planes out here.

BRUCE: You haven't been?

SUE: Where? What are you talking about?

BRUCE: The Grand Canyon.

SUE: No.

BRUCE: It's, uh . . . worth seeing.

SUE: Okay.

BRUCE: That's a big understatement. You're here for three months, right?

SUE: Roughly, yes.

BRUCE: You should go.

SUE: I probably should.

BRUCE: Definitely. Definitely.

SUE: You're insane.

BRUCE: It's like a four hour drive from here. It's nothing. I'm telling you—It's, uhh . . . you can't perceive the depth of the thing. Or I couldn't. Because I have nothing to compare it to. I've never seen anything that deep, you know? It's uhh, really moving. Makes you really think.

SUE: About what?

BRUCE: I don't know. Time, you know. Time. The great tremendous past.

SUE: Yeah, well. I have a hard enough time with the present.

BRUCE: It makes you feel pretty insignificant.

SUE: Why would you intentionally choose to feel insignificant?

BRUCE: It's liberating in a way, don't you think?

SUE: No. I don't. Sounds like it sucks.

BRUCE: You know what?

SUE: What?

BRUCE: You seemed more fun on our date.

SUE: I am fun. I am.

BRUCE: Okay.

SUE: I am so much fun. That's a ridiculous thing to say about me.

BRUCE: Sorry.

SUE: You should see how much fun I am.

BRUCE: Okay.

SUE: Okay, what?

BRUCE: Let's see it.

SUE: It's not like I . . . I don't just do fun on command.

BRUCE: Okay.

SUE: I was fun on that date.

BRUCE: You were.

SUE: Right?

BRUCE: So much fun, we're in Phoenix.

SUE: Yeah, well.

BRUCE: No. That night was a lot of fun for me.

SUE: Okay, then. See?

BRUCE: Yes. I stand corrected. You're fun.

    Pause.

SUE: So. The Grand Canyon.

BRUCE: Yeah.

SUE: It's . . . what? How old? It's . . . what? The earth is billions of years old . . . ?

BRUCE: 6,000.

SUE: What?

BRUCE: The earth is 6,000 years old. Roughly.

SUE: Uh.

BRUCE: Grand Canyon was created by the flood.

SUE: The flood.

BRUCE: Yeah.

SUE: The one with Noah.

BRUCE: Yep.

> *Pause.*

SUE: *(to no one in particular-)* Check.

BRUCE: It's a joke.

SUE: Oh. Well. I don't really know you, so . . .

BRUCE: It's a joke.

SUE: Okay.

BRUCE: I think the earth is 4 or 5 billion years old.

SUE: I thought I was old.

BRUCE: No. You're not old.

SUE: 4 or 5 billion?

BRUCE: I think so.

> *Sue ponders this.*

SUE: Okay, then. But. Did you know?

BRUCE: What?

SUE: I read this thing—there are these scientists who say that the science is there or will be there to time travel.

BRUCE: Sounds good.

SUE: You'd think, yes. You'd think. But here's the thing.

BRUCE: What?

SUE: If that's true, which some very reputable people say is true, then where are the time travel tourists?

BRUCE: What are they?

SUE: Where are the people from the future who come back here?

BRUCE: Not here yet.

SUE: Why not?

BRUCE: I don't know.

SUE: Well, I do.

BRUCE: Tell me.

SUE: Because they aren't coming back. They haven't which means they won't. Because if they had we would know. Which could only mean one thing.

BRUCE: What?

SUE: It could only mean that this world, at least as we know it, will not be around for that much longer.

BRUCE: Really?

SUE: Yes. It's the only conclusion. In fact, there was a heavily-advertised time travelers convention—it was at MIT on May 7, 2005, designed for time travelers to all come back on that date . . .

BRUCE: No one showed.

SUE: A lot of people showed.

BRUCE: Oh. Really?

SUE: But none were from the future.

BRUCE: They didn't come back because the world as we know it isn't even going to be around for that much longer.

SUE: That's right.

BRUCE: Wow.

SUE: Yeah.

BRUCE: If that's true.

SUE: I think it is.

BRUCE: Then that sucks.

SUE: I thought you like feeling insignificant.

BRUCE: Not that insignificant.

SUE: I think it's about time, don't you?

BRUCE: For what?

SUE: Earth is old. Time to move on. Let 'er blow up.

BRUCE: You really believe that?

SUE: I do. Did you read what happened today?

BRUCE: No. What happened?

SUE: It doesn't even matter, really. Same old shit. Pick a day, read the paper. Doesn't matter.

BRUCE: What happened today?

SUE: Doesn't matter. It's just all very clear that we don't really learn a thing and we just play out the same shit over and over, over the millennia, and frankly, the sooner we fuck the planet, the better for the bacteria that are itching to take over.

BRUCE: Wow.

SUE: And you say I'm not fun.

BRUCE: I can't believe I'm about to do this . . .

SUE: What?

BRUCE: I shouldn't be bringing this up.

SUE: What?

BRUCE: But I feel given the depths of your morbidity, I have no choice.

SUE: What?

BRUCE: And I am breaking all sorts of rules here . . .

SUE: Just tell me.

BRUCE: I'm that guy.

SUE: What guy?

BRUCE: The guy . . . from the future.

SUE: You're that guy?

BRUCE: I am that guy. Hi there.

SUE: Well. Wow. Welcome to the past.

BRUCE: Thank you.

SUE: I'm honored. You've come out to me.

BRUCE: You gave me no choice.

SUE: So what's the future like?

BRUCE: It's a lot like Battlestar Galactica. The original one.

SUE: Nice.

BRUCE: Yeah. It's not bad.

SUE: I'm glad to hear it.

BRUCE: Did you ever consider that maybe people from the future don't tell the people in the past who they are?

SUE: Why wouldn't they? I would.

BRUCE: I'll tell you why—people can't handle it. People can't handle very much in the way of outright truth.

SUE: I agree with you there.

BRUCE: If I went public, I'd end up in some subterranean holding cell in Quantico, Virginia.

SUE: Possibly.

BRUCE: So we do it on the down low . . . We just come in periodically to poke around, see what's going on.

SUE: Is that right? So why now?

BRUCE: Well. The truth?

SUE: Yeah.

BRUCE: Women from this era have a reputation for being kind of easy.

SUE: Oh yeah?

BRUCE: So guys come back looking for a little action.

SUE: A sex vacation in the past.

BRUCE: That's right. I hate to reduce it to this, but you're pretty much fish in a barrel.

SUE: Is that right?

BRUCE: In the future, men learn a great deal more about seduction which make us so efficient in this era.

SUE: You didn't seduce me.

BRUCE: That's how good I am.

SUE: Yeah, right.

BRUCE: If you see it, it ain't seduction.

SUE: Is that right?

BRUCE: It's a saying we have in the future.

SUE: So what other advancements do we have to look forward to?

BRUCE: Better batteries. Like, way better batteries that last hundreds of times longer.

SUE: That's positive.

BRUCE: Yeah, you won't believe the batteries of the future.

SUE: What else?

BRUCE: Turns out the Mormons were right.

SUE: Really?

BRUCE: Yeah. It was a big surprise to everyone. Except the Mormons. Latter Day all the way. It's another saying we have in the future.

SUE: Wow.

BRUCE: I'm kidding.

SUE: About being from the future?

BRUCE: About the Mormons. No, so far no God has made him, her or itself known. The big stuff is still mostly orchestrated by mankind. Things got really warm for a while. The size of the population became a lot more reasonable. Then the cold comes. Comes and stays.

SUE: What happened?

BRUCE: A massive meteor, smashing into the earth. Knocked off our axis. The electromagnetic field permanently altered. Nothing worked anymore. Nothing. Just a planet of very cold people, wandering around in the dark looking for food. As you can imagine, things got ugly.

SUE: Were you around for this?

BRUCE: This was way before me. After some very brutal thousands of
     years . . .

SUE: Still no God?

BRUCE: No God. Nowhere.

SUE: And you're telling me this why? To cheer me up?

BRUCE: I'm not done. People started to organize again. They did. It
     took a long time of warring and slavery and general brutality,
     but our better instincts came to fore.

SUE: See, I don't believe you.

BRUCE: No?

SUE: Our better instincts are merely a by-product of living a lucky life.

BRUCE: You think?

SUE: I do. We are all a hair away from being the savages we are at our
     core.

BRUCE: History proves you wrong. Future history. They started over.
     From scratch, they started over. The good guys organized and
     made it happen. And they had absolutely everything to relearn.
     Everything. It had all been forgotten. And they didn't do too
     bad. So you can stop stressing that it's all going to end.

SUE: Thanks. That's a load off.

BRUCE: Right? There is a reason to stick around.

SUE: I guess I have to take your word for it, being that I am merely
     from the present.

BRUCE: You do.

SUE: Okay. There's no Grand Canyon in the future?

BRUCE: I'm sad to say that there is not.

SUE: What happened to it?

BRUCE: It filled with sediment.

SUE: So you came all the way back here to see the Grand Canyon?

BRUCE: No.

SUE: Then what for?

BRUCE: To see you.

SUE: To see me.

BRUCE: Yeah.

SUE: Why me?

BRUCE: You seemed nice. At least on paper.
     Pause.

SUE: Maybe you are bad weird.

BRUCE: Oh—I joined a barbershop quartet. I would sing for you but it kind defeats the purpose without my guys here.

SUE: No worries.

Pause.

BRUCE: It's getting late.

SUE: Yeah.

BRUCE: We have to get up early.

SUE: Yeah. Where are you staying?

BRUCE: The Taurus.

SUE: Is that a hotel?

BRUCE: My car.

SUE: Oh. You don't have a room?

BRUCE: No.

SUE: Oh. How come?

BRUCE: I don't know. There's some sort of convention in town.

SUE: Time Travelers?

BRUCE: Yep. I really have no excuse for not having gone further back into the past to book my room . . . .

SUE: Stay at my place.

BRUCE: No, look, I told you I wouldn't bother you any more than briefly tomorrow.

SUE: Wait. You're actually going to say no to the Long Term Slash Short Term Inn & Lodge.

BRUCE: It does sound rather enchanting.

SUE: Right? They have a continental breakfast.

BRUCE: Hmm . . . Maybe if it were inter-continental.

SUE: Oh. It is. Muffins from the English.

BRUCE: Oh. Well. Toast from the French?

SUE: Absolutement.

BRUCE: Wow.

SUE: So . . . is that a oui?

BRUCE: For the Long Term Slash . . .

SUE: Short Term Inn & Lodge.

BRUCE: Inns I can do without. Hard to say no to a lodge though.

SUE: You are preaching to the choir.

BRUCE: Do they have hot chocolate?

SUE: No.

BRUCE: Okay, it's a deal.

SUE: Just don't try any of that sophisticated future seduction.

BRUCE: You got it.

SUE: Okay. You have to use your powers with a certain amount of re-
    sponsibility.

BRUCE: Of course.

> *Lights out.*

SCENE 4

> *Sue's housing. They are half dressed. No one is saying anything.*

BRUCE: It's just second nature, the whole seduction thing...

SUE: Of course.

BRUCE: Yeah. I can't really help it.

SUE: Right. At least we know I didn't get pregnant.

BRUCE: True.

SUE: I hope you understand that this is merely because I am lonely
    and in a new city.

BRUCE: Got it. Lonely. New city.

SUE: Or alone, rather. Which I don't mind.

BRUCE: Okay.

SUE: I'm alone. A little lonely. It breaks up the day.

BRUCE: Of course.

SUE: And nothing more.

BRUCE: It's okay—I'm on a sex vacation.

SUE: I forgot. Happy sex vacation.

BRUCE: Thank you. And thank you for participating.

SUE: Always eager to help a tourist.

BRUCE: So. Where are the cats?

SUE: With my mother. They're mine. But they live with my mother.

BRUCE: Can't even commit to the cats.

SUE: No.

BRUCE: Thanks for letting me stay.

SUE: It's no problem.

BRUCE: And you were right.

SUE: About what?

BRUCE: You are fun.

SUE: See?

BRUCE: You are.

SUE: I tried to tell you.

BRUCE: When you're not forecasting doom, you're okay.

SUE: Thanks.

BRUCE: You know. You and I, we're two for two.

SUE: How do you mean?

BRUCE: I mean, we've hung out a couple of times, and it's been fun.

SUE: Yeah. Tomorrow might put a dent in our numbers.

BRUCE: Doesn't it . . . .

> *But he trails off.*

SUE: Doesn't it what?

BRUCE: I don't know. We have a good time, you and I. Doesn't it seem to be a shame that we won't ever see each other again?

> *A beat.*

SUE: Let me ask you something.

BRUCE: Sure.

SUE: Are you just interested in me because I am being such a pain in the ass?

BRUCE: You mean, because you're playing hard to get?

SUE: You see, I'm not playing really.

BRUCE: You're just plain ole hard to get.

SUE: I suppose.

BRUCE: Well. That's a good question. Um. Probably partly.

SUE: You see?

BRUCE: But I think I would probably like you even if you weren't a pain in the ass, as much I enjoy pains in the ass.

SUE: My point is, here we are in Phoenix, Arizona, and I have been explicit with you that I am not interested in any sort of a relationship. And I keep putting you off and . . .

BRUCE: Was all this tonight putting me off?

SUE: Beyond that. I have not encouraged you and, being human, you find that attractive, or a challenge.

BRUCE: Perhaps I do.

SUE: But I'm just trying to remind you—take the game out of it and it's just people. And people, meaning me, are boring and petty and selfish, and if I were to sit here now with you and suddenly start twinkling about the eyes and asking you your favorite poem and movie and recipe and hanging on to your words as if they were the cure to cancer, then you would feel amused and emboldened for a while, until it became clear to you that there is no game in it at which point you would marshal your forces on the next nice ass that walks by.

BRUCE: Wow. You are . . .

SUE: What?

BRUCE: What is it you hope to get out of life? Really. Because I'm having a hard time imagining what it could be.

SUE: As few problems as possible. I want things to go smoothly. I don't want disappointment. I don't want to get my hopes up.

BRUCE: It's not all disappointment, you know.

SUE: It is. It is. It ultimately always is. You see, you say that to me, and fact is, that's bullshit, because you're gonna die. And how is your endgame anything other than a disappointment? To the people who love you? And in the interim, everyone is a terrified asshole, who given a few minor adjustments to their life, would so easily cut your fucking head off with a machete . . .

BRUCE: You think that?

SUE: Of course I think that. Of course. Our baser nature is our base nature. What in the hell have we learned? Really. Tell me.

BRUCE: And this is how your interest in nursing began?

SUE: No.

BRUCE: I was wondering.

SUE: It began when I was young and I needed a job to get me out of the house fast and they were hiring and paying for schooling and otherwise I may not have even made it this far. Don't get me wrong. My job requires compassion and that is something I actually have, believe it or not. In fact, I have so much compassion, I'm trying to save both of us from having to go through the annoyance and potential pain of an inevitably doomed relationship.

BRUCE: I don't need you to look out for me.

SUE: I think you do. I think you don't know any better. That's what I think.

BRUCE: Tell me why it's doomed.

SUE: It's doomed because I doom it. That's why. I don't even live anywhere. I don't. That's how I actually like it. And that's just one of many many reasons why I preemptively doom our relationship.

BRUCE: Let me just say this, I don't need you making decisions for me, out of whatever it is you think you have over me, your omniscience or whatever the hell you think it is you own.

SUE: I'm trying to save you some time and effort.

BRUCE: And furthermore. I'm not looking to get married to you. As you may recall, all I really said was that I thought it was a shame that we won't see each other again. And though it is obvious that I have some interest in you . . .

SUE: You drove to Phoenix to join me for my abortion.

BRUCE: Which is actually not really about you.

SUE: Fine.

BRUCE: And all I was saying was that it would be a shame. And I get you, I really do, and I get that you are trying to put me off, and I will confess to you that I may not be as incorrigible as you think, and that you are starting to have some success . . .

SUE: What do you mean?

BRUCE: That you are beginning to succeed in putting me off. You are winning that battle.

SUE: Okay, then.

BRUCE: It's working.

SUE: Okay.

BRUCE: I feel that I am beginning to like you less.

SUE: Great.

BRUCE: So—well done.

SUE: Thank you.

> *Pause. She begins to re-dress.*

BRUCE: Yes. Let's do that.

> *He puts on his other clothes—they do this in silence. They finish. Long pause.*

SUE: I'm sorry.

BRUCE: For what?

SUE: I'm just . . . sorry.

BRUCE: Okay.

SUE: Fact is.

BRUCE: What?

SUE: Fact is—I don't entirely dislike you.

BRUCE: I'm turning red from your effusions.

SUE: Will you let me talk in the way I would like to talk?

BRUCE: Okay.

SUE: I wouldn't be this stand-offish if it weren't for the fact that I like you too.

BRUCE: So this is what it feels like to be liked by you?

A beat.

BRUCE: All I was saying was—maybe next time you come see your mom or something, we could have a beer or something. Go bowling. That's really all I was saying.

A beat.

SUE: I like bowling.

BRUCE: I do too.

SUE: Me too.

BRUCE: That's all I'm saying. I just didn't want to drive out of here tomorrow without saying that maybe there could be a way to see each other again.

SUE: Okay.

BRUCE: And not will you marry me now.

SUE: Okay.

(beat.)

Are you going to make me shake on something?

BRUCE: No.

SUE: Okay. Good.

BRUCE: I'm saying the equivalent of "call me next time you are in town and perhaps we could go bowling."

SUE: Okay. That's fine.

BRUCE: Okay then.

SUE: I'm not a very good bowler.

BRUCE: Well. You don't have to be.

SUE: Are you?

BRUCE: Not particularly.

SUE: Good.

BRUCE: I get lucky sometimes.

SUE: I don't.

BRUCE: And that's the crux of it.

SUE: The crux of what?

BRUCE: Bowling. Sometimes you get lucky, sometimes you don't.

SUE: I guess so. Why are we still up? We have to get up early.

BRUCE: It's already early. Look outside.

> *She does.*

SUE: What should we do? We'd sleep for what—an hour?

BRUCE: I can't do that.

SUE: Me neither. Maybe we should just clean up and go out and get some coffee or something.

BRUCE: Catch the sunrise.

SUE: Yeah, okay.

BRUCE: Okay.

> *(pause.)*

Now?

SUE: Not just yet, no.

BRUCE: What are you doing?

SUE: Nothing.

BRUCE: Okay.

> *They both are still for a moment. Lights out.*

SCENE 5

> *The clinic. Sue and Bruce.*

BRUCE: Damn.

SUE: What?

BRUCE: You promised.

SUE: I promised what?

BRUCE: No Rolling Stone anywhere.

SUE: Oh, sorry.

BRUCE: I'll survive. How are you feeling?

SUE: Tired.

BRUCE: Me too. Nice place. Empty.

SUE: I know the nurses. The clinic doesn't actually open for an hour.

BRUCE: Aren't you fancy?

SUE: I am fancy. So is this worth the three-day drive?

BRUCE: I think so, yeah.

>*(pause.)*

In the future, having a child, you know, is so much easier.

SUE: Why is that?

BRUCE: Because most people travel back in time to take care of themselves as babies.

SUE: Really?

BRUCE: What better caretaker?

SUE: I guess so. Did you do that too?

BRUCE: I did. It's hard work.

SUE: I'll bet.

BRUCE: I was a big crier from day one.

SUE: You turned out okay.

BRUCE: Thanks.

SUE: Not too bad.

>*(pause.)*

I certainly admire anyone who has the balls to raise a child.

BRUCE: Me too.

SUE: And I'll tell you what would keep me from doing it.

BRUCE: What?

SUE: The simple fact that they could die before you.

BRUCE: Oh.

SUE: And therefore what is the fucking point? Because that is a storm I could not weather.

BRUCE: Wow.

SUE: I guess it doesn't happen a lot but it does happen. I work in hospitals, I can tell you. And you think it won't happen to you, but I can tell you this with one hundred percent certainty—everyone thinks that until it happens to them. Doesn't matter. No one is safe. I know. I've seen it.

BRUCE: I agree.

SUE: You do?

BRUCE: I do.

SUE: I thought you were my counterpoint on these issues.

BRUCE: You're right. No one is safe. No one.

SUE: That's right.

BRUCE: When I went to the movies with my wife years ago I certainly didn't think I would be the only one eventually coming home.

SUE: You're married.

BRUCE: I was.

SUE: Oh. What happened?

BRUCE: An accident. You know, you talk of our base natures and machetes and all that, but when it comes down to it most people are just getting hit by cars. Nearly 50,000 people last year died in auto accidents just here in this country.

SUE: I'm sorry.

BRUCE: Thanks.

SUE: When was this?

BRUCE: Years ago.

SUE: You never mentioned it.

BRUCE: There never seems to be the perfect moment for such a conversational tidbit.

SUE: And you thought, why not the abortion clinic?

BRUCE: Exactly. What else to do in the abortion clinic? When there's no Rolling Stone.

SUE: I'm sorry.

BRUCE: That's when I was told that having children would be an impossibility.

SUE: Oh, wow.

BRUCE: To which, I thought, well, as I have no wife to speak of, I don't think that's a big problem.

SUE: Right.

BRUCE: So I get you. No one is safe.

SUE: No.

BRUCE: And yet we have our lives to lead, don't we?

SUE: I guess so.

> *A pause. They are both alone in their thoughts for a long moment.*

BRUCE: It's kind of cowardly, really, when you think about it.

SUE: What is?

BRUCE: You know, cowering in the corner because of what might happen.

SUE: And what will happen.

BRUCE: Yeah, and what will happen.

SUE: If you're trying to get me riled up, it's not working. Because I'll agree with you on that point. I believe it is very definitely cowardly.

BRUCE: And that's okay by you?

SUE: It'll have to be.

BRUCE: It's not that I'm so brazen.

SUE: No?

BRUCE: No. Not brazen at all for a while. After the accident. No.

SUE: Of course not.

BRUCE: What does one do with that sort of information, you know?

SUE: A godless wilderness.

BRUCE: Well. Perhaps, yes.

SUE: It's hard not to come to that conclusion.

BRUCE: If God can't wake a sleeping truck driver, then what fucking good is he really?

SUE: Yeah.

BRUCE: Just a little tap on the shoulder. "Hey you, wake up . . . "
> *Pause.*
> But, you know, what are you gonna do? Not drive?

SUE: I try not to.

BRUCE: You still have to drive. And driving, despite it all, is a goddamn fun thing to do.

SUE: I don't know.

BRUCE: It is. It is. My trip out here. Was amazing.

SUE: I guess so.

BRUCE: I get it, Sue. I get it. Not much is safe. I get that. I definitely learned that little tidbit.

SUE: I'm sorry that you did.

BRUCE: But I get you. It's a terrifying prospect, having a child, isn't it?

SUE: I think so.

BRUCE: My wife and I had been deliberating about it.

SUE: Really?

BRUCE: Yeah. And, uh, after the accident. I just knew I didn't want to have kids anymore.

SUE: Yeah.
> *Bruce is lost in thought for a moment.*

BRUCE: But I don't know. I really don't know. I'm just thinking about all this .... What if I was just ... wrong ... about myself?

SUE: What do you mean?

BRUCE: And like I was saying, you have to live your life, you know?

SUE: That's what they say on the tv.

BRUCE: You have to drive a car to get where you want ...

SUE: Trains are pretty safe.

BRUCE: It's so fuckin' .... Here we are all alone at an abortion clinic in Phoenix, Arizona. Think about this.

SUE: Think about what?

BRUCE: What brought us together, you know?

SUE: We like the same bar?

BRUCE: No. I don't think so, no.

SUE: What else could it be?

BRUCE: Because I don't know. I mean, what are we doing here?

SUE: Abortion. Remember?

BRUCE: No. Bigger than that. What got us here?

SUE: The Taurus.

BRUCE: Do you see this?

SUE: See what?

BRUCE: What am I doing here? I came all the way here. I drove here. Here we are.

SUE: I didn't ask you to come.

BRUCE: You see this, right?

SUE: What are you talking about?

BRUCE: What I'm saying to you, Sue, is that perhaps what has happened ... is something extraordinary.

SUE: Nothing has happened.

BRUCE: They tell me I can't have kids. Suddenly, what? I don't want them? Of course I don't. Because I can't have them. And then ...

SUE: So what are you saying? You're saying now you do? You want children now?

BRUCE: Uh, you know ...

SUE: What?

BRUCE: Yeah.

SUE: Okay. That's your prerogative.

BRUCE: Do you see what I'm saying?

SUE: Your life, Bruce.

BRUCE: Maybe there are gifts, you know? Sometimes? Maybe there are.

SUE: What are you talking about?

BRUCE: You.

> *He points to her belly.*

Both of you.

SUE: Funny.

BRUCE: You know, if I suddenly did believe in miracles then this is one.

SUE: All right, Bruce. I get the joke.

BRUCE: I'm not joking. Look at me. I'm not.

> *Pause.*

SUE: You want what? That we . . .

BRUCE: I don't know.

SUE: What? What?

BRUCE: Okay. That we walk out of here . . .

SUE: Wait . . . that we walk out of here?

BRUCE: And we go get a cup of coffee, of decaf coffee, and have a conversation.

SUE: A conversation?

BRUCE: Yes. A conversation. Yes. About this situation. About us.

> *Pause.*

SUE: Bruce.

BRUCE: What?

SUE: And I am serious about this.

BRUCE: Okay.

SUE: Get the fuck out of here.

BRUCE: No. Why?

SUE: Get the fuck out. I am done with you.

BRUCE: No. Listen, all I'm saying is we talk . . .

SUE: As I'm sure you noted, there is security here, and as I am sure you will intuit, they will be siding with me the minute I start screaming for you to get the fuck out.

BRUCE: Just come with me so we can talk about the future.

SUE: There is no future. No future.

BRUCE: But, okay, if you don't want to be involved, maybe, I don't know, maybe I could take this child and raise him or her.

SUE: You're insane.

BRUCE: And can we go have this discussion somewhere other than an abortion clinic?

SUE: No. We need to be in the abortion clinic in order to get the abortion. I don't believe Starbucks offers abortions.

BRUCE: Because we kind of have to have it now. And I think we've been given this chance—this exceptional thing has happened . . .

SUE: No discussion.

BRUCE: Please. I need you to hear me out. Just hear me out . . .

SUE: . . . No . . .

BRUCE: . . . Let's just put the appointment off perhaps, for a day or two, let's just do that, okay?

SUE: No.

BRUCE: And let's just go outside, right now . . .

SUE: Stop. Bruce.

BRUCE: What?

SUE: You and I are done. With this conversation. With each other. For good. How do I know this? Because unless you walk out right now I'm going to scream . . .

BRUCE: Please don't.

SUE: Out.

BRUCE: Please.

SUE: *(loud-)* Leave me alone.

BRUCE: *(quiet)* Please.

SUE: *(louder)* Leave me alone.

> *Pause.*

BRUCE: Sue.

SUE: *(cutting him off-loud-)* Get out!

> *Lights out.*

SCENE 6

> *Bruce's apartment. Sue is at the door, in her coat. Uncomfortable. A long beat.*

SUE: I came back for the cats.

BRUCE: Okay.

SUE: Yeah.

BRUCE: Okay.

> *Pause.*

SUE: And . . . I wanted to stop by.

BRUCE: I just . . . never thought I would hear from you again. A restraining order, maybe.

SUE: Yeah, well. Here I am.

BRUCE: Here you are.

SUE: Hi there.

BRUCE: Hi.

> *She fishes around for something.*

SUE: Let me get that restraining order.

> *(beat)*

> I'm kidding.

BRUCE: I wouldn't blame you if you did.

> *A beat.*

> Come in, I guess. Do you want to come in?

SUE: Okay. I guess for a minute. Do you have a minute?

BRUCE: Yeah.

SUE: Or is this a bad time?

BRUCE: No.

SUE: Okay. You're not busy?

BRUCE: I'm just . . . . Nevermind.

SUE: What?

BRUCE: No. It sounds stupid.

SUE: What?

BRUCE: I'm making a casserole.

SUE: That's not stupid.

BRUCE: Who makes casseroles?

SUE: You.

BRUCE: Me. For one. Come in.

> *She walks into the apartment. A beat.*

> Do we . . . ? Can I take your coat? Is it . . . ?

SUE: No, that's okay. We can keep it brief.

BRUCE: Coffee, or . . .

SUE: No. Thanks. Look. Let me just get to it.

BRUCE: You do like to do that.

SUE: What happened a couple of weeks ago. That was fucked up of you.

BRUCE: I know.

SUE: It really was.

BRUCE: I know it was.

SUE: I didn't begin to expect that from you and I was taken aback and reacted the only way I felt I could. I wish it hadn't come to that, but it did. You are hard to deal with sometimes. You are hard to say no to. And I needed to say no to you.

BRUCE: I know you did.

SUE: Yeah. You don't just spring that on someone at an abortion clinic. You just don't do that, Bruce.

BRUCE: Look. Whatever you need to dish out, dish it out. You want contrition, I offer you contrition.

SUE: I'm not trying to punish you.

BRUCE: It's fine if you are.

SUE: And I know it was not an ordinary situation. We hadn't slept.

BRUCE: So what? It's no excuse.

SUE: I don't know.

> *Beat.*

BRUCE: You know what? I left that place just angry. But, you know, I had a three day drive coming back here, so . . .

SUE: So . . .

BRUCE: So I had time to think. And get a little sleep, you know?

SUE: Yeah.

BRUCE: And truth is, I was a lunatic out there, you're right. We hadn't slept. If I had had that thought any earlier than when I did, there in the clinic, I would've told you.

SUE: Yeah.

BRUCE: But I didn't. I, uhh, I'm sitting there and all of the sudden I have this bright idea, you know . . .

SUE: Yeah.

BRUCE: Which was not so bright . . .

SUE: Yeah.

BRUCE: It's just funny, really . . .

SUE: What?

BRUCE: How you have a whole life of knowledge and experience behind you, and suddenly you're willing to just drop it all. It's crazy.

SUE: No, I know.

BRUCE: I'm that much of a sucker? There's what? Suddenly miraculous events? A guiding hand out there? A greater meaning? I mean, there are just mounds of evidence in my life to suggest otherwise and there I am suddenly a sucker . . .

SUE: Don't be so hard on yourself.

BRUCE: I need to be hard on myself. Keep myself in check. I do. You know, it's simple, really, there are no miracles.

SUE: I guess not.

BRUCE: You know, and really, I wouldn't want there to be.

SUE: Why not?

BRUCE: Because the implications are just too terrible.
          Pause.
     So you know, I am very glad you are here . . .

SUE: You are?

BRUCE: I am. These past couple of weeks—I've been thinking about you . . .

SUE: Why?

BRUCE: Thinking I just wish I had the chance to tell you in person that I am very sorry for my behavior. But the dumbass that I am, you know, I still don't have a number for you, do you realize that?

SUE: I wasn't sure.

BRUCE: That's how ridiculous I am.

SUE: You're not ridiculous.

BRUCE: Saying that shit to you in the clinic. I'm standing there, saying let's talk about having a kid and I don't even have your phone number.

SUE: It's not important.

BRUCE: No. There are no miracles. Just the stupid shit that befalls us.

SUE: Yeah.

BRUCE: And so, I am so sorry.

SUE: It's okay. Me too. I'm sorry.

BRUCE: Let's just . . . can we just call this thing even . . .

SUE: Okay . . .

BRUCE: . . . and move on.

SUE: What do you mean?

BRUCE: Everything cancels out. We're even. Here we are, no better, no worse.

SUE: Okay.

BRUCE: Which is better than so many run-ins you have with people.

SUE: Yeah.

BRUCE: You see what I mean?

SUE: I guess.

BRUCE: And really, seriously, beyond apologizing to you I should thank you.

SUE: For what?

BRUCE: For actually being a grounding force for me.

SUE: Me being a grounding force for you?

BRUCE: That's right. I can be a victim of my own enthusiasm if I'm not careful.

SUE: I don't think that's necessarily a bad thing.

BRUCE: It can be. It absolutely can. For me. You know, if I don't keep my feet on the ground, I . . . I what?

SUE: You fall down?

BRUCE: Yeah. I fall down on my ass. Which hurts. And looks stupid to onlookers.

SUE: Yeah.

BRUCE: So thank you.

SUE: Okay.

BRUCE: So maybe not even even. I came out a little better in the end.
    (sticks his hand out-)
    Shall we shake on it for poetry's sake?
    Pause. She shakes.

SUE: Okay.
    A beat.

BRUCE: Thanks for coming by.

SUE: Yeah. Okay.
    But she doesn't go. A long pause. Nothing is said.

BRUCE: How did it go?

SUE: How did what go?

BRUCE: After I left the other day.

SUE: Oh.

BRUCE: Yeah. How did it go? Did it go okay?

SUE: Oh. Well. It didn't go.

BRUCE: Oh. What do you mean?

SUE: You had me very upset.

BRUCE: No, I know. I'm sorry again.

SUE: I know.

BRUCE: You didn't have the abortion?

SUE: That day.

> *(beat.)*

Not that day.

BRUCE: Oh. Yeah. Right.

> *Beat.*

SUE: Did you think otherwise?

BRUCE: When I saw you here, maybe for a moment, I thought . . .

SUE: Does that upset you?

BRUCE: That you had the abortion?

SUE: Yes?

BRUCE: It upsets me . . .

SUE: It does?

BRUCE: . . . in that I'm guessing it's a sucky thing to have to do.

SUE: Yeah. Well, it is.

BRUCE: But if what you mean is am I regretful, then no.

SUE: Yeah. Okay. Me too.

BRUCE: Yeah?

SUE: Yeah.

> *Pause.*

BRUCE: But it went okay?

SUE: It did, yeah.

BRUCE: Good.

SUE: Yeah.

> *Pause.*

BRUCE: Seemed like a good clinic.

SUE: Yeah.

BRUCE: Good security.

SUE: Yeah, well. Yeah.

BRUCE: Clean. It's a clean . . . All right, I'm just rambling.

SUE: Yeah.

BRUCE: Okay. I guess this is it, then.

SUE: Yeah?

BRUCE: Yeah. Nothing really tying us together anymore.

SUE: No?

BRUCE: I guess not.

> *A long pause. Again, nothing is said. And Sue is not leaving.*

You're still here.

SUE: Yeah.

BRUCE: Do you need more contrition? I have more. I can bring it on if you want.

SUE: I don't want any more contrition.

BRUCE: Then what else?

> *She doesn't answer.*

Am I missing something here?

SUE: You're content to just call it even, or whatever the hell you call it, and do your stupid handshake, which, incidentally I am so sick of, and go back to your casserole? Is that it?

BRUCE: Well. Sue. I guess.

SUE: You guess?

BRUCE: Are there other options?

SUE: I don't know. I guess not. Now that your feet are firmly concreted to the fucking earth . . .

BRUCE: You confuse me.

SUE: You think I confuse you? You should see what I do to myself.

BRUCE: What am I missing here? I was a stalker who got stupid. I am sorry. We shook and agreed to cut our losses. Right?

SUE: That's what this is, cutting our losses?

BRUCE: Don't you think we should? Since our third date involved an abortion clinic, screaming, and a scuffle with security?

SUE: I should've figured . . .

BRUCE: Sue.

SUE: Yeah?

BRUCE: We barely know each other.

SUE: So?

BRUCE: I don't even know your last name.

SUE: You don't know my last name?

BRUCE: No. I don't. I know you told it to me. But, no, I don't know it, okay?

SUE: That's just . . . fucking priceless.

BRUCE: Look. I don't know what's going on here. The last I saw of
   you, you were screaming at me. And here you are . . .

SUE: Here I am.

BRUCE: And so what it is you want?

SUE: To . . . . to . . . . I wanted to see you. To talk to you. You know, we
   met . . .

BRUCE: People meet all the time.

SUE: We've gone through all this craziness.

BRUCE: These things happen.

SUE: I know they do.

BRUCE: They just happen. All the time, in fact.

SUE: No, I know.

BRUCE: It's not extraordinary.

SUE: I know.

BRUCE: It never is. Anything that happens is not extraordinary.

SUE: I know. Just the, what do you call it, the stupid shit that befalls
   us.

BRUCE: Yeah . . .

SUE: But here it is. In our laps, nonetheless.

BRUCE: So what are you saying?

SUE: And maybe it's not extraordinary and it's certainly no miracle,
   but here we are, Bruce . . .

BRUCE: Yeah. Here we are. And . . .

SUE: I didn't come all the way here to get my cats . . .

A long pause.

BRUCE: You really think this might be a chance for us?

SUE: I don't know. Maybe. I don't know anymore. And why is it so
   hot in here?

BRUCE: I'm baking.

SUE: I know. Me too.

BRUCE: No, I'm actually baking. In the kitchen.

SUE: Right.

BRUCE: Should I . . .

SUE: What?

BRUCE: You must be getting warm in that coat.

SUE: So what are you saying?

BRUCE: I'm saying do you want me to take your coat?

SUE: No. No.

BRUCE: I know it's a little hot in here.

SUE: It's hot.

BRUCE: Do you want to take off your coat?

SUE: No.

BRUCE: Okay.

SUE: Do you want me to take off my coat?

BRUCE: If you're warm, yes.

SUE: I'm fine.

BRUCE: Or to stay for a little while. I can make coffee.

SUE: I like tea.

BRUCE: Okay. Me too.

SUE: You do?

BRUCE: Yeah.

SUE: Then why did we keep getting coffee?

BRUCE: I don't know.

SUE: It's stupid. I like tea.

BRUCE: Me too. I prefer it.

SUE: Me too. You ordered coffee.

BRUCE: Because we called it "meeting for coffee." So did you for that matter.

SUE: You were having coffee. So . . .

BRUCE: Do you want some tea?

SUE: No.

> *(beat.)*

Are you having some?

BRUCE: No. Yes. I am.

SUE: I'm okay.

BRUCE: I'm making some anyhow. What type of tea do you like?

> *He starts off but she stops him.*

SUE: Bruce. You know, it was tremendously misguided, but you were really laying it all on the line out there.

BRUCE: It turned into lunacy.

SUE: I guess it did. But at least it was something, you know. And it got me thinking. And for whatever reason, I went against everything that makes sense and I came up here to see you. And I'm here. And I like you, Bruce. In as much as I know you. Which, admittedly, is not a lot.

BRUCE: We like tea. Who knew?

SUE: Exactly. And if you don't want to sit around here and have one more conversation in the abstract about things that we just don't get, then I agree with you. I'm tired of that too.

BRUCE: Okay.

SUE: I'm getting sick of my own voice.

BRUCE: Me too.

> *(a beat-)*

Sick of my own voice. Not yours. You actually have a very pretty voice.

SUE: But you've taken a couple of stands with me and maybe it's time for me to take one too. Which is this: Bruce. I'm taking off my coat.

> *She does.*

BRUCE: Okay.

> *He takes her coat.*

SUE: Thank you. I was dying.

BRUCE: Let me turn off the oven.

SUE: Wait. Bruce.

> *He turns back to her.*

Do you like me? Because I like you. I like you.

BRUCE: I like you, Sue. I've liked you since the minute I met you.

> *A beat.*

Now what?

SUE: I don't know. What do we do?

BRUCE: I don't know.

> *A pause.*

SUE: We could bowl.

BRUCE: Bowl?

SUE: Bowling. Go bowling.

BRUCE: Oh.

SUE: Remember? "Call me when you're back in town and maybe we can go bowling?"

BRUCE: Yeah. I do.

SUE: I'm sorry. It's a stupid idea.

BRUCE: I'll go bowling with you.

SUE: You will?

BRUCE: I like bowling.

SUE: I remember.

BRUCE: Yeah.

SUE: We haven't even been on a date.

BRUCE: I know.

SUE: Not really. We can just go bowl a game or two, right?

BRUCE: Why not? Why the hell not?

SUE: Okay, then.

BRUCE: Okay. When?

SUE: I don't know. Now? Is now too soon?

BRUCE: Now?

SUE: Is that too soon? Tomorrow? The next day?

BRUCE: No. Now is good. Now is okay.

SUE: Okay, good. Good.
      (Pause.)
    Shall we just . . .

BRUCE: Yeah, no. We can just go.

SUE: Okay.

BRUCE: Let me, umm . . . I was going to say get my things, but one doesn't really need anything to bowl, do they?

SUE: Just ourselves.

BRUCE: Okay, then. Let me turn off my oven. And off to the bowling alley.
      He steps out for a moment.
      She pulls out a scrap of paper and a pen, and is writing something down as he returns.
    Are we ready?

SUE: Before I forget.
      She hands him the piece of paper.
    My number.

BRUCE: Oh, thanks. Right.
      (beat—he looks at it.)
    Holmes?

SUE: Sorry?

BRUCE: Your last name. It's Holmes.

SUE: Yeah. It is.

BRUCE: Sue Holmes.

SUE: And now I have to confess I don't know yours.

BRUCE: Really?

SUE: I don't know yours either, no.

BRUCE: After the shit you gave me.

SUE: Yeah.

BRUCE: It's James.

SUE: James.

BRUCE: Yeah.

SUE: Well, then.

BRUCE: Yeah.

SUE: Nice to meet you.

BRUCE: Nice to meet you too...

> *Sue sticks her hand out—they shake hands.*
>
> *Lights out. The end.*

Slasher

Allison Moore

PLAYWRIGHT'S BIOGRAPHY

Allison Moore is a displaced Texan living in Minneapolis. Her play, *Slasher,* premiered at the 2009 Humana Festival, and has received productions in Los Angeles, San Francisco, Dallas, Philadelphia, Atlanta, San Antonio and St. Louis. Other plays include: *End Times* (2007 Kitchen Dog Theatre, Dallas Critics Forum Award), *American Klepto* (2010 hotINK), *Hazard County* (2005 Humana Festival), *Split* (2005 Guthrie Theater commission), *Urgent Fury* (2003 Cherry Lane Mentor Project, Mentor: Marsha Norman), and *Eighteen* (2001 O'Neill Playwrights' Conference). She is a two-time Playwrights' Center Jerome Fellow, two-time McKnight Fellow, and Bush Artists Fellow. Moore's adaptation of Willa Cather's novel, *My Antonia,* for Illusion Theatre, premiered in February 2010. Her newest play, *Collapse,* will receive an NNPN Rolling World Premiere at Aurora Theater (Berkeley), Curious Theater (Denver) and Kitchen Dog (Dallas). BFA: Southern Methodist University. MFA: University of Iowa Playwrights Workshop.

ORIGINAL PRODUCTION

Slasher was developed with the generous support of a Bush Artist's Fellowship and a Playwrights' Center McKnight Advancement Grant. The play ran March 1–April 11, 2009 at the Actor's Theatre of Louisville's 2009 Humana Festival of New American Plays.

Frances McKinney . . . . Lusia Straus
Christi Garcia and others . . Christy McIntosh
Marc Hunter . . . . Mark Setlock
Sheena McKinney . . . . Nicole Rodenburg
Hildy McKinney . . . . Katharine Moeller
Jody Joshi . . . . Lucas Papaelias

Director . . . . Josh Hecht
Scenic Designer . . . . Paul Owen
Costume Designer . . . . Jennifer Caprio
Lighting Designer . . . . Russell Champa
Sound Designer . . . . Matt Callaghan
Properties Designer . . . . . . Doc Manning
Fight Director . . . . K. Jenny Jones
Stage Manager . . . . Robin Grady
Production Assistant . . . . . Melissa Blair
Dramaturg . . . . Amy Wegener
Casting . . . . Alaine Alldaffer Casting

It was subsequently produced in Los Angeles at the Zephyr Theatre October 29th through December 13th, 2009

CAST

Director . . . . Lee Sankowich
Jody Joshi . . . . Brendan Bradley
Marc Hunter. . . . . Tim Cummings
Sheena McKinney. . . . . Steffany Huckaby
Frances McKinney . . . . Suzanne Ford
Christi Garcia, Bridget,⎫
Marcy, Beth, Madison, ⎬. . . Deb Knox
Car Hop, News Anchor⎭
Hildy Mckinney . . . . Joanna Strapp

CHARACTERS

Sheena McKinney: 21, girl-next-door kind of pretty. Not book-
  smart, but a survivor.
Hildy McKinney: 15, Sheena's little sister. Smarter than Sheena,
  but less capable in a crisis.
Frances McKinney: 40-50, their mother. Angry, thwarted feminist with a questionable disability. Gets around her
  house with the aid of a li'l rascal scooter. Loud.
Marc Hunter: 35-40, a D-list director and recovering alcoholic
  and sex addict. Tells everyone he's younger than he is.
Jody Joshi: 23, an undergrad film school dude. Capable, knows
  his stuff, but kind of a kiss-ass.
Christi Garcia: 23-30, Assistant Director of the Holy Shepherd
  Justice League. Very put together, as if she's always ready
  to make a statement on camera. Not to be underesti-
  mated.
Bridget/Marcy/Beth/Madison: Attractive young women who are
  killed in various ways, all to be played by the actor playing Christi Garcia
Woman/Car Hop/Radio Announcer/News Anchor: Also to be
  played/voiced by the actor playing Christi Garcia

SETTING

In and around Austin, Texas, 2007. Frances' run down house; a
Hooter's-style bar; a Sonic drive in; another house where they film.

STYLE NOTE

As the play progresses, Sheena's life begins to resemble a horror
movie; acting and production choices should reflect this.

Slasher

PROLOGUE

Flash back, 1992. The construction site. Darkness. Night. Sound of rain.

WOMAN'S VOICE: No . . . . no, please . . .

> *A crack of thunder, and a flash of lightening reveals Frances, searching for the source of the voice.*
> *Another flash of lightening, and we see two shadowy figures—a woman and Marc. They are outside on the deserted construction site. Marc crouches over the woman, who lies in a compromised position.*

WOMAN: No!

> *A loud crack of thunder. The woman lets out a piercing scream. Frances, her face twisted in rage, gives a primal yell in response.*
>
> *Blackout.*
>
> *In the darkness, the sound of Frances falling violently.*

SCENE ONE

Present day. Sound of rain continues. Sound of a car door slamming.

HILDY: *(O.S.)* Wait!

SHEENA: *(O.S.)* Run!

> *Sound of the two girls squealing as they run through the rain. Sound of keys in the door. Lights up as the front door opens into the living room of an old house. Sheena and Hildy step into the house, shaking off the storm. They carry a bag of groceries and a box from a chicken joint. Frances*

lies awkwardly on the floor. She wears an old bathrobe and slippers. A motorized scooter sits empty on the other side of the room.

FRANCES: I've been waiting for you.

SHEENA: *(annoyed)* Jesus Christ.

HILDY: Mom! Are you all right?

SHEENA: What happened.

FRANCES: What do you think happened? Get my scooter.

Hildy gets the scooter.

SHEENA: Let her get it herself.

FRANCES: Thank you for your concern, Sheena.

SHEENA: The physical therapist showed you how to get up.

FRANCES: According to her I should be training for a damn marathon.

SHEENA: Walking ten minutes three times a day is not—

FRANCES: I FELL.

As Hildy helps Frances into the scooter, Sheena reaches into Frances' pocket, grabs a bottle of pills.

SHEENA: How many did you take?

FRANCES: Give me those!

(Sheena dodges Frances, counts the pills.)

I've been lying on the floor for three hours, all you care about is how many pills—

SHEENA: Is today the eleventh?

HILDY: Tenth.

(to Frances)

We got chicken?

FRANCES: It's not enough that I'm disabled, you have to humiliate me, too. Why don't you call Marshall Davis, huh? He would loooove to see me lying on the floor, not able to get up. He'd pay to see that. Get me flat on my back so everybody at city hall can take their turn—

SHEENA: Mother!

FRANCES: STEPPING ON ME. You can stop counting. I've been a good little cripple.

SHEENA: Today is the tenth, your prescription was refilled on the first—

FRANCES: So I took an extra—

SHEENA: FOUR extra—

FRANCES: Whatever—

SHEENA: Which is why you were passed out for three hours and forgot to tell me Hildy's practice was cancelled.

FRANCES: It was a choice between taking a couple of extra pills and screaming in agony for half the day! Now give them back.

Sheena hands Frances the pill bottle.

SHEENA: Did you hear from that attorney?

FRANCES: Coward. Ball sucker.

HILDY: You want ice tea?

FRANCES: No thank you, dear.

SHEENA: So he's not taking the case.

FRANCES: Didn't even have the guts to call me himself. Made his secretary do it for him.

SHEENA: Hildy?

HILDY: *(to Frances)* There's mashed potatoes?

Sheena gathers her things to leave.

FRANCES: She's probably not even his secretary. He just employs her so he can claim the blow jobs as a business write off.

SHEENA: Please eat something tonight.

FRANCES: Where are you going?

SHEENA: I picked up a bunch of shifts.

FRANCES: Well, there goes the dean's list.

SHEENA: How else are we going to fix the AC?

FRANCES: You wouldn't have to pick up shifts if they weren't paying you third-world wages-

SHEENA: They're not.

FRANCES: Two dollars and fourteen cents an hour is what women in Mexico make for pulling used limes out of Corona bottles.

SHEENA: I'm late.

FRANCES: You know why they get away with paying you that? Because most tipped workers are WOMEN. If you got the other servers together to protest, stage a walk-out-

SHEENA: We'd be replaced in a day and a half, and then *no one* in this house would have a job.

(to Hildy)

I'm closing tonight, do you have a ride in the morning?

HILDY: Yep.

FRANCES: They underpay you on purpose to force you to giggle and flirt and generally debase yourself so all the dickless little men will leave you a big tip!

SHEENA: I do NOT debase myself!

> *Immediate shift to:*

SCENE TWO

> *The bar. Sheena takes off her jacket revealing a tight v-neck t-shirt that reads 'Busters' in big letters across the chest. It's her uniform. She picks up a tray and quickly puts on a big smile for Jody and Marc who sit at a table in the bar.*

SHEENA: Hey Jody!

JODY: 'sup, Sheena.

SHEENA: Be right with you.

> *Sheena exits. Marc watches her go uncomfortably, like he's in a dentist's office.*

JODY: So you were saying?

MARC: I was saying, what I was saying is, that it's an allegory.

JODY: Absolutely—

MARC: Which is the case with most horror movies, the good ones, anyway. They tell us about our deepest fears, not just personally but as a society.

JODY: Definitely.

MARC: Take Hostel, right? The whole movie trades on this fear that super rich Europeans *get off* on torturing Americans.

JODY: Well, yeah, but, I mean. They do, right?

> *(Beat. Marc does not laugh.)*

> Just, illustrating your point—

MARC: That's good.

JODY: That we really think rich dudes are total sadists-

MARC: When you let that underlying fear inform every shot, *that's* when you transcend the genre. That's what separates the break-out hit from just another slasher flick—Texas Chainsaw Massacre being the original example.

JODY: Oh man, from the word go that film is unbelievable—

MARC: Because of the threat. That's what was so revolutionary.

JODY: Well, that and Tobe Hooper's insane editing—I mean, forty edits per minute—

MARC: Blah blah blah, fine. His editing is great, but it would have meant nothing if he hadn't—. At a time when the media's favorite whipping boy was the so-called 'Me Generation,' he makes a film that says: yes, young people do smoke pot and drink beer and have sex, *but they are innocent.* The threat comes from the adults.

JODY: I see what you mean.

MARC: And not adults like "The Man" or "The Suit," no no no no no. It's the *family.* The movie hits on this deep fear that the family structure itself is ultimately responsible for the most unspeakable violence and terror.

JODY: Absolutely.

MARC: This project I'm working on now, it's really about what happens to a man when he's forced to, to repress and even hate his own, natural, sexual desires.

JODY: Right.

MARC: He should be loving these women—they're beautiful young women—he *wants* to love them, but he's been told that sex is evil. And so he has to kill them.

JODY: Yeah.

> *Sheena re-enters and waits on them.*

SHEENA: I'm back.

MARC: You are.

SHEENA: What can I get for you?

MARC: Club soda and lime, please.

SHEENA: You got it.
> *(to Jody)*
And I already know what you want—
> *She starts to exit.*

JODY: Actually, can I, uh, just get an ice tea?

SHEENA: Um. Sure?

JODY: Thanks.
> *Sheena exits.*

MARC: You're a regular, huh?

JODY: Well, half the filmmakers in town hang out here, so if you want to know what's going on—

MARC: It's the hub.

JODY: Exactly.

MARC: When I was here there was a place off Magnolia, I hope to
    God it's been condemned. Can't remember how many times I
    found McConnoughey or Zellweger passed out on the bath-
    room floor there—

JODY: Right.

MARC: Oh wait, that was me!

JODY: Right.

MARC: Had a little tendency to, uh, overindulge—

JODY: I've been there, brother.

MARC: But you don't drink anymore?

JODY: Oh. I'll have a beer now and again, just—

MARC: Just not now.

JODY: Well, this is a meeting, right?

MARC: Is it? I mean, you called me, buddy.

JODY: All right, okay, so. So I heard through the grapevine that you
    need a first assistant.

MARC: Interesting. What else did you hear?

JODY: Nothing, really.

MARC: Uh-huh.

JODY: Well, just that you've got a 21-day shooting permit up in Round
    Rock that started today, but Jenna Long pulled out of her con-
    tract yesterday and took most of your investors with her. But
    since you're on the hook with the Texas Film Commission and
    you've already paid up your insurance and deposit on cameras,
    you're planning to shoot anyway.

MARC: Wow.

JODY: It's a pretty small town.

MARC: Let's assume what you've said is, more or less true. Why
    should I give you the job.

JODY: I'm ready, dude. In the past two years I've shot and cut five
    short films, three of them horror.

MARC: But you've never worked on a feature.

JODY: Well—

MARC: Because, see, here's the thing: if we miss a shot, Jody, if we
    have to do extra set-ups because someone's not paying atten-
    tion, I'm literally throwing money away.

JODY: I hear you, brother—

MARC: Not *my* money. But money that I worked very hard to raise. This film gets made in the next twenty days, or it does not get made—and it not getting made is not an option.

JODY: I'm Johnny on the spot—

MARC: You graduate already?

JODY: Um, technically, no, but—

MARC: You're still a student.

JODY: I'm just missing, like, a math class—

MARC: *You can still access the editing room at the University?*

JODY: Oh. Oh! Yeah. Definitely. Access is easy, brother.

MARC: The first assistant is gonna have a lot of responsibility.

JODY: I can handle it.

MARC: And it's gonna be old-school. I'm talking twenty-three hours a day and being grateful for that one hour off. So I need to know: how bad do you want this.

JODY: I'd sell my mom for it.

MARC: Is your mom hot?

JODY: Not really.

MARC: It's a joke.

JODY: Right.

MARC: Sort of.

JODY: Um—

MARC: I'm joking about your mother, specifically—I mean unless you're lying to me and she's one of those really hot moms—

JODY: No.

MARC: Because I have a rule now about not dating anyone under 30, so.

JODY: Oh.

MARC: It's a recent thing.

JODY: I mean, that's cool, man—

MARC: It is. It is cool. You should try it.

JODY: Sure.

MARC: I'm telling you, once you date a woman who is 32 or 33, 35 even? How old are you?

JODY: Twenty three.

MARC: Talk to me when you've lived in LA for fifteen years.

JODY: So does this mean—

Sheena brings their drinks.

SHEENA: One soda with lime and one ice tea. Can I get y'all anything else right now?

MARC: I'm so sorry I didn't mention this before, but—is it Sheena? I like kind of *a lot* of lime.

SHEENA: Oh—

MARC: I should have said something when I ordered—

SHEENA: Let me get you another one.

MARC: You don't mind?

SHEENA: Not at all! You just want one or two or—

MARC: One will be fine. Thank you.

> *(Sheena exits, he watches her go.)*

God, I miss Texas. You have no idea.

JODY: So, the location is in Round Rock?

MARC: It's dynamite. It's suburban and rural all at the same time. I swear to God, find the right location, and you're halfway there.

JODY: I just saw your film, um, *Initiation Rites*? And the locations in that are—

MARC: You what.

JODY: Your movie, from last year?

MARC: How did you, where did you get it.

JODY: I downloaded it.

MARC: Great.

JODY: Did I do something wrong—

MARC: They said they were never going to release it—

JODY: I was just online, and—I mean, you directed that, right, it's yours?

MARC: Did I direct it? Yes, if you can call it "directing" when you're forced to cast five of the six principals with relatives of the investor, and then deal with his demands that entire scenes be reshot to show his girlfriend at a more flattering angle—

JODY: Yo, I didn't mean to—

> *Sheena brings the lime, Marc puts up a finger to stop her.*

MARC: Which I would have done in the first place, if she'd HAD a flattering angle.

> *(to Sheena)*

The way you walked across the bar just now to deliver a slice of lime to an agitated but I assure you a very grateful customer—

you displayed more intention in that simple action than the lead so-called actress in *Initiation Rites* did for a single moment in the entire movie.

SHEENA: She must've really sucked.

MARC: That, Sheena, is the understatement of the year. The entire film was a waste, except for maybe one shot.

JODY: *The scene in the woods!* With the low angle shot looking up at her. I mean, right?

> *Beat. Marc sees that Sheena's interested.*

MARC: Go on.

JODY: It was right after, what was her name—

MARC: *"Gabriella."*

JODY: Right. She's just buried the guy. She takes a step, and the camera is right there. Her bare foot sinks into the mud and you slowly pan up her body. There's blood and dirt caked on her arms and legs, and the trees are towering up behind her. And it's like: she's as powerful and as silent as those trees.

MARC: That's the one.

JODY: It's a great shot.

SHEENA: It sounds cool.

MARC: *(to Sheena, this is all for her)* We got on location and it just came to me. That's the thing about directing, you gotta be open all the time, filming in your head constantly, "what if we shoot it this way, what if we put the camera there—"

SHEENA: Right.

JODY: That is so true—

MARC: *(still to Sheena)* To make a great film, you prepare, you prepare, and then you throw it all out the window and fly.

JODY: Right on, brother.

MARC: Don't say 'brother,' it makes you sound like an asshole.

JODY: Um—

MARC: Scream for me.

SHEENA: Excuse me?

MARC: I'm sorry, I'm being rude. Marc Hunter, I'm a film director.

SHEENA: I figured that out.

MARC: I'm going to be shooting a movie here in town and it just so happens that I need to recast a couple of roles.

SHEENA: Um, I'm not an actress.

MARC: Why don't you let me be the judge of that.

SHEENA: You want me to just scream? Right here in the bar.

MARC: I don't want you to 'just scream.' I want you to scream like . . . . like you're all alone in a house. You're house sitting, friends of your parents. You thought it would be fun. Make your boyfriend a fancy dinner, make love to him in front of the fireplace. But your boyfriend won't be there 'til late and you're upstairs in that king-sized bed, all alone when you hear a noise: drip, drip, drip. It's coming from the attic. You call your boyfriend, he says it's probably just a leak. Get a bucket, he says, and he'll deal with it in the morning. So you find a bucket and a flashlight and ascend the creaking stairs into the deep darkness of the attic. You reach the top of the steps, pull on the light string, and click: the bulb is burned out. You don't want to go, but you have to now. You take a step, flash the light in front of you, and you see a pool of blood, it stretches back to an old wheel chair that's been tipped over, blood gathering beneath it, and there it is, drip, drip, dripping right in front of you and you look up to the rafters and you see it:

SHEENA: *(Screams. It's a knockout.)*

MARC: Yes!

JODY: Wow.

MARC: You were right there, you really saw it—

SHEENA: Holy crap—

MARC: You're brilliant! Pretty but not too pretty, with that believably innocent quality—but at the same time I totally buy that you'd put up a hell of a fight—

JODY: Oh yeah!

MARC: You are the perfect Last Girl.

SHEENA: The last what?

MARC: The Last Girl. The last one to be killed. You're not SAG, or AFTRA are you?

SHEENA: What?

JODY: No.

MARC: *(He hands her his card.)* Email me your address, I'll get you a contract tomorrow. Shooting starts Thursday morning.

SHEENA: But, I have class. And I work and—

JODY: So ditch!

SHEENA: I can't just quit my job.

MARC: Well, Sheena, I hate to tear you away from all this, but, um: I'm offering you a role in a feature film.

SHEENA: How much do I get paid?

MARC: The non-union rate is five-hundred a week. Principal shooting starts Thursday, and it goes without saying that you need to be 100 percent available, because as it turns out, time actually is money, and we're already behind schedule.

SHEENA: I want ten grand.

JODY: What?

SHEENA: Ten grand, plus a percentage of gross.

MARC: I'm sorry, the non-union rate is—

SHEENA: I make $500 a week here.

MARC: All right, okay, fair enough. I'll tell you what: we can do $800 a week.

SHEENA: No.

MARC: We don't normally negotiate this kind of thing—

SHEENA: If I'm the last girl to get killed, that means I'm in most of the movie.

JODY: That's true.

MARC: *(to Jody)* Shut up.
          (to Sheena)
    I'll give you fifteen-hundred dollars a week, But that's it—

SHEENA: Ten grand, plus a percentage of gross.

MARC: Only investors get gross!

SHEENA: Then I want twenty grand.

MARC: Okay, did no one ever explain that when you negotiate, the high bidder generally comes down toward the low bidder until you reach a compromise somewhere in the middle?

SHEENA: You just hired a girl in a bar with no experience to play the last girl in your movie? Shooting starts the day after tomorrow, you're already behind schedule and I'm guessing every day you spend looking for a new last girl is gonna cost you a hell of a lot more than twenty grand.

MARC: I'll give you ten grand.

SHEENA: Twenty.

MARC: Ten, plus one percent net—

SHEENA: No—

MARC: Two percent net—

SHEENA: I don't believe in net—

MARC: Fifteen grand, and that's my final offer.

SHEENA: Done.

MARC: Thank God—

JODY: Holy shit—

SHEENA: I'm in the movie?

MARC: Welcome to *Bloodbath*.

SHEENA: Oh my God! I can't believe it! I'm so excited! I have to, I have to go quit my job!

>   *Sheena exits. Marc slams his club soda, gets up.*

MARC: I have to get out of here, I have to explain to my one remaining investor what the hell just happened.

JODY: But, wait! You never actually said—

MARC: You're in. You'll get gas money, cold tacos on the set and two points net—and don't even think about negotiating.

JODY: You are not gonna regret this, broth—Marc.

MARC: Stop by my hotel in the morning and pick up the script. And start tracking down a meat hook, the biggest claw-foot bathtub you can find, and a wheel chair.

>   *Sound of whirring.*

>   *Immediate shift to:*

SCENE THREE

>   *Frances' house. Frances whirs by on her scooter. A knock is heard. She opens the front door to reveal Christi, who stands holding a clipboard.*

CHRISTI: Hi, how are you doing today?

FRANCES: That depends, are you Mormon?

CHRISTI: Um, *no*—

FRANCES: I like the Mormons. You can say anything, they just smile.

CHRISTI: I'm Christi Garcia, I'm Assistant Director of the Holy Shepherd Justice League? We're in the area to let people know about an important issue that—

Frances slams the door in Christi's face, cutting her off. Christi knocks again. Frances opens the door.

CHRISTI: Are you aware that there's an abortion clinic being built across the street from the mall? It's going to be six blocks from LBJ high school.

FRANCES: Sounds convenient.

Christi hands her a flier.

CHRISTI: Holy Shepherd is staging a protest tomorrow, all the information is right here—

FRANCES: What's to protest? Get an abortion, stop for an Orange Julius, still make it to cheerleading practice.

CHRISTI: Cynicism comes from a lack of hope, Mrs . . . ?

FRANCES: *MS.*

CHRISTI: It comes from deep despair. I am living proof of what young people can accomplish when they reject our any-thing-goes culture and embrace the values of self-respect and chastity.

FRANCES: I bet you're a big hit at parties.

CHRISTI: I refuse to stand by and let the cancer of immorality spread unchecked. When you decide you want to take action, when you're ready to help create a better society—

Frances slams the door in her face once more. There is another knock.

FRANCES: Look, I already—

(She opens the door, Jody is standing there with a script.)
You're definitely not a Mormon.

(NOTE: if Jody looks very clean cut, please change Frances' line to: "Oh good, a Mormon!")

JODY: Um, I'm looking for Sheena? I need to drop this off for her. Is she here—

FRANCES: What is this.

Frances grabs the script from him.

JODY: The script, for the movie? Are you her mom? Marc asked me to drop it off and—

FRANCES: *Bloodbath.*

JODY: Yeah.

FRANCES: A Film by Marc Hunter.

JODY: It's actually not bad—

FRANCES: Marc Hunter—

JODY: A couple of clever twists, and—

FRANCES: Marc with a 'C'—

JODY: He's the—

FRANCES: Smarmy, beady-eyed hustler who went to school here?

JODY: Hey, you know him!

> *Frances zips into the house, taking the script. She pops a handful of pills.*

JODY: So, okay, I mean, you are Sheena's mom, right? Sheena lives here?

FRANCES: Get out.

> *Frances starts to charge him.*

JODY: I'm going, I'm going!

FRANCES: Wait!

> *(He stops)*

What exactly is Sheena doing with this movie.

JODY: She's in it? She's, like, the main girl.

FRANCES: I see.

JODY: She's gonna be amazing. You should hear her scream.

FRANCES: Oh, I will.

> *Immediate shift to:*

SCENE FOUR

> *Sonic. The car. Sheena in the driver's seat. She leans out to order into the drive up box. Hildy sits next to her.*

DRIVE UP VOICE: *(garbled mess)*

SHEENA: Hi, two chicken strip dinners, an order of chili cheese fries, and two diet cokes please.

DRIVE UP VOICE: *(more garbled mess)*

HILDY: Get something for mom.

SHEENA: I did. I'm going out, genius.

HILDY: With who?

SHEENA: None of your business.

> *(Sheena puts on a pair of very hip sunglasses.)*

I do have a life.

HILDY: When did you get those?

SHEENA: Today. I needed a new pair.

HILDY: That why you were so late?

SHEENA: Actually, I was late because I was getting the muffler replaced. The muffler on this car that takes you everywhere—not that you even noticed that you couldn't hear me coming four blocks away.

HILDY: Oh. Yeah, it is a lot quieter!

SHEENA: Look, you need to start taking more responsibility.

HILDY: I already clean the whole house.

SHEENA: For rides, for getting yourself to and from places. I'm not gonna be around forever, so you need to get used to it.

HILDY: What's going on.

SHEENA: What's going on is that I'm 21 years old, I'm supposed to have my own life, not be taking care of you all the time. I'm not your mother.

HILDY: I know that.

SHEENA: Plus I've been cast in a movie.

HILDY: What?!

Car hop arrives with bags of food and drinks. Sheena passes them off to Hildy, gives the car hop a bill.

CAR HOP: Two chicken strip dinners, one chili cheese fry, two diets, nine forty-seven.

HILDY: You're lying!

SHEENA: Here's ten, keep the change.

CAR HOP: Thanks.

Car hop exits.

HILDY: You're a marketing major!

SHEENA: So?

HILDY: Seriously?

SHEENA: *Yeah.* The director is in from LA. He came in to Buster's last night with this film guy I kind of know and the next thing, he's offering me a part.

HILDY: It's not porn, is it?

SHEENA: NO!

HILDY: I'm just asking.

SHEENA: It's a horror movie, all right, and I'm the lead, I'm the last girl.

HILDY: The last what?

SHEENA: The last girl, the last to be—I'm basically the main character, so I have to be on the set all the time. You're gonna have to
get rides and figure out dinner and stuff.

HILDY: Have you told mom?

SHEENA: *No*, and you're not going to either.

HILDY: She's gonna freak.

SHEENA: She is a freak.

HILDY: You know how she gets about horror movies—

SHEENA: Which is why no one is telling her.

HILDY: You don't think she's gonna notice you're gone all the time.

SHEENA: Not as long as her prescription doesn't run out.

HILDY: When she finds out, I want to be there to see it.

SHEENA: Do you know how many girls would kill for a chance like this?

HILDY: Oh, sorry, I assumed you were going to *be* killed—

SHEENA: I'm serious!

HILDY: Or forced to saw off your own arms, or get gutted by a maniac
or whatever—

SHEENA: *They're paying me fifteen thousand dollars, okay?* Fifteen grand
that's gonna fix the AC and pay for your SAT prep course, and
get me the hell out of here when I graduate so I don't end up
working at Buster's for the rest of my life. So I don't really care
right now about mom's "feminist critique of the horror genre."
Because let me tell you something: *It cannot be exploitation when
they are paying me this much money.*

HILDY: This is gonna be so rad.

SHEENA: You know what? Tell her. I don't care. She can't stop me. I
mean, seriously, she hasn't left the house for almost a year.
What's she gonna do?

> *Immediate shift to:*

SCENE FIVE

> *Frances' house. Hildy and Sheena step into the house holding their
> cokes and the Sonic bag. Frances sits on her rascal, ready for battle.
> She holds the copy of the script.*

FRANCES: You.

HILDY: Uh-oh.

SHEENA: What is that?

FRANCES: This?

She rips a single page from the script.

SHEENA: Don't!

FRANCES: Oh, I thought you didn't know what it was.

SHEENA: Where did you get it.

FRANCES: I was actually hoping that you DIDN'T know—

SHEENA: Give it to me—

FRANCES: Because this, *this* is a chronicle of female degradation, one hundred and five pages in which a virginal young woman named "Sloan" is terrorized—

Frances rips another page.

SHEENA: Mother!

FRANCES: *(and another)* sexually objectified—

SHEENA: Stop!

FRANCES: *(and another)* TORTURED AND RAPED AFTER BEING BATHED IN ANOTHER WOMAN'S BLOOD.

HILDY: Gross.

FRANCES: No, Hildy. "Gross" is a booger. "Gross" is vomit, or feces. *This* is a contagion in which the most reprehensible acts are packaged as entertainment—not just entertainment, but as TITILATION, so that men like Marc Hunter will continue to think that it's HOT to see women RAPED AND KILLED! I am going to track him down and cram every single page down his throat, page after page until his dangly little uvula is castrated by a thousand paper cuts and he chokes on his own blood! Or maybe I'll just burn it.

Sheena makes a quick grab for the script, but Frances zips away on her scooter. A chase.

SHEENA: I won't let you!

FRANCES: Where are the matches!

SHEENA: I am doing this movie!

FRANCES: OVER MY DEAD BODY!

SHEENA: I can arrange that!

FRANCES: I will lock you in the closet before I let that happen! I will force-feed you the collected works of Betty Freidan! I will not allow you to be tortured and humiliated—

SHEENA: I WANT TO BE TORTURED, OKAY?

FRANCES: What did you just say.

SHEENA: I want to be tied up, and look scared and scream my head off, and you know why? BECAUSE IT'S A MOVIE.

FRANCES: I am not hearing this.

SHEENA: I AM IN A MOVIE! I'm the STAR! And I didn't just get the part! I NEGOTIATED! I demanded more money and I GOT IT! YOU'RE SUPPOSED TO BE PROUD OF ME!

FRANCES: I'm supposed to be proud you want to be degraded?

SHEENA: IT'S NOT REAL, MOTHER! I'M IN CONTROL!

FRANCES: You're actually retarded, aren't you?

SHEENA: You know what? I'm outta here.

> *Sheena bounds up the stairs, sound of drawers opening and closing. Frances comes to the foot of the stairs, talking up at Sheena.*

FRANCES: I always knew you weren't smart, but I didn't think you were actually STUPID. Have you learned NOTHING? Watching me bang my head on the glass ceiling, day after day—

> *Sheena reappears at the top of the stairs*

SHEENA: You haven't worked in years.

FRANCES: I HAVE CHRONIC FATIGUE!

SHEENA: You want to stop me from making this movie? Here's your chance: Come up here and stop me.

> *An expectation.*

FRANCES: Don't mock me.

SHEENA: I dare you. Walk up these stairs and admit that there's nothing wrong with you, and MAYBE I won't do the movie.

HILDY: Sheena, what are you doing?

SHEENA: The choice is yours, mom.

HILDY: You know she can't go up stairs.

SHEENA: Oh yes she can. She just doesn't want to.

FRANCES: That's not true.

SHEENA: I want you to admit that you're a lazy, bitter drug addict—

HILDY: Sheena, stop it.

SHEENA: Who would rather rail about injustice than GET A JOB—

FRANCES: You're beyond cruel.

SHEENA: What's cruel is pretending you're too tired to even walk across a room, and forcing your daughter to support you so you

can spend all your time screaming that you've been discriminated against.

SHEENA: I HAVE been discriminated against—

SHEENA: The city gave Marshall Davis that cleaning contract because
you couldn't do the job.

FRANCES: I DID the job.

SHEENA: You took a whole day to clean one floor!

FRANCES: Hello! I'm DISABLED, of course it's going to take me
longer.

SHEENA: You are such a victim! God! You talk about how people are
so afraid of strong, powerful women "like you." But no one is
afraid of you, and you know why? Because you don't DO ANY-
THING! Ever since dad left you've done nothing! Well I'm actually DOING something now, and you can't stop me.

Sheena disappears onto the second floor.

FRANCES: Oh, so this is your big statement? Well, I've got a question
for you: Who controls the film? Who controls the money, huh?
I'll give you a hint: it's not you! You and the rest of your gener-
ation, you're all too busy getting boob jobs and counting carbs
to notice that WOMEN ARE STILL ROYALLY SCREWED.
They pat you on the head, tell you discrimination is over. Who
needs equal rights when you've got the WNBA? They trot out
Condoleeza Rice once a month like she's the EQUALITY
BONG so you're all too stoned to notice that WE STILL
ONLY MAKE 76 CENTS ON THE DOLLAR!

*Sheena barrels down the stairs with a bag of clothes and
climbs over Frances like she's a piece of furniture.*

SHEENA: Get out of my way.

FRANCES: I am not going to let you—OW!

HILDY: Stop it!

FRANCES: You are NOT taking my car.

SHEENA: It's MY car, mom. I bought it after you totaled the last one
ramming into Marshall Davis' Expedition!

HILDY: Where are you going?!

FRANCES: If you do this movie, I am disowning you, Sheena. I'll never
speak to you again.

HILDY: Mom!

SHEENA: Fine.

HILDY: Sheena!

SHEENA: She's all yours.

HILDY: You can't leave. What am I supposed to do?!

SHEENA: You're the genius. Figure it out.

FRANCES: They've turned my own daughter against me.

SHEENA: No, you did that all on your own.

    Immediate shift to:

SCENE SIX

    Lobby bar. Sheena approaches Marc, who sits at a table with a club soda and an open bottle of beer.

SHEENA: Marc, I'm so sorry to keep you waiting—

MARC: It's okay.

SHEENA: I know it sounds lame, "the dog ate my script," but seriously, if you met my dog—

MARC: It's not a big deal. I've got another copy up in my room.
    (Catching himself)
Which I will bring down to you. Here.
    He hands her the beer.

SHEENA: This is for me?

MARC: Well, it's not for me.

SHEENA: You are so nice, and I feel like such a loser! We're supposed to talk about the movie, and acting, and I haven't even read the script—

MARC: No, no, it's better this way. Because here's the thing: I don't want you thinking too much, Sheena. That's the biggest mistake actors make. Over-preparation.

SHEENA: Really?

MARC: Acting is all about being in the moment. They shouldn't even call it "acting." They should call it *reacting*. Because that's what you're doing.

SHEENA: Right.

MARC: It's very instinctual. And that's what you've got. Losing Jenna Long and, honestly, a good chunk of the budget with her, that was, hard to take. But now? I really think you're gonna be better.

SHEENA: Me?

MARC: Absolutely. That's why I wanted to shoot in Texas. I mean, who needs the L.A. attitude when I can find such an unspoiled, untainted, unbelievably attractive, young actress right here.

SHEENA: Um, wow.

MARC: I mean it's also cheaper—it's a lot cheaper. But to this day some of the best work I ever saw and ever did happened right here. Matt McConnoughey didn't know what he was doing any more than the rest of us. We just did it, you know? Filming out of the back of some shitty van, trespassing on construction sites. That's what I'm after with this one.

SHEENA: You know Matthew McConnoughey?

MARC: I know a lot of people.

SHEENA: Oh my God.

MARC: In L.A., that's all anybody cares about: who do you know, who's attached to your project. It has nothing to do with *vision*. You should move there. As soon as you can.

SHEENA: What?

MARC: I mean, if you're at all interested in having a career as an actress, which I think you could.

SHEENA: Really?

MARC: Absolutely. But if you're gonna do it, don't wait.

SHEENA: Well, I have to finish school.

MARC: No you don't. I mean, do whatever you want, but LA is obsessed with youth. And I hate to say it, but it's especially true for women. The women who wait, or God help them, the ones who go to grad school and THEN move to LA when they're 25? They either end up teaching pilates or doing porn.

SHEENA: 25 isn't old.

MARC: How old do you think I am.

SHEENA: I don't know, like, 30?

MARC: I am. I am thirty. Which is old for a man in LA, but it's still not as old as a 25-year-old actress.

SHEENA: That's crazy.

MARC: The only unknown 25-year olds who work get cast as the fat friend. And you, Sheena, are not a fat friend.

SHEENA: There's actually a "fat friend" category?

MARC: Um, *Yeah.* It's pretty competitive. There aren't that many fat roles, and, well, nobody wants a fat Pilates instructor, if you know what I'm saying.

SHEENA: *They cast the fat friend in porn?*

MARC: *Niche porn.*

SHEENA: You're making this up.

MARC: I've got pay per view. We can move this conversation up to my room and I'll prove it to you.

    Beat. Did he say what I think he just said?

SHEENA: What?

    Beat. Is she into it? No? No, definitely not.

MARC: *That's reacting.* God, you're perfect, so in the moment—

SHEENA: Wait, I was?

MARC: You're gonna be amazing on camera. I want you to remember this, Sheena, this exact moment. How you were open and listening and just ready to react. If you do that on set? I promise you: I will capture it, and you will blow everyone away. Will you trust me enough to do that?

SHEENA: Yeah, I will.

    They look at each other. A moment of connection. Marc begins to caress her, almost unconsciously. Sheena is unsure how to react.

MARC: How's your beer, is it good?

SHEENA: Yeah, I like Shiner.

MARC: Me too.

SHEENA: Oh, I thought you didn't drink.

MARC: I don't. You want another?

SHEENA: That's okay—

MARC: Let me get you another—

SHEENA: Marc, are you trying to get me drunk?

MARC: No! God, no—

SHEENA: I'm just teasing—

MARC: No, I need to attack this head on. I can feel that there's a little attraction happening?

SHEENA: Um—

MARC: But this is a strictly professional relationship, I have absolutely sworn off all, romantic entanglements with women under thirty.

SHEENA: Okay.

MARC: Period. So I've come clean about that. If I hadn't, you know, my sponsor would've crucified me.

SHEENA: I'm so sorry if I was doing something that made you think—

MARC: It's understandable.

SHEENA: I really didn't mean to—I just had this big blow out with my mom, so it's been kind of a crazy day. Almost everything I own is in this bag, I have no idea where I'm even staying tonight, so I'm just a little, whatever—

MARC: You don't know where you're staying?

SHEENA: But starting now, I am one hundred percent professional, Marc. I'm gonna be open, and in the moment, and I will do absolutely everything you tell me to do.

MARC: Well, that's, music to a director's ears.

SHEENA: Good. So should we go up to your room now?

MARC: Um—

SHEENA: I mean, I have to get the script, right?

Immediate shift to:

SCENE SEVEN

Frances' house. Night. She sits in her scooter at the table. She's lined up all her pills across the table. A mallet is nearby.

FRANCES: Marc Hunter. You like to watch. You like to hear women scream, don't you. I should have taken you down when I had the chance. Come on, Frances.
    (She counts the pills)
Onetwothreefourfivesixseveneightnine . . . . Seventeen. Seventeen little lovelies, lovely blues. This was all part of their plan, wasn't it? Keep her doped up, keep her quiet! You have to get rid of them, Frances. Think about him. Sadistic little prick, it all happened because of him and his movie. Just do it. Do it. DO IT!
    Frances swings the mallet, screaming and smashing the pills to bits. Hildy runs down the stairs.

HILDY: Mom!

FRANCES: AAAAAAARRRRRGGGGHHHHHAAA!

> *Hildy watches as Frances smashes all the pills in a flurry of banging. An expectation.*

HILDY: Why did you just hammer all of your pills?

FRANCES: Because I'm not taking them anymore.

HILDY: What.

FRANCES: I'm done. Finished. Cold turkey.

> *Frances suddenly puts her face to the table and takes a full snort of the pill powder.*

FRANCES: Get me the dust buster!

HILDY: What are you—

FRANCES: Now, before I change my mind!

> *Immediate shift to:*

SCENE EIGHT.

> *The set. A suburban kitchen. Marc is agitated, pacing. Jody is on his cell phone. Walkie talkies dangle from both Marc and Jody's necks.*

MARC: Where is he?

JODY: *(to Marc)* He says the directions he got were—

MARC: How far away is he?

JODY: *(into the phone)* How far are you from the set—?
> *(to Marc)*
> He doesn't know, he's looking for a place to ask directions but—

MARC: Why didn't he call when he realized he was lost—

JODY: *(overlapping)* He kept thinking it was gonna be—

MARC: Instead of WAITING until he was already late to call—

JODY: *(into the phone)* I know, man, it's cool, it's just—

MARC: IT IS NOT COOL.

JODY: *(into the phone)* Okay, okay, yeah, Perdenales is like—

MARC: Hang up the phone.

JODY: *(into the phone)* I think you're too far south, man, you're—

MARC: *(Shouting into his walkie talkie)* I SAID HANG UP THE PHONE.

JODY: *(into the phone.)* I'll call you back.

*Jody hangs up. Sheena has entered, wearing her film cos-
tume—a form-fitting tank-top with a bright cropped hoodie,
and short shorts.*

SHEENA: It all fits.

MARC: Great, yes. You look great.

SHEENA: Thanks.

MARC: You look really—. All right, Jody, you're going to stand in for
Brian, we're gonna mark through the scene. I'll get all the shots
I can of Sheena, while you get back on the phone and see if you
can get that idiot here before we get further behind.

JODY: Got it.

MARC: So. You open the door, the first shot is the two of you crossing
the threshold, your magical weekend getaway. Brian, you find
the light switch—

JODY: Over here—

MARC: Yes, and the lights come on and you both look around slowly,
slowly. Sloan, you're nervous, but you're not scared—

SHEENA: Not yet—

MARC: Definitely not. You're excited, you're apprehensive, you want
him to like you.

SHEENA: Right.

MARC: Brian, you're mostly thinking about how smart you are for getting the keys from your uncle's buddy so you can fuck Sloan's
brains out.

JODY: Got it.

MARC: But in a sweet way. Hit this mark, we'll do a nice 360 around
the two of you, thinking all of these things, so we see how harm-
less and normal the place looks.

JODY: Right.

MARC: Then Brian, hit your mark here for the line, "See? What did I
tell you?"

JODY: Right.

MARC: Sloan you stay right here, still a little apprehensive.
     (Marc demonstrates for Sheena)
"Are you sure he said it was okay? You hardly know this guy."
     (to Jody)
Brian.

JODY: *(in a leading man voice)* "He gave me the key, didn't he?"

MARC: Yes. Grab hands.

JODY: "Don't worry, he's out of town until Monday. We've got the place all to ourselves."

SHEENA: *(imitating Marc's vocal quality and body language)* "Until everybody else gets here."

MARC: Good.

JODY: "It'll be fun."

SHEENA: "I know. I just wanted this weekend to be . . . special."

JODY: "It will be. I promise."

MARC: And the shot goes back to Sloan as Brian moves to the next room.

JODY: "Come on, check it out."

MARC: *(to Sheena)* The camera's still on you, scanning your face, you decide to follow your man, and walk out of the shot.

    Jody's phone rings.

JODY: It's him.

MARC: Go.

    Jody steps away to answer the phone.

MARC: Once he's gone—

SHEENA: Look, before Jody comes back—I just wanted to say thanks, again, for letting me crash in your room last night.

MARC: Don't mention it.

SHEENA: You totally saved me, and I really didn't intend to impose, or make you uncomfortable—

MARC: I was, totally comfortable. I mean it's not like we were sleeping together!

SHEENA: NoI I know!

MARC: I mean, they give you two beds, someone may as well use the, the other one.

SHEENA: I just I wanted to say thanks. I got a hold of my friend Heather, I'm gonna stay with her now—

MARC: Great. That's great—

SHEENA: So it won't happen again.

MARC: Well, you know, any time you want to you can always, always—. Let's skip ahead. Madison calls, she's having car trouble, they're gonna be late. You and Brian have been playing hide and seek. It's sexy, it's playful—at some point you lose the jacket?

SHEENA: *(She takes off the jacket.)* Right.

MARC: So you're exploring the house. Something seems strange, and now you can't find Brian. Is this part of the game? Maybe. You step in here to look, hit this mark.

SHEENA: *(in her movie voice)* "Brian? Come on, where are you?"

MARC: The room is empty. You notice the family photos: a stern minister with a very young Victor and the beautiful Elise, *who you realize looks almost exactly like you.* You see the framed newspaper clipping about Elise's death. A cold wind blows through the room. You shudder, and turn and see: the door to the porch is mysteriously open. You hit this mark here. Now you're getting worried.

SHEENA: "Brian?"

MARC: You hear a noise. You go to the porch, but it's not coming from there. What is it? Your senses are on high alert, your nipples should be like rocks.

SHEENA: What?

MARC: Skip it. You shut the door, shivering. You listen, trying to figure out where the noise is coming from. You hear it, coming from in here. But that can't be, that's impossible. Hit this mark—

SHEENA: "Come on, this isn't funny."

MARC: Open the door and—

> Sheena opens the door to reveal Bridget, a brunette. She's virtually naked and her neck and wrists have been slit.
> (NOTE: Some productions have concealed Bridget in a giant freezer, with Bridget spilling out onto the floor like a corpse. Others have used a closet, with Bridget hanging upside down as if she's been trussed up there to let her blood drain. I'm sure there are other possibilities as well.)

SHEENA: *(screams)*

MARC: *YES!*

SHEENA: Oh my God.

BRIDGET: Hey. I'm Bridget.

MARC: Oh, I'm sorry, did you guys not meet yet?

SHEENA: No.

MARC: Bridget's dead girl number one.

BRIDGET: The unsuspecting realtor who gets it in the first ten minutes.

SHEENA: Right. Nice to meet you.

MARC: *(to Sheena)* That reminds me: You're not claustrophobic, are
   you?

SHEENA: Um—

> *Immediate shift to:*

SCENE NINE

> *Frances' house. Frances is on the phone. She digs through an old tool-
> box as she waits to leave a message. Some tools she considers and then
> discards back into the toolbox. When she finds a tool she likes, she sets
> it out on the table, like a surgeon assembling her instruments.*
>
> *Just as Frances begins to leave the message, Hildy enters with a
> sad-looking pair of soccer shoes. When she hears Frances speak, she
> stops short, unseen by Frances. As Hildy listens, she slowly backs away,
> becoming more and more anxious.*

FRANCES: Mr. Hunter, this is Belinda Chapman from Channel 5
   News. I'm a, real *fan* of your work, all the way back to your ear-
   liest days here in Austin.

> *(She finds a hatchet, hefts it in her hand, sets it on the table.)*

   Oh yes. And I would LOVE to interview you about your new project. *Bloodbath?* I have to say, it sounds like a real crowd pleaser.

> *(She snaps a large needle nose pliers in then air, adds them
> to her selected tools.)*

   So, I thought we'd meet at the set. I think that'd be best. I really
   want to get an up-close look at your—

> *(She revs a cordless drill.)*

   artistic process. I am really looking forward to this. You name
   the time, Mr. Hunter. And I will be there.

> *Hildy pulls out her phone.*

> *Immediate shift to:*

SCENE TEN

> *Break room—the set. Sheena and MarcY. Sheena is still in
> her costume, and now has mud streaks up her legs. MarcY
> is a redhead who appears to have had half her face burned
> off. The other half of her face is perfect. They drink diet cokes*

> *and eat chips. An occasional scream is heard—filming continues nearby.*

MARCY: God I can't wait to get home and wash this stuff off.

SHEENA: I bet.

> *A scream is heard. They continue their conversation.*

MARCY: Amanda's good, though. I mean this stuff she did on my face, with the burns—

SHEENA: It's, amazing.

MARCY: It totally looks like someone held me down on a hot griddle. Which is good, because, you know, I was held down on a hot griddle!

SHEENA: Right.

> *Sheena's phone rings, she silences it.*

MARCY: So when do you get killed?

SHEENA: Um, later. At the end, actually.

MARCY: You're the last girl?

SHEENA: Yeah.

MARCY: Wow, that's gotta be cool. How do they do it?

SHEENA: I get impaled, I think.

MARCY: Awesome. Save the best for last, right?

SHEENA: Marc said it might change, but I think I get to take Victor down with me.

> *(Her phone rings again, she silences it.)*

He's been keeping me chained up while he kills everyone else, because I look like his dead sister?

MARCY: Uh-huh.

> *More screaming, Sheena talks over it.*

SHEENA: After he washes me in all the blood he's collected, he wants to put me in one of Elise's old dresses. That's when I make a break for it. He comes after me and we end up crashing through the railing, and I fall and get impaled on the same spike as Brian. Victor freaks, 'cause he wasn't gonna kill me, he was gonna keep me? So it's like I'm Elise dying all over again. And while he's trying to keep me from bleeding out, I grab his knife and gut him!

MARCY: Cool!

SHEENA: *(Her phone rings again.)* Ugh.

MARCY: Someone really wants to talk to you.

SHEENA: It's my sister. She's been calling all day because my mom is, my mom is crazy.

MARCY: I totally know what you mean.

SHEENA: No, I mean, she's literally *crazy*. And I feel bad my sister has to deal with her, but, I just, I need a break from it all.

> (*Sound of a chainsaw. A woman screams, "No, no, please!"*)

I need to have some normalcy for once, you know?

MARCY: Totally.

SHEENA: My sister's probably freaking out about some stupid thing my mom is saying she's gonna do. But she never actually DOES anything. She's all talk. And if I answer, I'm just gonna get sucked back in.

MARCY: Then I say don't do it.

SHEENA: I deserve to have some fun, right?

MARCY: Hell yeah! Oh, crap.

SHEENA: What?

MARCY: *(Marcy pulls something out of her mouth.)* Part of my burn flaked off.

SHEENA: Let me see.

MARCY: Amanda's gonna kill me.

SHEENA: Oh, I'm sure she can fix it.

MARCY: I better go. I'll see you.

SHEENA: Yeah.

> *Sheena's phone rings again, she silences it.*
>
> *Immediate shift to:*

SCENE ELEVEN

> *Hildy, on the phone in a tight light—she is hiding somewhere in the house.*

HILDY: Sheena? Look, I know you're busy being mutilated and all, but seriously, mom has flipped her can. She stopped taking her pills, Sheena. Mom is SOBER. She got dad's old tools and set up target practice with the staple gun, and now she's making me help her build explosives! She wants to blow up the guy who's directing the movie. She keeps talking about how she's not gonna be a joke on the ten o'clock news this time? I seriously think she's gonna do something so please pick up your freakin' phone!

FRANCES: *(O.S.)* Hildy!

HILDY: I'm freaking out, I don't know what to do and I need new soccer shoes by Friday! Call me.

FRANCES: *(O.S.)* Hildy come here!

Hildy sneaks out of her spot and enters the living room where Frances sits, in her scooter.

HILDY: I'm right here, mom.

FRANCES: Where?

There is a board with wires sticking out of it on the table now, along with an assortment of tools and plastic bottles—a ridiculous attempt to make a bomb. Frances is a wreck, she's twitching and shaking. The rumpled remains of the script, and the Holy Shepherd flier are strewn about. Hildy stands out of Frances' line of vision, packing her backpack, putting on her bike helmet.

HILDY: I was looking for more plastic.

FRANCES: Get it and let's finish.

HILDY: Um, I have to go to school, mom.

FRANCES: Screw school!

HILDY: You're shaking.

FRANCES: Just ignore it.

HILDY: And sweating a lot—

FRANCES: It'll stop in a minute.

HILDY: I really think I should call Dr. Mosier—

FRANCES: NO! That pill-pushing prick. He's practically been force-feeding me narcotics for the last fifteen years! Trying to keep me from DOING SOMETHING. Well, NOT ANYMORE.

HILDY: Okay, mom: I know this is not really about fixing the toaster.

FRANCES: Keep working.

HILDY: You could go to jail for building a bomb.

FRANCES: Bomb? Who said anything about a bomb.

HILDY: The instructions you printed off the internet say it. Look, I know you're upset about Sheena and the movie, but I mean you've already got a deferred sentence for trying to run over Marshall Davis after he got the cleaning contract—

FRANCES: I THOUGHT I WAS PRESSING THE BRAKE.

HILDY: If you try to blow up this director they are gonna put you away.

FRANCES: Do you know how many crimes go unsolved each year? How many criminals are never brought to justice? Murderers and rapists—

HILDY: Mom—

FRANCES: HUNDREDS. THOUSANDS. Half the time the police don't even LOOK.

HILDY: I think they're gonna look for a bomber.

FRANCES: If they'd been looking, they would have caught him before it happened again! Then that self-righteous dyke getting on the news saying I should have done something. Well NOW, I am going to DO SOMETHING. And this time, NO ONE is going to be LAUGHING!

(Hildy has quietly taken the key to Frances' scooter.)

What are you doing. Hey! HEY!

Hildy stands out of reach, holding the key.

HILDY: I'm taking your key, I swear this is for your own good.

Frances reflexively presses the button on her chair; nothing happens. A moment of horror.

FRANCES: *Give it back.*

HILDY: I'm going to school.

FRANCES: Give me my key!

HILDY: Promise you'll just stay here until I get back, okay?

FRANCES: Hildegard McKinney—

HILDY: *I don't think you're faking.* Okay? I know Sheena does, and a lot of other people. My friends, and most of my teachers. Coach Conner—

FRANCES: That health Nazi always hated me—

HILDY: But if you were only pretending to be disabled, that would mean that all this time—my whole life basically—you've never been there. That you've never come to any of my soccer games or the awards assembly or anything, not because you couldn't but because you didn't want to.

FRANCES: Hildy, you know that's not true—

HILDY: *(overlapping)* And I know that's not true! You want to be a good mom, it's just. You're in a lot of pain. Right?

An expectation.

FRANCES: I hurt *so much.*

HILDY: I know.

FRANCES: I never wanted to be like this. They did this to me. You see that, don't you? Things were supposed to get better—

HILDY: They will—

FRANCES: No, no, they won't, not unless we do something—

HILDY: I'm taking your key, okay?

FRANCES: We have to stop them, Hildy—

HILDY: Because then you'll be safe here. Because you can't go any-where without your chair, right?

FRANCES: You're so smart, I know we can do it—

HILDY: So I'm putting a bottle of water, and, and a Hot Pocket on the table for you—

FRANCES: We can finish it!

HILDY: I'll just be at school—

FRANCES: Don't leave me!

> *Hildy turns on the radio.*

HILDY: You can listen to the news, and when I get home—

FRANCES: We have to take a stand—

HILDY: I'll be back, I swear.

FRANCES: Hildy, don't go, don't—

> *Hildy exits.*

FRANCES: Hildy! Stupid internet instructions! Think. Think, Frances.

RADIO: . . . In breaking news, a bomb went off this morning at the site of the proposed Emma Goldman clinic on Payne Avenue. Anti-abortion protesters organized by Holy Shepherd Church gath-ered at the site last night in an effort to prevent the clinic from opening. In a statement released earlier today, church leaders denied any involvement in the bombing. Fortunately, no one was injured. In other news . . .

> *Frances springs into action. She grabs the phone cord, pulls it to her. She finds the Holy Shepherd flier, dials the number, waits for someone to pick up.*

FRANCES: Yes, may I speak to—

> *(she refers to the sheet of paper)*

Christi Garcia? Thank you, I'll hold.

> *Immediate shift to:*

SCENE TWELVE.

The set. Beth, a blonde in soccer mom clothes strides onto the set where Marc is getting Jody in to costume and instructing him.

MARC: *(to Jody)* Keep your face front, so we get a good shot of the mask, that's the most important thing.

JODY: Right—

BETH: Where the hell is Tyler?

MARC: He's been replaced, all right?

BETH: Jesus Christ.

MARC: Why is this so baggy?

JODY: Dude, Tyler was a lot bigger than me, but maybe I can—

MARC: Lose it. Just go with the mask.

JODY: Yeah.

> *Sheena enters, watches.*

MARC: When you start pushing her through the saw, make sure you really sell it, I want to see how much effort it takes to cut through her skull.

JODY: Got it.

SHEENA: Where's Tyler? Why is Jody dressed like Victor now?

BETH: Didn't you hear? It's amateur night.

MARC: *(to Beth)* It's gonna be fine!

BETH: Sorry, Mr. Scorsese.

> *(to Sheena)*

I'm so moving to LA, just as soon as I finish grad school.

MARC: Let's get set up for the take. Get your mask on, Sloan's Mom, get into position.

> *Jody puts on a creepy mask, while Beth/Sloan's Mom slips her arms through two ropes attached to a table so that she appears to be tied down.*

JODY: Do you want me to say the lines?

MARC: Yeah—just keep the scene going. We'll dub it later if we have to.

> *(Marc's phone rings. HE hands it to Sheena)*

Damnit—this is that reporter again. Find out when she's coming for the interview.

SHEENA: Sure—

> *Sheena stuffs the phone in her armpit and runs for an exit.*

MARC: *(into his walkie)* Standing by.

JODY: *(grabbing his walkie from his back pocket)* Standing by.
> *(He stuffs it back in his pocket.)*

MARC: And action!

BETH/SLOAN'S MOM: I know you have my daughter, and you won't get away with it!
> *Sound of the circular saw starts as Sheena steps off the set into a tight spotlight. Lights go out on the set, but we continue to hear the sound of the saw and screaming as filming continues.*

SHEENA: *(into the phone)* Hello? Hello?
> *(She's missed the call.)*

> Crap.
> *(She looks at the number to redial and sees:)*

> Oh my God . . . .Mom?!?
> *Immediate shift to:*

SCENE THIRTEEN

> *Frances' house. Sound of knocking. Frances crawls or rolls across the floor to the door. She opens it, revealing Christi, who carries her clipboard and some brochures.*

FRANCES: What took you so long?

CHRISTI: I was a little tied up.

FRANCES: Well don't just stand there, come in.
> *Christi awkwardly steps over Frances.*

CHRISTI: I must say, I was surprised you called me, Ms. McKinney.

FRANCES: You're not the only one.

CHRISTI: The Lord works in mysterious ways.
> *(She watches Frances struggle for a moment.)*

> Can I help you up, or—

FRANCES: I'm FINE.

CHRISTI: All right then. I brought some information about Holy Shepherd, and of course, the information about the Justice League that you requested. I also wanted to let you know about our pick up service, Riders to Joy? We have two transport vans that are fully handicap accessible and—

FRANCES: Are you driving one now?

CHRISTI: Um, no ma'am. I'm driving my personal vehicle?

FRANCES: That's all right, that'll work.

CHRISTI: Excuse me?

FRANCES: Look, let's cut to the chase. I called you because I want to stop this.

> *(She hands Christi the script.)*

It's despicable.

CHRISTI: *Bloodbath.* These movies are just awful.

FRANCES: We have to stop them. Every other minute there's a Law and Order with a prostitute dead in an alley, a CSI with a stripper face down in a vat of Jell-O—

CHRISTI: You're shaking a little, are you okay?

FRANCES: Sometimes I think if I see one more "artistic" shot of a beautiful young woman who's been beaten or tortured or raped, I will go completely crazy.

CHRISTI: Don't you worry. The Justice League has a plan.

FRANCES: What are we gonna do.

CHRISTI: We have a letter you can send to your local TV stations and movie theatres—

FRANCES: No no no—

CHRISTI: When advertisers hear from consumers—

FRANCES: Nobody pays attention to that stuff—

CHRISTI: When they see an effect on the bottom line—

FRANCES: I'm talking about fire bombs!

CHRISTI: What.

FRANCES: Why the hell do you think I called you? I heard about the bombing this morning—

CHRISTI: Ms. McKinney—

FRANCES: You people know how to get shit done, and you get away with it, too!

CHRISTI: Pastor Dan issued a statement, Holy Shepherd had NOTH-ING to do with that—

FRANCES: I want to kill him. The director, the producer, everyone who's involved—

CHRISTI: We do not advocate the use of violence as a means to—

FRANCES: You don't have to pretend with me—

CHRISTI: The Justice League is not—

FRANCES: By any means necessary! We may not agree on everything, but you and I both know that letters won't change anything. We have to *do something* to get their attention. My daughter has been brainwashed by this, this trash, and I'm gonna lose her. We have to stop them. We have to save them.

CHRISTI: What did you have in mind?

FRANCES: I know where they're filming. I got the director's number off the script, and said I was from Channel Five. Then he sang like a canary. The house is half a mile from your church. All I need is a ride.

An expectation.

CHRISTI: Is that mess of wires supposed to be a bomb?

FRANCES: You tell me.

Split scene: the set. Sheena runs into an isolated place, she has twigs sticking out of her hair, like she's been running through the woods.

JODY: *(O.S.)* Sheena?

SHEENA: *(calling off to Jody)* Just a second!

(to herself)

I have to check my messages.

Christi and Sheena dial their phones.

FRANCES: Who are you calling?

CHRISTI: My friend Piper. Her dad's an explosives expert at the ATF?

(She waits for Piper to pick up.)

Since Pastor Dan hired me, I've implemented a three-hundred and sixty degree strategy that includes outreach, publicity, utilization of the courts, and covert ops.

SHEENA: *(as she listens to Hildy's message)* Oh my God.

FRANCES: *Covert ops.*

CHRISTI: *(to the phone)* Hey Piper, it's Christi, call me back, 'k?

SHEENA: *Oh my God!*

Christi hangs up.

FRANCES: You're like a perky little general.

CHRISTI: That's what it takes to battle evil. And we're gonna strike at the source.

SHEENA: *Oh my freakin' God!*

Immediate shift to:

SCENE FOURTEEN

The set. Sheena runs to Jody.

SHEENA: Jody! Look, I need your help—

JODY: As soon as Marc is done with Madison, you need to be in position for the chase—

SHEENA: Listen to me. Marc thinks someone from Channel Five is coming.

JODY: Yeah, I talked to her earlier.

SHEENA: Did you tell her where we are, she *knows* where the location is?

JODY: Yeah.

SHEENA: Crap. I have to go.

JODY: What?!

SHEENA: I'm sorry but this is—

JODY: They're gonna be done any minute!

SHEENA: I think my mom wants to kill Marc!

JODY: What?

MARC: *(O.S.) (coming through the walkie around Jody's neck)* Quiet on the set!

SHEENA: I should have answered my phone—

JODY: What are you talking about?

SHEENA: He's the guy! He's—seriously, she thinks he ruined her life!

JODY: Marc?

SHEENA: Yes! He was making this movie—he must have been in college. He snuck onto my dad's construction site because he was filming there at night—

JODY: Right.

SHEENA: There'd been a whole series of rapes that summer. It was all over the news. My mom was obsessed, she was part of this women's action group? So one night my dad doesn't come home—probably because he's off with his secretary. My mom goes to the construction site to try to find him. When she gets there she hears this woman screaming. She sees all these people standing around, so she calls the cops—

JODY: Because she thinks—

SHEENA: Yes! And then she calls the TV station and says: the Austin serial rapist is here, right now! The cops are about to nab him, here's the address!

JODY: Nooo—

SHEENA: The TV crews get there first, and all they find is Marc and a bunch of kids filming this scene. It becomes a big joke on the 10 o'clock news. And that night another woman is raped! The cops say if my mom hadn't called in a false report they would've caught the guy.

JODY: Whoa.

SHEENA: And this bitch from the women's group gets on the news and says if my mom really thought a woman was being raped, she should have done more to stop them. My mom completely loses it, my dad runs off with his secretary and now I'm making a movie with the SAME GUY.

JODY: Holy coincidence, Batman.

SHEENA: She's making my little sister try to build a—she's gonna try to kill him.

JODY: Okay, isn't your mom, like, in a wheelchair?

SHEENA: Look, I will be back as soon as I can—
> *(Sheena turns and runs smack into Christi.)*
> *(screams)*

CHRISTI: There's gonna be a lot less of that going on now.
> *(She gives a card to Jody)*
> Christi Garcia, Assistant Director of the Holy Shepherd Justice League.
> *Marc comes running in behind her.*

MARC: I told you, this is a closed set.

CHRISTI: I just wanted to let the rest of your crew know that filming is about to shut down.

JODY: What?

CHRISTI: Holy Shepherd has filed an injunction barring you from using this property on behalf of the owner.
> *She produces a document.*

JODY: We have all the permits!

CHRISTI: Mr. Parrish didn't understand the nature of the movie you all would be making here.

MARC: He understood the money I paid him to use this dump!

CHRISTI: We'll have you shut down by Monday, so it really would be best for you to just leave now.

> *(to Sheena)*

You know, you don't have to take your clothes off to make people like you.

SHEENA: Excuse me?!

CHRISTI: But first you have to like yourself.

MARC: Look, unless you flash a badge in the next three seconds—

CHRISTI: Mr. Parrish is a member of Holy Shepherd—

MARC: *(to Jody)* Call the cops, dial 911, RIGHT NOW.

> *Jody dials.*

CHRISTI: There's no need, I'm leaving. But I'll be back. Judge Monson is scheduled to hear the case first thing Monday morning. He's a very fair man. I should know. He's my Uncle.

> *(Hands Sheena a card.)*

When you're ready to treat yourself with respect, close your legs and call me.

> *Christi exits as Sheena shouts after her.*

SHEENA: Hey!

MARC: Sheena, find Amanda, tell her we're skipping ahead—

SHEENA: Marc—

MARC: Tell her she has to do all of Madison's make-up and wounds for the meat hook scene *now.*

JODY: The meat hook scene?

SHEENA: Marc, I have to go home.

MARC: What?

JODY: That's almost at the end of the movie!

SHEENA: I know it's bad timing, but—

MARC: No one's going anywhere.

SHEENA: But it's an emergency!

MARC: You leave, I will come after you for delay of production and take every cent you've got.

> *(to Jody)*

Jody, anything that can be shot someplace else, take it off the schedule. Make sure we've got all the exteriors—

JODY: Look, I'm all about working fast, but—

MARC: Good—

JODY: We've only been shooting for two days!

MARC: We have to work faster—

JODY: We barely have enough footage to cover 20 minutes of film—

MARC: So get moving!

JODY: Just call your investor and ask him to—

MARC: *There is no investor!* All right? I am financing this entire movie with a three-hundred-thousand dollar second mortgage on my six-hundred square foot condo, most of which is already spent! And I will be damned if I am going to be homeless at thirty-seven years old!

SHEENA: You're thirty-seven?

MARC: NO! Now we are going to shoot enough film in the next forty eight hours to edit together SOMETHING that I can sell to a video distributor, even if it kills me. So until the cops show up to shut us down, *nobody leaves the set.* Now move!

> *Immediate shift to:*

SCENE FIFTEEN

> *Split scene. Sheena steps downstage into a spotlight, pulls out her phone and dials as Hildy enters the house, wearing her backpack and bike helmet.*

HILDY: Mom? Mom?

> *(She sees the empty scooter.)*

Crap!

> *Her phone rings. She answers it.*

HILDY: Oh my God, Sheena—

SHEENA: I just got your messages and—

HILDY: I swear to God, I didn't think she could leave—

SHEENA: What?

HILDY: You said it yourself, she hasn't left in a year, and I had to go to school—

SHEENA: What's happening?

HILDY: She's gone! She's not here—

SHEENA: What?!

HILDY: I really didn't think she could do it, I even took her key! Her scooter's still here, but she's gone—

SHEENA: She was building a bomb and you left her alone?!

HILDY: I had a chemistry quiz!

SHEENA: Okay, all right. She couldn't have gotten very far, right? She doesn't have money for a cab, I have the car. Even if she's planning to blow up Marc, she'd have no way of getting here, right?

> *Hildy finds the flier from Holy Shepherd.*

MARC: *(Off Stage)* Sheena! Get in here!

HILDY: This is weird.

SHEENA: What?

HILDY: It's just, this flier. It's from some church group, she circled the phone number over and over.

SHEENA: Oh my God, what's the name of the church?

HILDY: Holy Shepherd? It's for something called the Justice League.

SHEENA: Crap.

MARC: *(O.S.)* Sheena!

> *Immediate shift to:*

SCENE SIXTEEN

> *Break room—the set. Madison, a perky blonde, sits alone in a prop wheelchair, listening to her headphones. She sings to herself, an up-beat pop song like "Love Shack" by B-52s. She has what appears to be a gigantic meat hook going through her back and out her chest.*

MADISON: *(singing)* . . . the love shack is . . . . we can get to-ge-ther-er . . .

> *Frances appears behind Madison, doing a commando-style crawl, advancing on Madison.*

MADISON: *(in a low voice)* Love Shack Baby.

> *Frances has outfitted herself with an old tool belt containing various tools that could be used as weapons. Frances crawls up behind Madison, waiting for her opportunity.*

MADISON: *(still singing)* Bang bang bang on the door baby . . . I can't hear you.

> BANG BAN-GGGAAAAAHHH!!!

> *As Madison's mouth opens wide, Frances stuffs a bandana in it, stifling her scream.*

> *Immediate shift to:*

SCENE SEVENTEEN

The set. A tight light follows Sheena, as though she is being tracked by a camera. They are filming. She runs a few steps, trips and falls.

SHEENA/SLOAN: *(in her movie voice)* "No!"
>*She turns back towards her pursuer, pushing herself away from him. Jody, dressed as Victor, advances menacingly towards her, wearing his signature mask. Sheena remains on the floor, backing herself into a corner.*

SHEENA/SLOAN: "No, no please—"

JODY/VICTOR: "Oh yes."
>*Victor reaches Sheena, grabs her—*

SHEENA/SLOAN: *(screams)*
>*She struggles to get away, but Victor handcuffs Sheena to an old radiator. She whimpers and cries.*

SHEENA/SLOAN: "No no no no"

JODY/VICTOR: "You shouldn't have worn this. You knew daddy wouldn't like it."
>*In a swift movement, Victor rips Sheena's shirt down the center, leaving her stomach and chest exposed except for her bra.*

JODY/VICTOR: "Now it's time for your bath."
>*The light follows Victor as he turns to a bathtub of blood. Above it is an empty harness where Madison is supposed to be.*

MARC: CUT. Where the hell is Madison? She's supposed to be in the shot!

JODY: I told her to get in position ten minutes ago—

MARC: *(calling)* Madison!

SHEENA: You want us to reset—

MARC: *NO.* Stay where you are, we can take it from the reveal—
>*(calling)*
> Madison IF YOU DON'T GET ON THIS MEAT HOOK IN THE NEXT 60 SECONDS—
>*All the lights go out.*

JODY: What the—

SHEENA: Oh my God.

MARC: Great. This is just great.

SHEENA: Marc, there's something I should tell you.

MARC: Did you see the fuse box in the laundry room?

JODY: I'm already on my way—

SHEENA: No! Wait, please—

MARC: GO.

> *Jody exits.*

SHEENA: Marc, you have to unlock me.

MARC: Just STAY WHERE YOU ARE.

SHEENA: Seriously, I have a really bad feeling about this.

> *(Marc laughs.)*

I didn't tell you before because I didn't want you to think I was crazy, but—

MARC: *(He laughs more.)* You have a *bad feeling* about this?

SHEENA: Listen to me—

MARC: I lost my star, all my investors, quite possibly the only piece of property I'l ever owned, and you have a BAD FEELING?

SHEENA: I THINK MY MOTHER IS HERE!

> *The lights flick on. Frances is there, in the wheelchair. She wears a hockey mask, a la Jason from Friday the 13th, her hand on her holstered cordless drill.*

SHEENA: *(screams)*

FRANCES: Hello, Marc.

MARC: Who are you?

SHEENA: Mom, please!

MARC: Wait, this is your mother?

> *Frances takes the mask off.*

FRANCES: We'll see who's laughing in five minutes.

MARC: I'm sorry, you can stay for a couple of takes, but you've got to keep quiet and stay out of the way.

FRANCES: You'd like that wouldn't you?

SHEENA: Nobody wants you here, so just leave!

FRANCES: Keep us all tied up and whimpering, like Sheena.

> *(to Sheena)*

You're really in control now.

SHEENA: I *am* in control!

MARC: Do I know you?

FRANCES: If it weren't for me, you wouldn't even have your pathetic little career—

SHEENA: We'll call the police.

FRANCES: You'd still be working construction, but thanks to all the free publicity—

MARC: Wait a minute—

FRANCES: I should have done this fifteen years ago.

MARC: *(it dawns on him) You!*

FRANCES: That's right. The middle of the night, a woman is dragged to a construction site, beaten and raped—

MARC: It was a movie!

FRANCES: I forgot, it's all okay because it isn't REAL. It's in SERVICE of the STORY. Isn't that what you said to Channel Five? "It's not about depicting violence against women, it's about telling the story!"

MARC: Well, yeah!

FRANCES: DID YOU EVER STOP TO THINK THAT MAYBE WE NEED SOME DIFFERENT STORIES?!?!

> *Marc attempts to leave the room, Frances maneuvers to stop him, revving the drill.*

FRANCES: Oh no you don't. I want justice, and this time I'm gonna get it.

SHEENA: You can't stop us!

FRANCES: I've already taken down everyone else in the place.

MARC: What.

FRANCES: Your bloody little bimbos, that punk who came to the house—

SHEENA: What did you do?

FRANCES: The make up girl? She was spunky.

MARC: *(calling)* Jody!

SHEENA: Mother, they will put you away for this!

MARC: I'm calling the cops.

> *Marc starts to dial, Frances trips him, his phone goes flying. She points the drill at him like a gun.*

FRANCES: DON'T MOVE!

> *(Marc holds his hands up in spite of himself. Jody creeps into the room unseen by Frances. He has several bleeding cuts on his arms, and duct tape wrapped around his head. Sheena sees Jody, they silently make a quick plan.)*

I can't let you do this, Sheena. You were supposed to finish what we started. But you just take whatever they force on you and then pretend it's what you wanted in the first place!

SHEENA: It IS what I want!

FRANCES: You're dragging us all back down!

SHEENA: I am pulling myself up! You know why there are so many horror movies? BECAUSE PEOPLE LIKE THEM! That's it!

(Marc see Jody.)

It's not some huge conspiracy to degrade women, or keep women down. Because the last time I checked, women have all the same rights as men! If a woman doesn't get a job, it's because she's not as qualified! If she gets paid less, it's because she didn't negotiate as well. And let me tell you something else:

(Sheena gives a sign to Jody and Marc.)

The WNBA is on the verge of bankruptcy, not because people are afraid to see women as strong and powerful, but because CHICK BASKETBALL IS BORING!

Jody and Marc spring on her. Marc grabs the drill as Jody tapes her mouth shut.

FRANCES: HEY! HEY—

(as they get the tape over her mouth)

MRWRUGH! HOMRWMIGITIZ!

MARC: Tie her hands up.

JODY: Hold her down!

Jody ties her hands.

MARC: Hurry. Just hold still! You're not going anywhere.

FRANCES: MURMIGURMITO!

JODY: There. That should hold for a little while.

They have finished the job. Frances sits in the wheelchair, hands bound, gagged with tape. She is seething, but for once, she is silent. Marc moves her out of the way.

MARC: We'll deal with her later.

SHEENA: I'm not stupid, mother, I know what I'm doing.

JODY: All right. I'm gonna untie Madison and call the cops.

MARC: No.

JODY: What.

MARC: We're gonna keep going.

JODY: Dude—

MARC: We'll just let her calm down.

JODY: She wrestled me down on a bed of carpet tacks!

MARC: WE ARE FINISHING THE MOVIE. Get Madison, and get reset for the shot.

> *Jody exits.*

SHEENA: Marc, I am so sorry.

> *Marc goes to her, crouches down next to her, tenderly.*

MARC: Are you okay?

SHEENA: I'm fine. I'm just embarrassed, all of this is happening because of me.

MARC: You don't have anything to be embarrassed about.

SHEENA: You really think we can leave her tied up there while we shoot?

> *They look at Frances. She tries to scream.*

MARC: Yep.

SHEENA: When we get a break, I'll call her doctor.

MARC: All right. Now get ready to be impaled.

> *Jody enters with Madison, her meat hook is ridiculously crushed, her costume comically askew.*

JODY: Um, we've got a little bit of a problem.

MARC: Okay, okay, Amanda can fix this.

JODY: Dude—

MARC: AMANDA!

JODY: She left! She was a little traumatized, you know?

MARC: All right. All right, Madison, honey, you doing okay?

MADISON: Yeah, I guess—

MARC: Good.

> *Marc rips her hook off.*

MADISON: Ow!

MARC: Here.

> *Marc takes the knife off his belt, swiftly cuts the straps off her tank top so she looks like she's wearing a tube top.*

MADISON: *(as he cuts her straps)* Oh! Oh!

> *He gets a bottle of blood, squirts it on her.*

MARC: Okay, what else?

> *(He grabs a short, spiky wig.)*

Put this on!

> *She puts the wig on. Marc and Jody futz with her costume and hair for a second. They stand back and look at her.*

MARC: What do you think?

JODY: You don't think anyone's going to recognize her from earlier?

MARC: She's gonna be a corpse in 15 seconds.

JODY: She looks great.

MARC: PLACES.

> *Jody pulls on Victor's mask as They scramble to get into position.*

MADISON: What are we doing?

JODY: I have no idea.

MADISON: Okay.

MARC: Madison, we'll start with you. Victor, you're gonna drag her over, show her off to Sloan, and then kill her.

JODY: Got it.

SHEENA: What about the scene where Victor tells Madison about Elise?

MARC: Nobody cares! Give me FEAR, give me TERROR, give me BLOOD. And no matter what happens, NO ONE STOPS. Everybody ready?

> *(They nod.)*

And . . . . ACTION.

> *Filming begins. Everyone tries to follow Marc's directions. Jody/Victor holds Madison around the neck, threatening her with a prop knife. She struggles to get away from him.*

MADISON: *(in her movie voice)* "Get off me, let me go!"

> *Jody/Victor drags her over in front of Sheena/Sloan.*

MARC: Get her closer.

MADISON: "Help me, please, help me!"

MARC: Reach out to her, she's you're only hope, that's it.

SHEENA/SLOAN: "Just let her go!"

MARC: Do it!

> *Jody/Victor slices Madison's neck, blood shoots out like a geyser.*

MARC: And Madison: death shake!

> *Madison shimmies her shoulders and chest.*

SHEENA/SLOAN: "NO!"

MARC: Madison, keep reaching for Sloan, keep reaching, try to speak—and Victor drop her!

> *Jody/Victor drops Madison with a thud.*

MADISON: Ow!

JODY: Sorry.

MARC: Keep going. Move in on Sloan.

Jody/Victor moves toward Sheena/Sloan. She tries to back away, but she's still handcuffed to the radiator. Frances watches intently.

SHEENA/SLOAN: "No, please, no—"

JODY/VICTOR: *(in his movie villain voice)* "Now it's just us."

SHEENA/VICTOR: "Please, just let me go!"

He shows off the prop knife.

JODY/VICTOR: "You're all mine."

SHEENA/SLOAN: "No, please!"

MARC: Smear some blood on her chest.

SHEENA: Um—

Jody and Sheena both look at Marc. Jody tentatively smears the blood on Sheena's chest, being very careful to not touch her breasts.

JODY/VICTOR: "I can . . . do whatever I want."

MARC: Really rub it in.

Jody/Victor rubs more vigorously, but still in the "safe zone."

SHEENA/SLOAN: "Don't touch me!"

MARC: Now grab her by the hair.

JODY: *(totally breaking from his Victor character)* Um, what?

MARC: I said grab her!

SHEENA: You could grab my arm, and—

JODY: Like here?

MARC: Grab her hair and pull her up—

SHEENA: Just give us a second to figure this out—

MARC: Shut up and give me the mask!

SHEENA: What?

MARC: I said give me the mask!

JODY: Okay.

Marc takes the mask from Jody, puts it on.

SHEENA: I'm sorry, what are we doing?

MARC: *(to Jody)* Just keep her in the frame.

JODY: Got it.

SHEENA: Marc—

MARC: And don't stop filming.

SHEENA: Wait, what are we doing?

MARC: Whatever we have to.
> *(to Jody)*
> Ready!

JODY: Action.
> *Marc/Victor moves in to Sheena/Sloan with the prop knife. Sheena tries to resume acting, but as the threat of Marc's actions becomes more real, all artifice drops away.*

SHEENA/SLOAN: "Please, no!"

MARC/VICTOR: Why didn't you listen to me?

SHEENA: "I should have—"

MARC/VICTOR: You should have stayed home with me instead of going off with that boy—

SHEENA: "I'm sorry!"

MARC/VICTOR: Liar!
> *Marc/Victor grabs Sheena's hair on the top of her head and pulls her up to her knees by her hair.*

SHEENA: Ow! You're hurting me!

MARC/VICTOR: Just like you hurt me.
> *Marc/Victor cranks her head back so she is looking up at him, he caresses her face.*

MARC: You were the only one who understood me—

SHEENA: Please—

MARC/VICTOR: Who believed in me—

SHEENA: You're really hurting me—

MARC/VICTOR: And you left!
> *He gives her head another rough jerk.*

SHEENA: *(screams)* Stop!
> *Marc has completely strayed from the script.*

MARC: You're so beautiful.

SHEENA: Stop it, just stop—

MARC/VICTOR: Everyone telling me no, telling me it's not right—

SHEENA: Fucking let go of me!

MARC/VICTOR: Telling me I wasn't good enough—

SHEENA: You're really hurting me—

JODY: Um, okay, maybe we should—

MARC/VICTOR: But not this time—

SHEENA: Stop the camera, stop!

MARC/VICTOR: I SAY WHEN WE STOP.

He throws her down forcefully and straddles her, pinning her to the ground. He tosses the prop knife aside, takes out his knife from his belt. Sheena is crying now.

SHEENA: No!

JODY: I don't think this is in the script—

SHEENA: What are you doing?

MARC/VICTOR: I just needed something a little, sharper.

SHEENA: No, stop—

JODY: Maybe we should stop for second—

MARC/VICTOR: *(To Jody)* KEEP FILMING.

(To Sheena)

Now you have to stay very still. I would hate for something bad to happen.

Marc runs the knife along Sheena's neck.

SHEENA: Okay, okay, I'll be still.

MARC/VICTOR: That's my girl.

(He runs the knife between her breasts.)

First we have to get you out of these clothes.

SHEENA: No, stop, Marc—Jody? Stop!

MARC/VICTOR: *Just react.*

He takes his knife, puts the point of it under the center of her bra, as though he's going to slice it open. Frances suddenly springs up from her chair. She has worked one of her hands free, and she runs, full-force, at Marc. They wrestle. Jody jumps in and tries to pull them apart. Frances fights fiercely.

MADISON: *(whispers to Sheena)* Is this part of the movie?

SHEENA: No!

Frances knocks Jody out, turns her attention back to Marc. Madison slowly moves toward the door.

MARC: I've had enough of you!

Marc knocks Frances to the ground. He grabs her ankle, pulls her toward him.

MARC: Oh no you don't!

SHEENA: JUST STOP!

MADISON: Someone let me know about the call time for tomorrow, 'k?

MARC: Madison get back here!

Frances grabs the cordless drill and attacks Marc.

MARC: *(to Frances)* What the fuck!

MADISON: Okay, see ya!

> *Madison exits. Marc and Frances struggle, Frances gets the drill very close to Marc's face.*

MARC: No no no no no no—

SHEENA: Leave her alone!

> *Marc pushes Frances back. With his hands clasped over her own, he turns her hands so that the drill is now facing Frances. She tries to back away, but Marc is too strong. HE pushes the drill dangerously close to her neck.*

SHEENA: CALL THE POLICE!

MARC: What's the matter? Nothing to say now? I remember you! Screaming all over the news, trying to make it sound like I was the villain! Well nobody listened then, and nobody's gonna listen now, so just shut up!

> *Jody is finally able to get up. He sees Marc, rushes over to help Frances, but stumbles into Marc, which sends the drill plunging into Frances' neck.*

MARC: What . . . No . . .

> *Marc releases his hands, Frances' hands remain on the drill, which is still in her neck. Jody reaches over pulls it out of her.*

JODY: Holy shit. We've gotta . . .

> *Jody takes the tape out of her mouth. A puddle of blood begins to appear all around Frances' head and neck. It is dark, different from the movie blood. Frances makes terrible gurgling noises.*

MARC: I was just holding it over her—I wasn't—

SHEENA: Oh my God—

JODY: Give me something to put on it.

MARC: I didn't—

SHEENA: What's happening?

> *Marc hands him a t-shirt.*

JODY: Call an ambulance.

SHEENA: Is she okay?

JODY: Call them, now!

> *Marc dials 911. Jody tapes the t-shirt to her neck with his gaff tape. The blood keeps coming.*

MARC: I need an ambulance, there's been an accident.

SHEENA: What's happening—

JODY: *(to Frances)* Just stay still, don't move. Holy shit, there's so much blood.

MARC: I think her neck is broken, she's bleeding—

SHEENA: SOMEBODY UNLOCK ME!

JODY: Oh my God, she's bleeding out.

SHEENA: She'S MY MOTHER! UNLOCK ME NOW!

> *Jody rushes to Sheena, fumbles for the key.*

MARC: 12695 Rancho Vista Way.

SHEENA: Oh my God, hang on, mom. Just. I'm sorry, I'm sorry I said all those things the other night, I love you mom, I do. I just want to be happy, that's all! I don't want be angry at everybody all the time. I never meant to hurt you, please—WHAT THE HELL IS TAKING YOU SO LONG!

JODY: The key won't work!

> *Frances looks at her watch. She sits, starts to stand. Blood has soaked through the t-shirt taped to Frances' neck and is pouring down her chest.*

MARC: Jesus Christ! She's getting up!

JODY: No, don't move—you'll lose more blood—

FRANCES: Shhhhhh, Sheena—

SHEENA: Mom?

> *Frances is up, takes a few staggering steps towards Sheena, who is still locked to the radiator. Frances tries to motion to Sheena to get down.*

MARC: Ma'am, just sit back down—

SHEENA: Don't touch her!

FRANCES: Sh Sh Sh Sh Sh Sheena—

JODY: Please sit back down—

SHEENA: Mom, please! You're gonna die if you don't sit down, please please—

> *With her last remaining strength, Frances throws her body over Sheena's. A bright light flashes across the stage, along with the Sound of a huge explosion.*
> *Blackout.*
> *Sound of sirens.*
> *A TV News Anchor appears in another area. She may be backed by video clips of Sheena leaving a hospital in a wheel chair pushed by Hildy, surrounded by flashing cameras.*

NEWS ANCHOR: Authorities are still baffled by a bombing last week
that left several people injured and one presumed dead. Austin
resident Frances McKinney is believed to have died when a
bomb was detonated at a residence in Round Rock. No body
was recovered at the scene, but police say it would be impossible
for anyone to have survived both the explosion and the ensuing
fire. The home was being used as a location for the upcoming
horror movie, *Blood Bath*. In a movie worthy twist, police say
the bomb was planted by McKinney, whose daughter, Sheena
McKinney, stars in the forthcoming movie.

> *Perhaps another video clip of Pastor Dan, speaking at a
> podium, with Christi Garcia behind him, nodding in agree-
> ment.*

Round Rock residents gathered last night for a prayer vigil to
end violence organized by Holy Shepherd Church. Church
leaders say they are planning to boycott the movie, but the
movie's distributors don't appear to be worried. They've scheduled a press conference in town tomorrow, where they're expected to announce that film will be released in August. For
WTEX Channel Five News, I'm Belinda Chapman.

SCENE EIGHTEEN

*Frances' house. Sheena enters wearing a short, low-cut black dress, her
hair in a towel. She walks with a lumbering thud—one foot is in a
cast, the other foot is bare.*

SHEENA: I can't find my shoe.

HILDY: It's right here.

SHEENA: Not those, my black ones.

HILDY: The ones with the huge heels?

SHEENA: They're here somewhere—

HILDY: You can't wear those.

SHEENA: Watch me.

HILDY: You're not even supposed to be walking this much. The doctor said you're supposed to be taking it easy, not—

> *Sheena has found the shoe and shoved her good foot into. She
> stands teetering a little.*

SHEENA: *I am perfectly fine.*

Beat.

HILDY: Are you seriously wearing that to the press conference.

SHEENA: What's wrong with it?

HILDY: Nothing, for Shakira.

> *Sheena takes off the shoe, carries it as she lumbers around the living room. She goes to the front door, opens it to look for the limo, leaves it open.*

SHEENA: Well what else am I supposed to wear? I can't get pants on over my cast! This is the only other black I have!

HILDY: Oh, right! You're in mourning. I forgot, what with all the interviews, and your agent—

SHEENA: What is your problem?

HILDY: Nothing, why would I have a problem with you promoting a movie that our mother killed herself trying to stop—

SHEENA: You don't need to remind me what happened, I'm the one she was trying to blow up, remember?

HILDY: She saved your life!

SHEENA: Only at the last minute! Only because she tried to kill me in the first place—

> *(Sheena starts to cry.)*

Crap.

HILDY: I'm sorry. I didn't mean to—. You know you don't have to do this.

SHEENA: I'm doing it.

HILDY: They can still have their press conference without you, just—

SHEENA: *This is the biggest opportunity I'm ever gonna get. All right?* This is gonna pay off the house, pay for your college. That agent says he's got three movie offers for me already because of all the publicity. So if this is what I have to do to take care of both of us, that's what I'm gonna do.

> *(Sound of a honk.)*

Crap. Tell them I'll be right there.

> *Sheena lumbers off. Jody appears in the doorway. He wears a large stabilizing neck brace, and carries a cactus.*

JODY: Hey.

HILDY: Hey.

SHEENA: *(O.S.)* I just need two seconds!

HILDY: Hair.

JODY: Right. I brought a cactus.

HILDY: Yeah.

JODY: Just to say, I'm sorry, for your loss.

> *He gives it to Hildy.*

HILDY: Thanks.

JODY: You coming to the press conference?

HILDY: I take the PSAT tomorrow?

JODY: Oh.

HILDY: I think it's a little more important.

JODY: Definitely.

MARC: *(O.S.)* Hildy!

HILDY: Plus someone has to look after Sheena's charity case.

JODY: Right.

> *Marc enters on Frances' scooter. He wears a bathrobe. He's
> got an awkward bandage over one eye and ear, and he's a
> little deaf from the blast.*

MARC: *(to Hildy)* The fridge is EMPTY. Don't you EAT anything in
this house?

HILDY: I think we have pickles?

MARC: What?

HILDY: YOU WANT SOME PICKLES?

MARC: Jesus Christ, I want FOOD. What the hell is he doing here?

JODY: This is so weird.

> *Sheena appears. Her hair is done.*

SHEENA: Hey Jody.

JODY: Sheena. You look amazing.

SHEENA: Really?

JODY: Definitely.

MARC: What's going on?

SHEENA: He can't hear you, just ignore him.

JODY: For real?

MARC: Why are you so dressed up?

JODY: Look, Sheena, I'm really sorry, about your mom, and everything—

SHEENA: Thanks.

JODY: Things got so crazy at the end, and—

> *Sound of another honk.*

SHEENA: It's okay. Let's do this.

MARC: You're doing something for the movie, aren't you?

JODY: He doesn't know about the press conference?

MARC: What are you doing, you're doing an interview?

SHEENA: Don't say anything.

MARC: HEY! Answer me!

SHEENA: *(loudly, so he can hear)* I am letting you stay here out of the kindness of my heart until your insurance settlement comes, but do not think for a second—

MARC: I wouldn't NEED to be here if YOUR MOTHER hadn't tried to BLOW US ALL UP!

SHEENA: *(to Hildy)* Will you be okay here?

MARC: Fine, go. We'll see who's the big star after my interview next week on Dateline NBC. Oh, they're very interested in my side of the story.

SHEENA: What are you talking about?

MARC: It seems you forgot to tell everyone how you got the part. How you came to my hotel room. Spent the night with me—

HILDY: What?

SHEENA: Nothing happened!

MARC: Oh, that's not how I remember it, Sheena.

SHEENA: *(to Hildy)* Hildy, get your stuff, you're coming with us.

HILDY: Good.

    Jody helps Hildy gather her stuff.

MARC: They say you make it sound like a Lifetime movie. "Innocent co-ed trying to support her family gets exploited by evil director!" But nobody's gonna believe that when I'm done with you.

SHEENA: I'm through feeling sorry for you! I won't let you hurt me again.

    Sheena pulls out her phone, dials 911.

MARC: Hurt you? You got exactly what you wanted. Hell, you negotiated. You sold your tits and ass for fifteen grand.

    (Sheena adjusts her dress, trying to make it more modest.)

Look at you. You're still selling it. I think you'd better start learning Pilates.

SHEENA: *(on the phone)* Hi, there's an intruder in my house? He keeps saying he lives here.

Sheena waves Jody and Hildy out the door. Jody stops, grabs the cactus for good measure, then exits.

MARC: You can't leave me here, HEY!

SHEENA: Yes, he's a white, male, about 40?

They are gone. Marc shouts after them.

MARC: You fuckers! Oh, fine, get in your limo! Live it up! We'll see who gets the last laugh!

(He slams the door.)

This is not over. This was MY movie, MY comeback. I'm gonna get on 60 Minutes. 48 Hours. *Doctor Phil.*

(HE zips back over to the door, to shout after them again.)

I'll go to the National Fucking Inquirer—

Marc opens the door and sees: Frances. She's covered in ash and dried blood, but she's strong and powerful. Lights shift. Marc tries to back away, but his scooter won't work. She unsheathes a knife.

MARC: No. No no no no no—

FRANCES: *Oh yes.*

Frances raises the knife.
As Marc lets out a long girly scream:

Blackout.

End of play.

Rights and Permissions

357